CELEBRATING THE AUTHENTIC AGING SELF

The Art of Aging

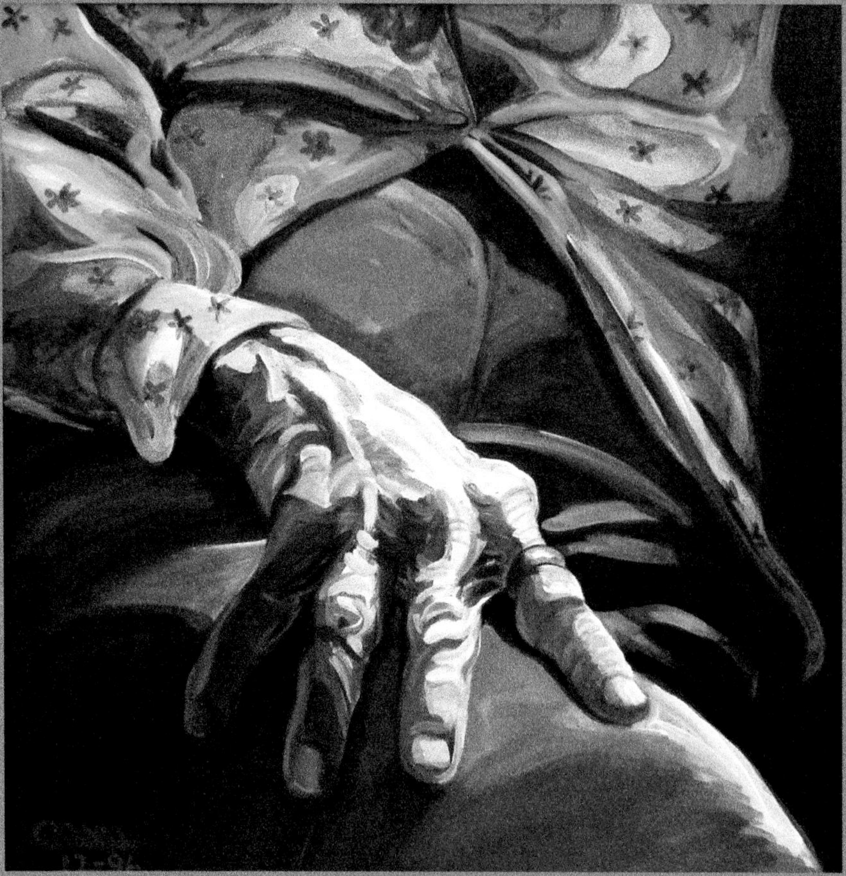

Aunt Kitty's hands

Every person's life is their work of art. The way they live, day by day, is the medium they use to express their artistry. Only in the latter stages of life is a person's work of art brought to fulfillment.

CELEBRATING THE AUTHENTIC AGING SELF

The Art of Aging

ALICE AND RICHARD MATZKIN

Youth is a gift of nature, but age is a work of art.

—Stanislow Jersey Lec

First Sentient Publications edition 2009

A paperback original

Cover design by Kim Johansen, Black Dog Design
Cover art by Alice Matzkin
Book design by Kim Johansen, Black Dog Design

Library of Congress Cataloging-in-Publication Data

Matzkin, Alice, 1939-
The art of aging : celebrating the authentic aging self / Alice and Richard Matzkin. -- 1st Sentient Publications ed.
p. cm.
ISBN 978-1-59181-081-0
1. Matzkin, Alice, 1939- 2. Matzkin, Richard, 1943- 3. Aging in art. 4. Older people in art. 5. Aging--United States--Miscellanea. I. Matzkin, Richard, 1943- II. Title.
ND237.M34M38 2008
700.8928'5--dc22
2008042788

Printed in the United States of America

10 9 8 7 6 5 4 3 2

SENTIENT PUBLICATIONS
A Limited Liability Company
1113 Spruce Street
Boulder, CO 80302
www.sentientpublications.com

To our parents who gave us life, love, and talent.

To all the elders who inspired us.

To Baba Muktananda, who tried to give us wisdom.

ACKNOWLEDGMENTS

We would like to thank our publisher at Sentient Publications, Connie Shaw, for her sage editorial advice. We also appreciate the valuable editing of Doug Adrianson, the late Hope Frazier, and our good friend, Carol Royce Wilder. Thanks to Maureen O'Brien for our serendipitous meeting and her valuable guidance. Thanks to Marilyn and Jerry Wennstrom for opening the door. Thanks to Kim Johansen for creating a beautiful book design.

Table of Contents

Introduction
9

Why Old People?
13

Women of Age: Portraits of Wisdom, Beauty and Strength - Alice
17

Naked Old Men - Richard
65

Naked Truth - Alice
87

Lovers - Richard
107

Declining Years: Aunt Kitty from Age 89 to 97 - Alice
119

Reflections on Being with Our Parents in Their Old Age and Death - Alice and Richard
129

On Becoming Elders - Alice and Richard
139

Afterword: *Alice and Richard Matzkin and Their Art – A Love Story* - Alice and Richard
151

To know how to grow old is the master work of wisdom, and the most difficult chapters in the great art of living.

—Henri Frederic Amiel

Introduction

TIME IS A PATH. IT LEADS IN ONE DIRECTION—FROM THE PAST TO THE FUTURE. We must all journey on this path, where the one and only constant is change. Our voyage takes us from birth to old age, and eventually to death. In the later stages of life's journey the path becomes steeper, rockier, and increasingly difficult to tread. Though the route gets more challenging as time goes on, the view can be magnificent.

We are two artists, husband and wife, who are in our mid and late sixties. Over the last dozen years we have been working on a series of art projects related to aging. Having entered the youth of old age, we have used our art as a vehicle to explore our experiences and feelings about growing older. This book documents our journey so far. Looking back, we ponder our progress. Looking forward at the road ahead, we contemplate our future with curiosity and hope, but not without fear and trepidation.

The Art of Aging is several books rolled into one. It is an art book, it is a personal odyssey, it is an educational book, and it is an inspirational book—one that kindles hope for a positive and meaningful old age.

As an art book it presents art projects related to the subject of aging by two people who have been blessed with gifts that allow us to envision and create art. When we gaze at these pages, we can honestly say we are awed by the beauty and power of the art that has been created through us.

As a personal odyssey the book reveals our ongoing efforts to come to terms with our fear and curiosity about the process of aging, growing old and dying, and ultimately, our desire to live meaningful lives. As artists we each embarked on this journey, one using hands to mold clay, the other putting paint to canvas. Though we have used the medium of art, ours is not just a personal quest. It is a universal human journey, one that all conscious beings, as they confront their mortality, must make.

This is also an educational book. Through our personal odysseys with the art projects and through living into our sixth decade, we have come to a degree of understanding about what it means to enter into the stage of being an elder. In this book we share what we have learned with words; in addition, the book's message is conveyed on a visceral level through the images.

Finally, we hope that our book is an inspiration to others. In contrast to all the anti-aging articles in magazines and the anti-aging books on the shelves of bookstores, which view aging as a fearsome disease, this book is pro-aging. In the process of working through and beyond many of our fears and apprehensions about getting older, we are left mainly with a sense of promise, rather than despair. We have grown to the conclusion that old age does not necessarily have to be a time of dissolution and depression. We have found our older years to be a time of ripening and fruition, and have discovered elders in their eighth, ninth, and tenth decades who are reaping a bountiful harvest. These remarkable elders—family, friends, and generous strangers—serve as models and mentors who inspire us and help us envision what can be possible if one treats aging as an art.

Who are these elders who have mastered the art of aging? They are people who have used their accumulated life experience, both painful and pleasurable, to enrich their life and the lives of those around them. They have arrived at a place of peace and acceptance. They allow themselves to fully experience their present moment. They have retained a sense of excitement and curiosity. They have concern for others and give generously of themselves. They are able to face the end of their lives with equanimity and a sense of completion. Some of these elders grace the pages of this book and their inspiration is the mastery we aspire to in the coming years.

At our present age, we have arrived at a wonderful point in life—our golden years. We have grown beyond mid-life, often considered an unsettling period of yearning and turmoil. For many, the mid-forties to the end of the fifties is a time of questioning earlier decisions, feeling regret for paths taken or not taken, and attempting to grasp at fading youth. We have navigated beyond those turbulent waters and accepted our life as lived so far, appreciating the gift of our present moment. We are also engaged in the inner work that is laying the foundation for our future, the potentially difficult challenges of old age. Our art projects, and this book, are part of that inner work.

There is an art to aging well that goes far beyond the simple piling up of year after year. Everyone does that without effort. However, to become a master of the art of aging is to mature, to ripen, to live to the last breath with meaning and passion and curiosity. Aging well is like creating a work of art. A fine art piece doesn't just miraculously materialize. Artists must love their creations into being, meticulously working and reworking the image on canvas or in clay until it fits the image they have in their mind. So it is with creating a beautiful old age. It takes vision, dedication, and constant attention. This is important, necessary work at any age. Creating a good old age is work that takes a lifetime. The most important moment to begin that work is right now. The choices a person makes in the present will influence what their future will be like. We believe that if people turn their attention to the process of growing older rather than trying to hide, delay or deny it, they will discover far greater riches and serenity in their older years.

The Art of Aging is a contemplation of our experience on the path of growing older. We have observed the aging process in ourselves and others, thought about it, read about it, painted and sculpted it. These years have been rich and productive. Our projects, both the artwork and the writing, have been a labor of love for us. At times hard labor, at times joyful, the work has opened us, informed us, inspired us. We offer our words and our artwork in the hope that they will touch others and help move them to become masters of their own art of aging.

Anyone who keeps the ability
to see beauty never grows old.

—Franz Kafka

Why Old People?

FEW ARTISTS OF NOTE HAVE MADE OLD PEOPLE A SIGNIFICANT THEME IN THEIR ART. There are exceptions. Rembrandt produced many portraits of older people, including many beautiful self-portraits as an elder. To a lesser extent Daumier and Rubens featured elders in their work, as did Goya and da Vinci. Of course, the old were not absent in the art of the past. Elderly men often appeared in religious paintings, representing God, or as various biblical personages. Classical sculptures depicting mythic themes from antiquity sometimes featured bearded older males with massive torsos, striking heroic poses. The abundance of sculpted busts and painted portraits of older people that reside in museums attests to the desire of rich old men to have their likenesses, and those of their family members, preserved for posterity. Portraits and sculptures have always been ways of honoring important people and events or commemorating historical figures, and these were usually senior members of society. However, we are not aware of any other artists who have spent years exclusively depicting elders in their work, as we have.

So, why have we chosen old people almost exclusively as subjects of our artwork? The main reason is that the aging process held, and holds, profound personal interest for both of us. Since we are in rhythm with each other and are both concerned about getting older, it would not be unexpected that we would both use art as a way to work through unresolved feelings about aging. As we stood gazing into the doorway to old age, the specter of aging

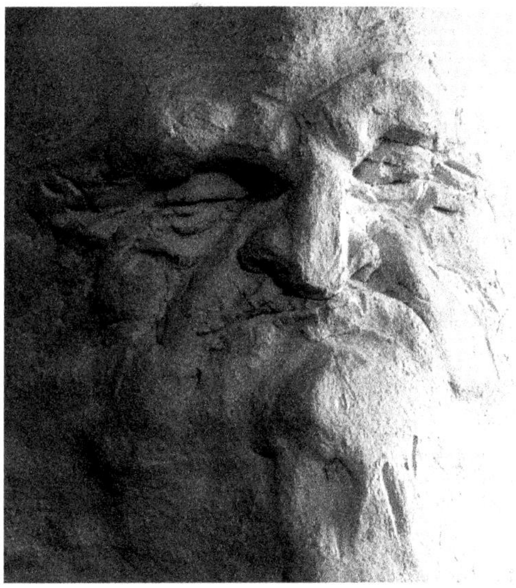

and death became more real for us. Our parents, friends, and relatives were getting older, and our own bodies were as well. We felt threatened by the process we were undergoing, yet also curious. The fear and curiosity we were experiencing were translated onto canvas and clay. Our art became a healing tool—an attempt to make sense of the changes that were occurring in our bodies and minds.

We found that the aesthetic aspects of working with older subjects appealed to us both. The crisscross of wrinkles, sagging skin, and miscellaneous bulges and folds on an older body provide much more interesting material to paint and sculpt than the smooth, unblemished surface of the young.

Besides being more interesting from an aesthetic angle, an older face and body express soul. There is history written there—catastrophic losses, toughness, endurance, courage, dignity, hard-won wisdom. These and other human qualities are more clearly seen on the faces of elders than in any other age group. We find this expression of character deeply moving. It takes time to evolve, like the patina that forms on a fine piece of furniture after a lifetime of use.

The beautiful qualities in the alluring face of a young woman and the rugged handsomeness of a young man are self evident. But, you must look more deeply to discover the beauty in a weathered old face. When you suspend traditional rules of beauty, and observe without judgment, the aged beauty will reveal itself.

When we were younger, we were blind to the beauty and depth of older persons. Our fears and prejudices permitted us to see only the surface—the aged features, the infirmities, the differences in dress, interests, and ideas. We tended to avoid close connections with old people, as if age was contagious.

Since we have gotten older, we have come to see elders in a different light. Elders are the keepers of the values of previous generations. They are a living window into the past. Alice's stepfather was present at the attack on Pearl Harbor. Her mother danced to Ellington and Basie in Harlem during the forties. What stories they have to tell. There is a proverb, "When an old person dies, a library disappears." With their years of accumulated life experience, elders have access to wisdom that the young are not privy to. By honoring elders we can tap into that wisdom and deepen and broaden our lives.

Being around the elderly has also helped sober us and caution us about our own coming old age. For a while, we were part of an entertainment troupe that visited assisted living facilities, convalescent hospitals, and Alzheimer's units. These were depressing places where the elderly were warehoused to wait out the remainder of their lives. Our performances were gratifying in that they brought some light into the resident's lives, but they were also deeply disturbing experiences for us. Everywhere, we saw hopelessness, helplessness, boredom, and sadness. We realized that we needed to wake up, take care of ourselves, and grasp the moment, because in a few short years we might end up living there.

We learned much from our art projects. As we painted and sculpted old people, our anxieties about our own aging rose to the surface where they could be more easily experienced and understood. We became aware of our preconceptions and watched them begin to melt. As we spoke to our subjects, we were able to contemplate their lives and their words and appreciate the satisfaction of a life well lived, the necessity of a positive outlook and the importance of accepting the inevitability of change. These experiences over the past dozen years, plus the maturity that these years of living bring, have radically changed the way we look at aging. This change is documented in our art and in our writing of this book.

It's not how old you are,

but how you are old that matters.

—Chinese Proverb

Women of Age

Portraits of Wisdom, Beauty, & Strength

ALICE

I WAS FIFTY-FIVE YEARS OLD, LOOKING AT MYSELF IN THE MIRROR with horror. Where did these lines and wrinkles and sagging skin and gray hair come from? My hands had become my mother's hands, my body, my grandmother's body. The change seemed to have happened overnight. It was just yesterday that I was young and wrinkle free. Where did the time go? Who was this old person with graying hair looking back at me, and what was her future?

I became afraid and confused. This wasn't the me I thought I was. I began to spend a lot of time thinking about death and the rotting of my body. Not only was my outside surface crumbling, but all the organs, bones, tissues, and cells on the inside were decomposing too. I was fixated on people in various stages of dying and objects in their process of deterioration. I had become so focused on death and dissolution that I forgot about living life. Fear of the future was making me neglect the most precious moment of my life: now.

My outlook needed immediate change! I realized that if I was going to live my life in a happy, satisfied way, I had to go beyond my terror of growing old and dying. It was crucial for me to start focusing on living and seeing the positive side of growing older—to stop fighting the inevitable, and begin to embrace the physical and mental changes that were taking place right before my eyes.

Those changes—the sagging skin and wrinkles, physical evidence of my fleeting youth—were what troubled me most. Aging would inevitably take its toll on my face and body. But I could not let it take its toll on my mind. I needed to enlarge my definition of beauty in aging so that it included my whole being rather than only the outer few millimeters of the surface of my body.

What I needed were female mentors—women older than I who were living their old age the way I wanted to live mine. By their example they would provide me inspiration and hope. If I could find beauty in their aging faces, then certainly I could find beauty in my own. If I could absorb their wisdom and spirit, surely I could tap into my own.

Being an artist I had the perfect medium at my fingertips. I would use paint and canvas to work through my fears. In my mind, I thought that seventy years old was a reasonable entry into old age. I decided I would seek out women in their seventh decade and older who were living productive, generous lives, and paint their portraits. My objective was to focus on what they were accomplishing in the present, rather than what they had accomplished in the past. I interviewed these women and asked, "What makes life worthwhile?" "What is it like being an older person?" "What message would you give women that would enlighten and inspire them?"

Finding the women was easy. As soon as I spread the word about the project, friends and acquaintances phoned me and stopped me in the street to nominate some older woman they admired. The media was also helpful. Newspapers, radio, and television occasionally carried stories of women in their seventies, eighties, and nineties who were actively contributing to society. When I discovered a woman who inspired me, I would call her, tell her about my quest, get a feel for her, and let her get to know me. Sometimes I would give her written materials describing the project. Almost every woman I contacted was willing to participate.

Each meeting was an adventure. Richard, my supporter, collaborator, friend, and cameraman, would accompany me. We would sit and talk with the women a while to grow comfortable with each other. Then I photographed them. When it was time for the interview, Richard manned the video camera.

I was always excited when I returned to my studio, sifted through the photos, and began the process of putting color and form on the canvas. It was fascinating to watch these wise, intelligent and committed women emerge in paint—and for me to again experience the reflection of their wisdom, beauty, and strength.

The women I painted and interviewed for the project are of such diversity that they resist classification. They are of different races, have varied temperaments, and pursue a wide array of interests. Yet from my impressions of being with them and from the content of the interviews, a similarity of ideas and characteristics emerged. All the women share these qualities: They are *passionate, generous, focused in the present*, and *attractive.*

Each of these women has a *passionate sense of purpose.* Each has a commitment to some interest, cause, or creative endeavor that plays an important part in her life. Choosing not to witness life from the sidelines, these women are fully immersed in their endeavors. Their impassioned involvement keeps them from being bored, and therefore, none are boring.

These are the kind of people who openly give of themselves. They all espouse and demonstrate love and *generosity of spirit.* They do not reserve their generosity for family and friends, but share themselves with the community.

Though many of the women are of advanced age and have led fascinating lives, their focus is not on the past. Their concern is with now, with maximizing the quality of their *present time* and creating the best life possible. Some spoke of death, but without regret or fear. I believe this is because they had lived and are now living full and meaningful lives. It seems that they are not intending to leave much of their lives unlived.

Despite their age, every one of the women possesses a vivaciousness and *physical appeal* that seems unrelated to her years. They have a sparkle in their eyes that shines through their lines and wrinkles. Their beauty, though not conventional, is earned through years of living—and is uniquely their own. I believe it is not solely a physical phenomenon; rather, their attractiveness is a reflection of their inner state.

It became very clear to me that it is meaningless to relate age to the number of years lived. There are young people who are old at forty, and old people who are young at ninety. To call this ageless quality youthfulness is a misnomer and reflects age bias. The quality these people share is freshness—an approach to life that is open, vibrant, and adventurous, not concerned with what was, but with what can be. Freshness is a mental attitude. It has very little to do with one's life circumstances. These wonderful women share all the problems faced by people their age, yet their passion, generosity, and present focus keep them fresh. That is a key idea I learned from the women, and is reason for my optimism about my later years. I do not have to be a *victim of my age!*

I know that good genes and lots of luck can be a dominant factor in living a long and healthy life, but they have little to do with leading a happy and fulfilling life. For that, a positive mental attitude, as these women demonstrate, is an essential ingredient.

My experience of the wisdom, courage, intelligence, generosity, creativity, and passion with which all these women live their lives has changed my attitude about my older years. I now know that it is possible to have a fruitful and creative old age. I can appreciate my lines and wrinkles and sagging skin knowing they are the story of my years and only the outer surface. What is most important is how I feel inside.

The good news is that this group of women is only the tip of the iceberg. The world is filled with amazing older women. Just look around and see for yourself.

NOTE: *At this writing, many of the vital women I met and painted have now passed away. Just another reminder of the preciousness of life!*

"I am 103 years old and I have never been happier in my life."

Beatrice Wood at 105 (nine days before her death)

POTTER, SCULPTOR, WRITER

"When I am not in my studio creating, I would like to be president and change the world."

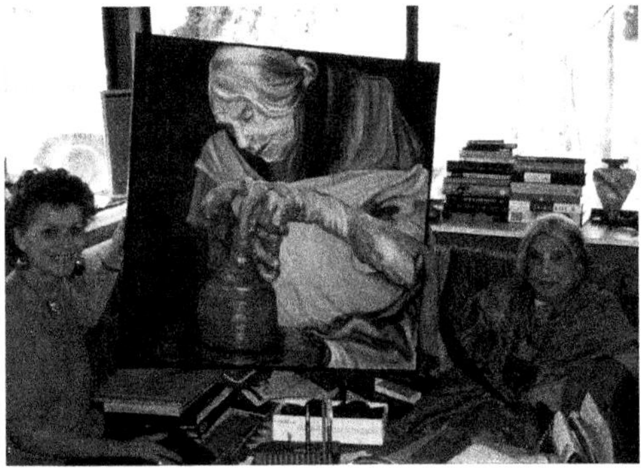

Beatrice Wood at 100 with Alice (with painting from The National Portrait Gallery, Smithsonian Institution)

THE FIRST TIME I MET BEATRICE SHE WAS ninety-eight years old. She was a neighbor, living a couple of miles down the road. Her house was on top of a hill with a gorgeous view of fields and mountains. Walking into her studio and home was always a treat. Beatrice would be sitting in her fuchsia and turquoise room amid her lusterware pots and outrageous, sometimes scandalous and political sculptures, dressed in a gorgeous sari, adorned with ethnic earrings and necklaces and bracelets, a smile on her face. She was feminine, vivacious, generous, intelligent, kind, sensual, and funny. Here was a woman who dared to be herself.

Beatrice was one hundred the first time I photographed her working in her studio. She ignored me as I worked. She was totally focused and caught up in the creative process. As she threw piece after piece on the potter's wheel, the pot and her arm and her hand were like one unit.

When I interviewed and videoed Beatrice at 103 for the *Women of Age* project, she was still going into her studio each day and creating pots and sculptures and drawings. In the afternoon she would write. Laughingly, she exclaimed that by the time she was 105, she would be compost for her rose garden.

We attended her 105th birthday. She was wheeled outside to a resounding chorus of "Happy Birthday" sung by two hundred adoring friends. She was dressed in a gorgeous bright pink sari, with lots of jewels, and her smile was radiant. From her turquoise couch she lovingly and silently exchanged greetings with each guest.

She left this world peacefully nine days later.

It was powerful for me to see, from Beatrice's 105-year-old example, that the well of creativity never runs dry.

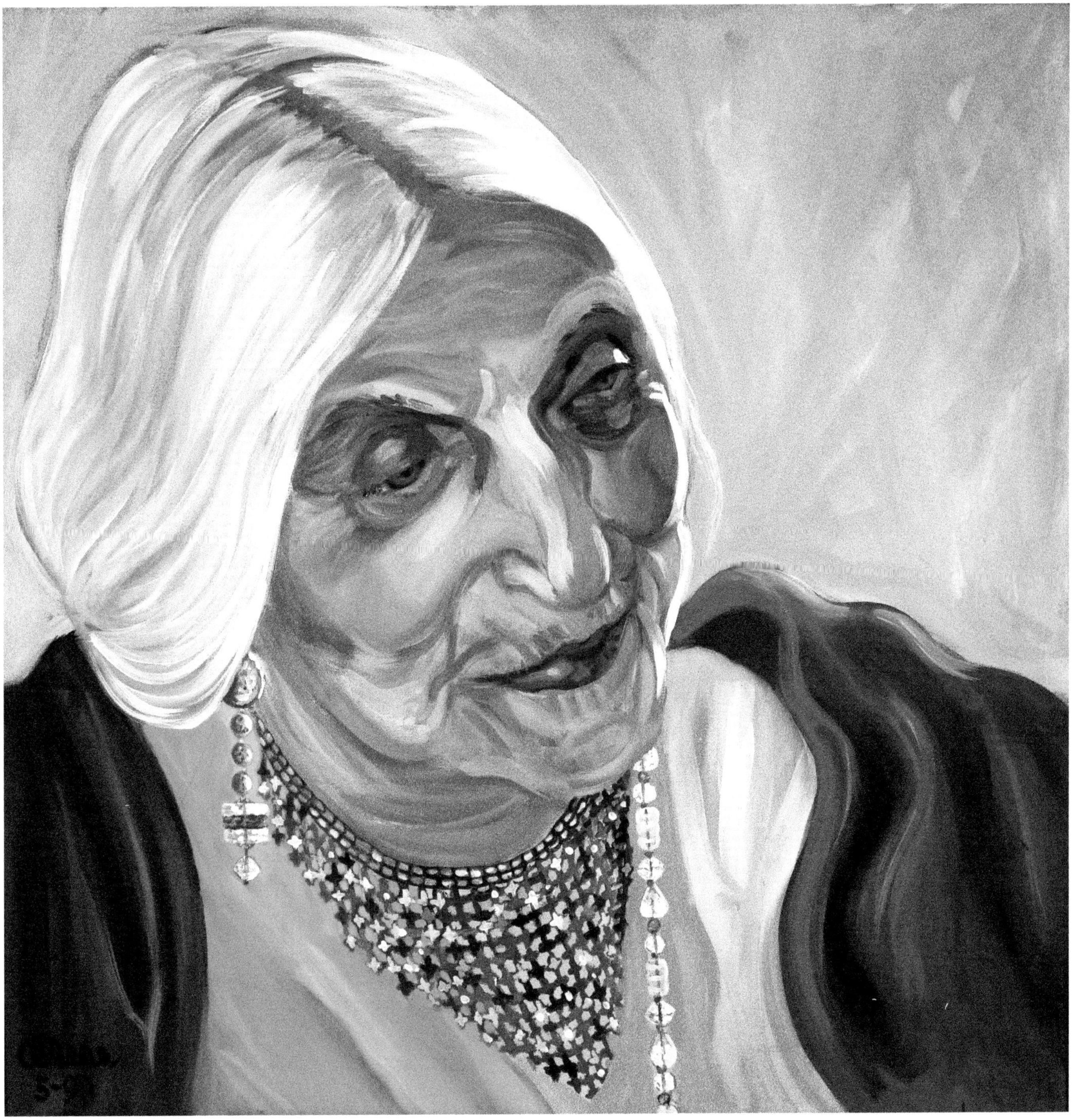

Painting of Beatrice Wood at 105, nine days before her death

"I think that love and compassion for yourself
and other human beings is most important."

"We try to laugh and love and lift—

to brighten someone's life."

Happy Lucky Fawn at 81

YOGINI, DANCER, ENTERTAINER

"You are never too old to realize your dreams."

AFTER READING ABOUT HAPPY LUCKY FAWN in a senior newspaper, I called her on the phone. Immediately, we felt a warmth between us and made a date to meet. On the given day, Richard and I waited in the lobby of her apartment building. Suddenly the elevator doors sprang open and out swept a graceful, smiling, and vibrant Happy, dressed in a dark red velvet leotard. A lively energy emanated from this eighty-one year old woman.

After retiring from her job twelve years earlier, introverted and overweight, Happy signed up for a yoga class and discovered that she was limber, graceful, and a talented entertainer. As a celebration of her emergence from her introverted shell, she legally changed her name to *Happy Lucky Fawn. Happy* because she is happy most of the time, *Lucky* because she has been happily married to her husband, Earl, for fifty-five years, *Fawn* because she discovered she was graceful.

Happy continues to learn and grow. At senior centers she is studying tap, ballet, and Polynesian dance, as well as taking classes on how to be a clown. She and Earl are actively involved in senior issues, and regularly entertain at retirement homes and senior centers.

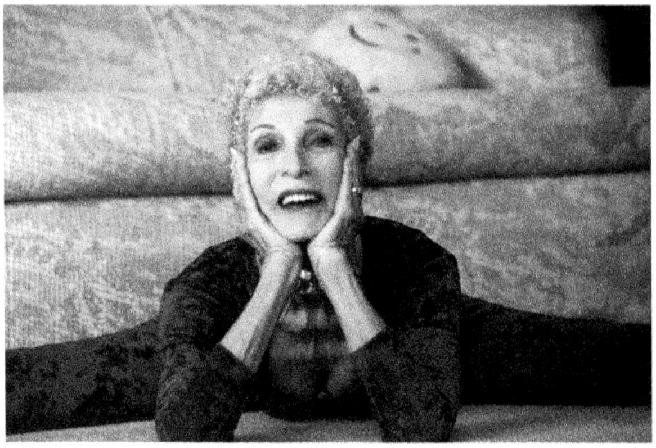

Happy Lucky Fawn at 81

"It is important to enjoy the now moment—live to the fullest and thank God that you are here and have the opportunity to do things."

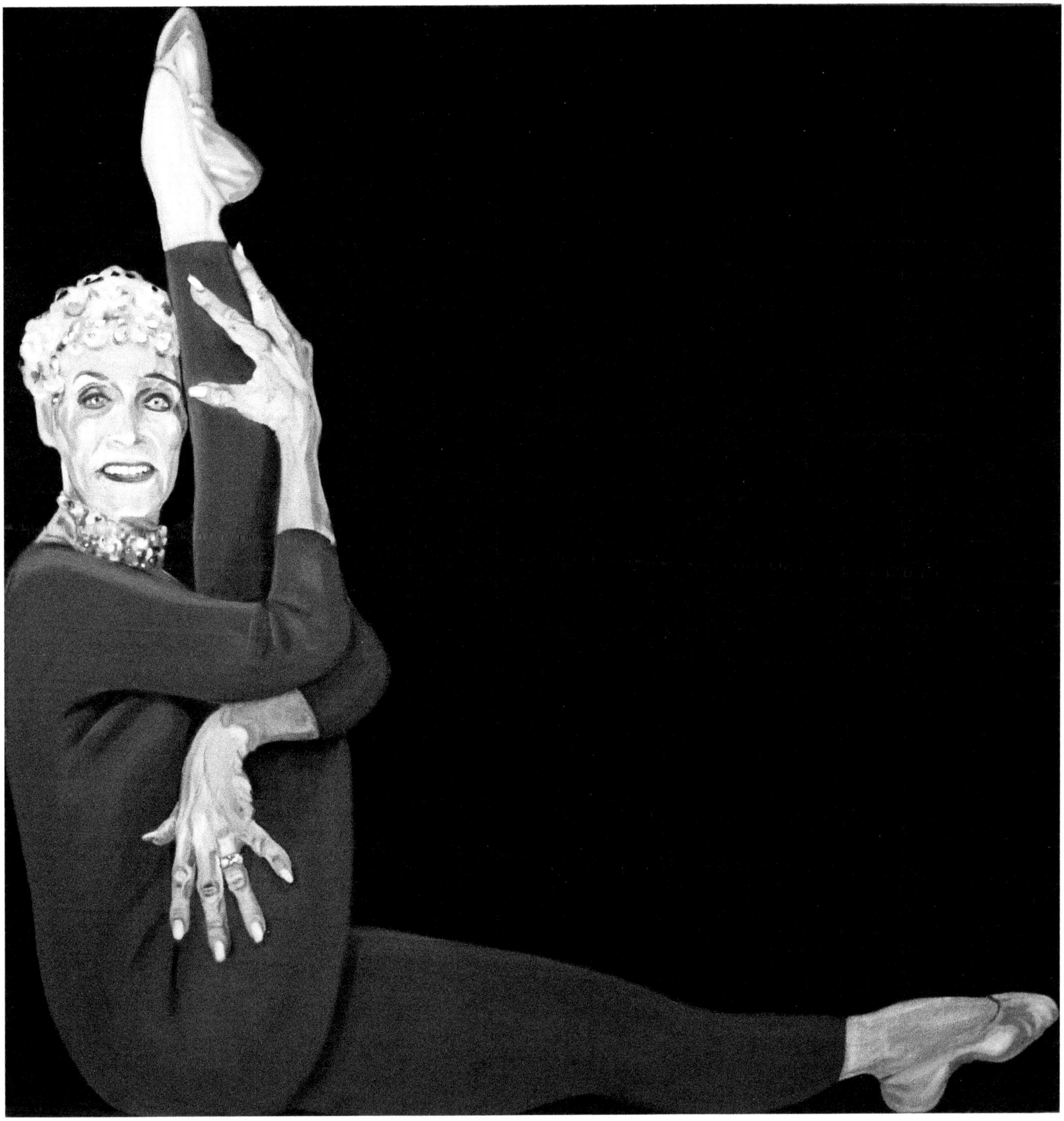

Painting of Happy Lucky Fawn at 81

"Getting older is not getting old."

"Have some interest in life, and with that one interest you should do better than anyone else could, in your own estimation."

Pablita Velarde at 79

PAINTER, AUTHOR

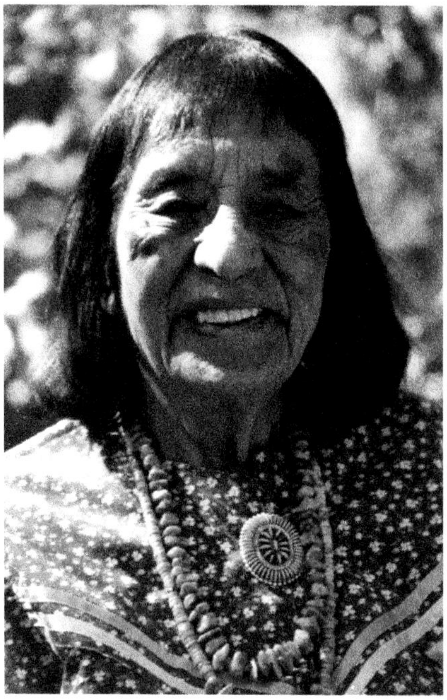

Pablita Velarde at 79

RICHARD AND I WERE VACATIONING IN THE Santa Fe, New Mexico, area when we stopped in a gift shop at the Anasazi ruins and saw a video about Pablita Velarde, a well-known Pueblo Indian painter. I found a telephone booth, looked her up in the phone book, and called her. When she answered, I told her about my quest. She graciously invited us to her home the next day.

We were warmly greeted by Pablita and welcomed into her living room. There we spent the next few hours in the company of this humble and strong woman. She spoke about how Pueblo women were traditionally the tribal potters, but she was given the gifts of painting and writing. In spite of strong opposition from family and tribe, she broke with tradition and expressed herself with paint and canvas. She still makes some of her own paint from the minerals and plants she finds in nature. When her book with paintings depicting stories told to her by her grandfather won top awards, and her paintings illustrating those stories began being displayed in museums across the United States, the tribe granted her a well-deserved acceptance.

I felt drawn to her creativity, and to her independence and dogged determination in following her calling to be a painter instead of a potter.

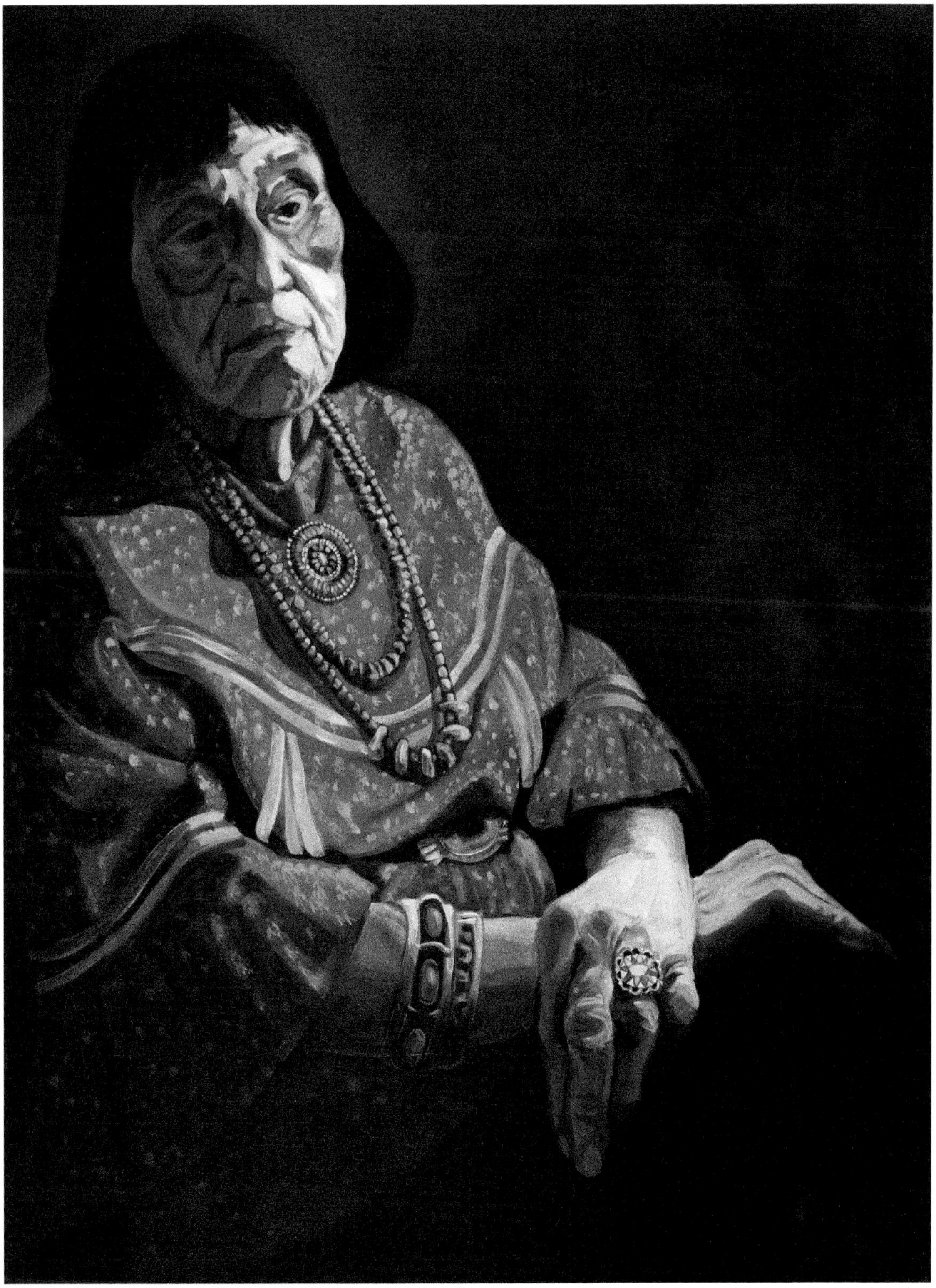

Painting of Pablita Velarde at 79

"I don't think about getting old.

Maybe I have a few more wrinkles, but I do the same things I used to do when I was younger."

Liz Bevington, aka Skateboard Mama, at 75

ATHLETE, BON VIVANT

LIZ BEVINGTON, KNOWN TO EVERYONE AS Skateboard Mama, is a local legend. For almost thirty years she has been skateboarding, rollerblading, and bicycling up and down the boardwalk of California's colorful Venice and Santa Monica beach areas.

On a beautiful, sunny day, we met in Venice Beach. Suddenly, bursting out from the middle of the crowded boardwalk, emerged a blonde, muscular, suntanned grandmother, riding a skateboard with a large, colorful sail attached. Her exuberance washed over us. She was filled with lust for life and a pure physical energy that most people half her age would envy. Her face was joyful as she whizzed around and around in a giant parking lot, weaving in and out of parked cars, demonstrating her strength and skateboard skills. After that strenuous show, she jumped on a bicycle and rode fast without holding the handlebars, while pumping weights with both hands. She told us that after a half-day of work as a house cleaner, she rides for hours at the beach, then goes to a local pub, has a couple of beers, visits with friends, and dances the evening away. I was exhausted just watching her!

I loved her positive outlook on life, her daring, and her absolute joy. Here is a woman who fully inhabits her body. It was inspiring to see such a strong, athletic, and fearless elder.

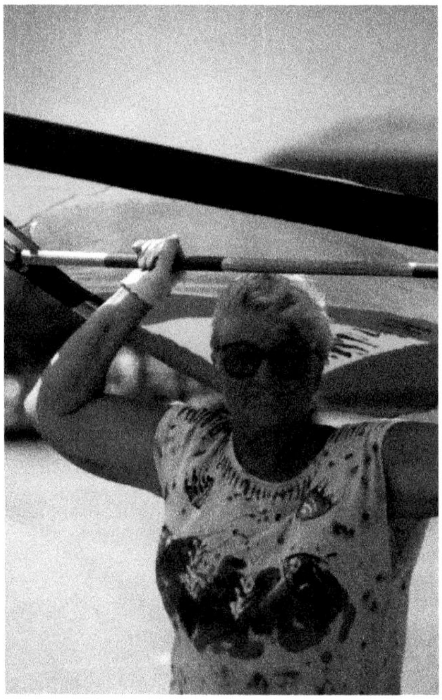

Liz Bevington aka Skateboard Mama at 75

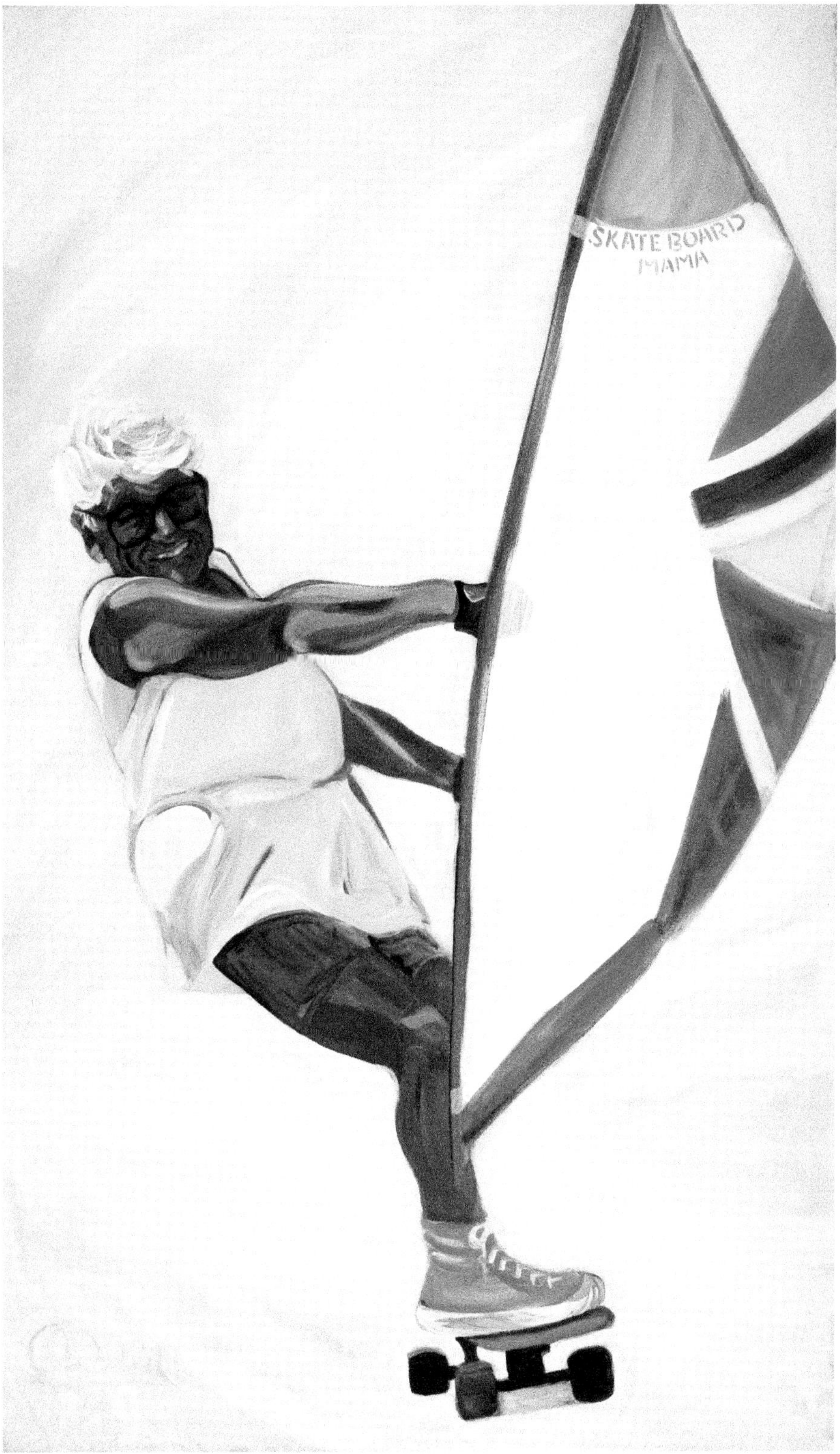

Painting of Liz Bevington aka Skateboard Mama at 75

"We have to give to life. We have to get from life."

Margaret Dixon at 73

PRESIDENT OF AARP

WE WERE ABOUT TO TRAVEL TO WASHINGTON, D.C., when I heard that AARP, an organization that advocates for the elderly in the United States, had a president who was a woman, an African American, and a senior citizen. Here was someone who had obviously defied the prejudices of sexism, racism, and ageism, and her story inspired me. I phoned her, and we arranged to meet a couple of weeks later.

Margaret graciously welcomed us to her elegant office overlooking the Capitol. Immediately we felt relaxed and at home with each other and had an enjoyable visit. I loved that she had risen to the position of president after serving first as a volunteer.

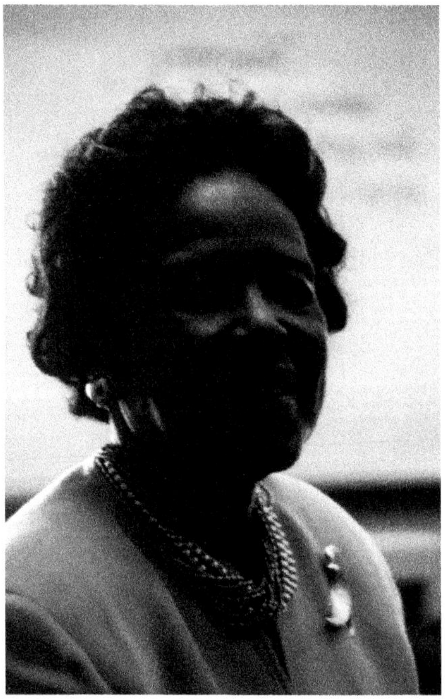

Margaret Dixon at 73

"Be happy,

be active,

have fun."

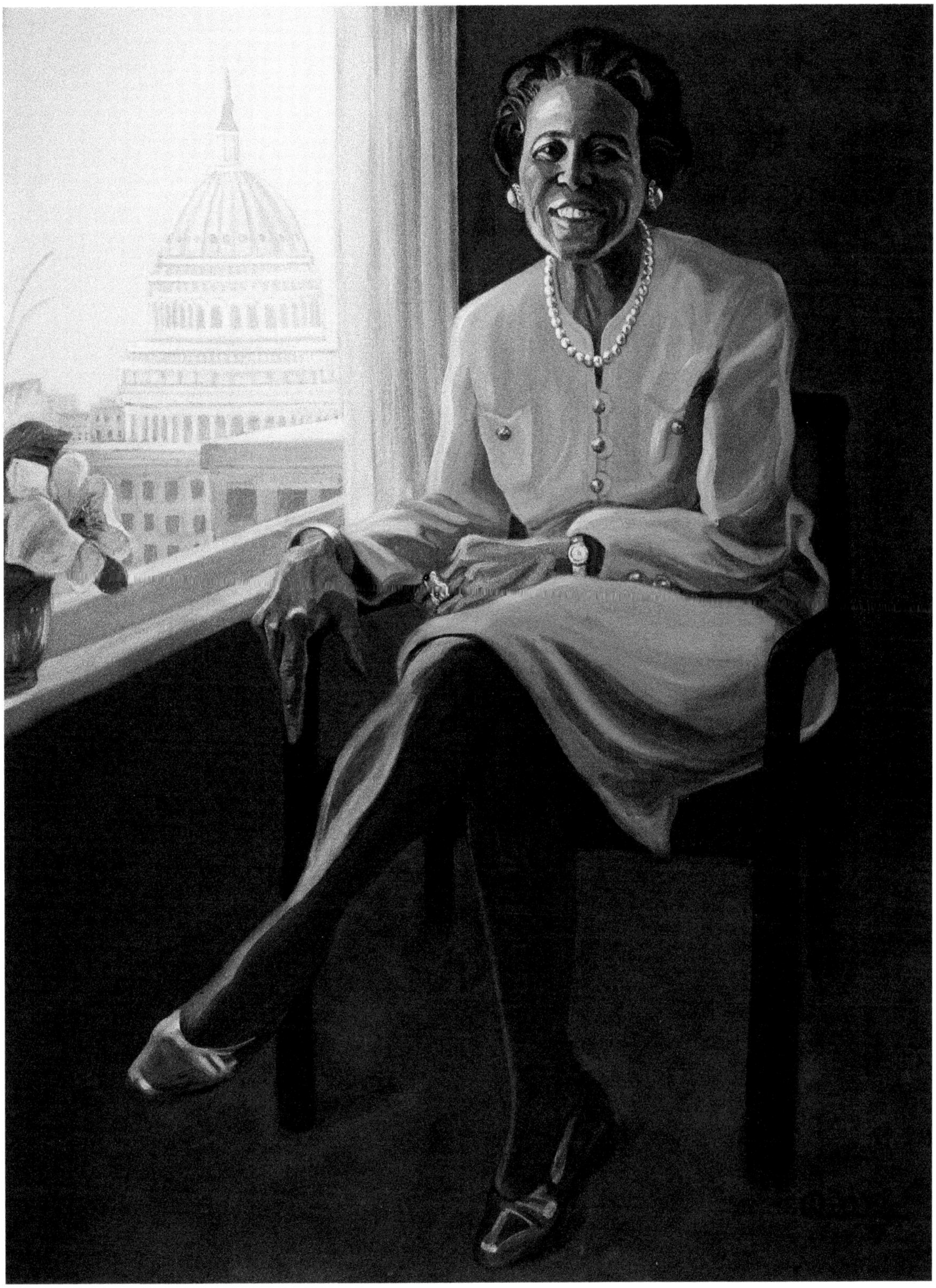

Painting of Margaret Dixon at 73

"I am part of something larger than myself and that makes life worthwhile."

Betty Friedan at 75

ACTIVIST, AUTHOR, MOTHER OF THE FEMINIST MOVEMENT

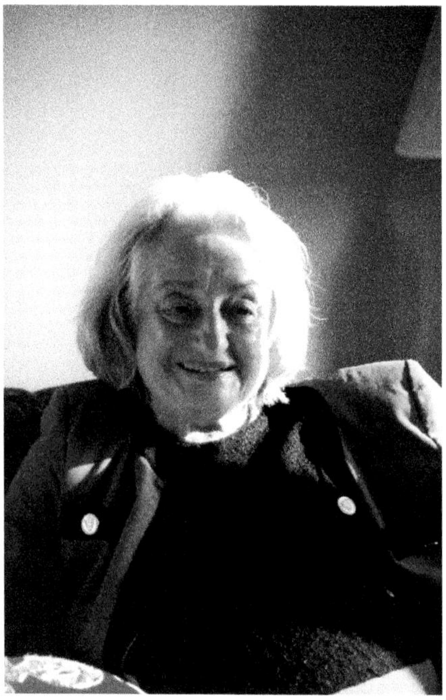

Betty Friedan at 75

I ADMIRED BETTY FRIEDAN FOR ALL HER contributions to the empowerment of women, so I looked up her phone number in Washington, D.C., phoned her, and asked if she would be part of my project. She agreed, and we made an appointment to meet at her apartment the following week. As scheduled, Richard and I arrived at 9:00 in the morning and knocked on her door. She brusquely opened it and yelled for us to be quick because she was very busy. In less than fifteen minutes, I conducted an interview, took 108 photographs (I managed to get one good picture of her as she was reflecting on the things that made life worthwhile), and was summarily told to get out! As the door slammed behind us, Richard and I stood frozen in the hallway, and stared at each other dumbfounded.

After that encounter, I felt reluctant to include her in my project. However, one morning six months later I woke up with the thought to paint her portrait. I realized that I had to let go of my judgments and the unpleasant experience of meeting her, and focus on my original reason for calling—my admiration for her lifelong passion and commitment to the cause of women's rights and her contributions to freedom and justice for women.

I painted the portrait of Betty in three and a half hours—record time, just like the interview. The National Portrait Gallery of the Smithsonian Institution purchased it, and it is now on permanent display in an exhibition entitled *20th Century Americans.*

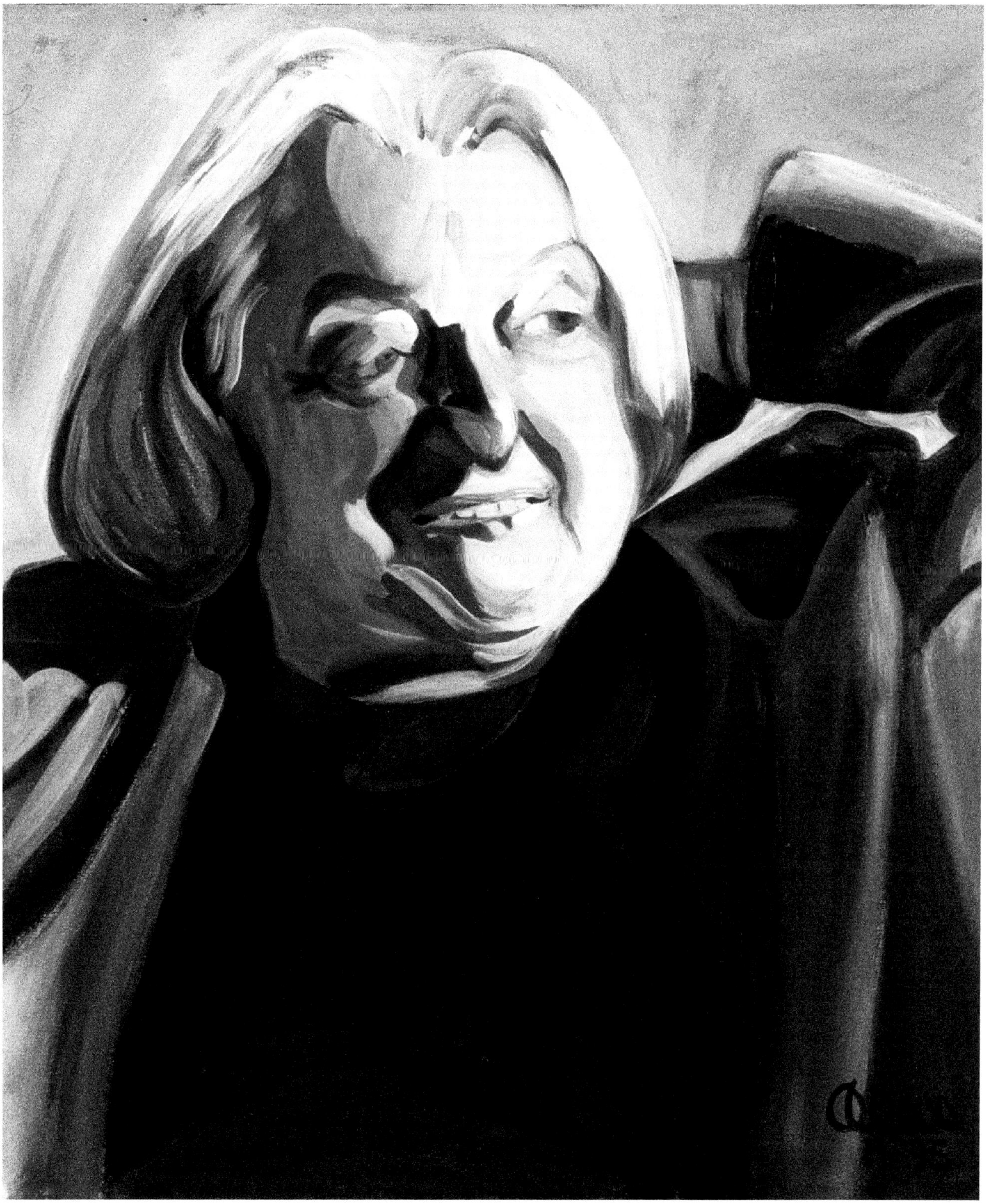

Painting of Betty Friedan at 75

"It's all in the loving touch."

Auntie Margaret (Kalehuamakaneoluluuonapali Ahuala Keilii) Machado at 81

Healer, Master Teacher of Hawaiian Lomilomi Massage

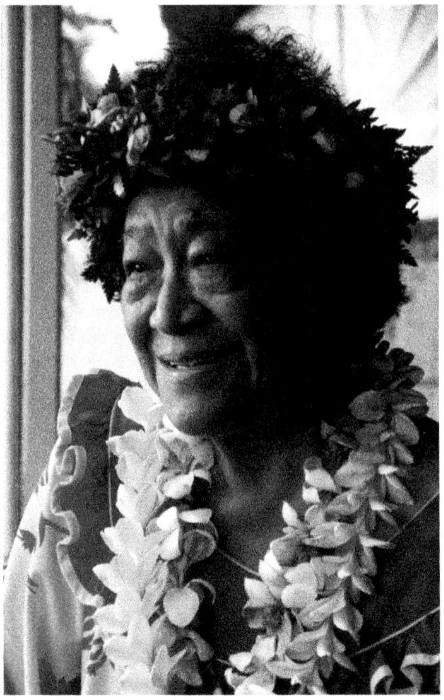

Auntie Margaret at 81

When we went to Hawaii, the locals recommended that we meet Auntie Margaret. (In Hawaii, the women elders are called Auntie.) She is a renowned teacher of Lomilomi, the ancient Hawaiian art of massage and healing bodywork. Auntie Margaret's school is in a small old wooden fisherman's house right on the picture-postcard-perfect, palm-tree-studded beach at Kealakekua Bay on the big island of Hawaii. People from all over the world come to learn this traditional form of healing from her. They bring their tents and camp at the school, cooking in the communal kitchen.

Auntie Margaret greeted us on the porch with a smile on her face, wearing a colorful Hawaiian muumuu. Around her neck and in her hair were many garlands of fragrant flowers, which had been given to her by students. She exuded warmth and naturalness. We sat on the porch overlooking the ocean for a long time, enjoying each other's company, the soft breezes, and peaceful setting. Auntie spoke about how important it is for people to be touched in a loving way. We were blessed and honored when Auntie Margaret blessed us both with a healing, and we were able to share her love through the touch of her hands.

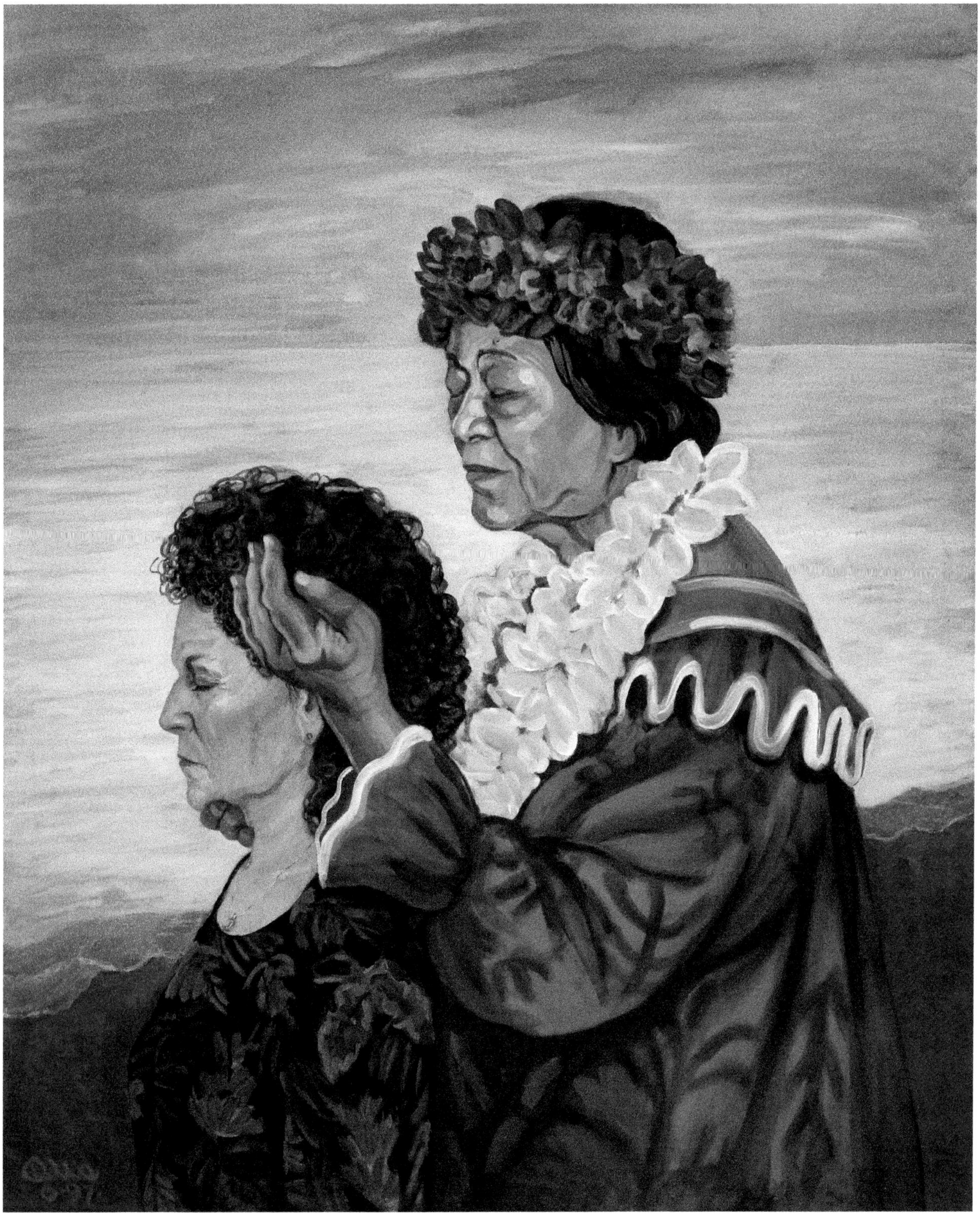

Painting of Auntie Margaret at 81

"I have so many things I am interested in,
I don't know what to leave out."

Edith Stauffer at 87

PSYCHOTHERAPIST, AUTHOR

"Life is wonderful,
people are wonderful.
I enjoy every day."

EDITH LIVES IN THE SAME TOWN WE DO. After hearing about her and the wonderful work she does, I knew that I would love to meet her, so I called and we made a date. We were lucky to find her at home because, at eighty-seven years old, she still travels the world giving lectures and workshops on the topic closest to her heart: unconditional love and forgiveness. She teaches that by loving ourselves and each other just as we are, and by forgiving ourselves and others, we can have happy and peaceful lives.

We spent several hours engaged in lively conversation with Edith in her charming office above a garage with windows overlooking her beautiful flower and vegetable garden. Here she spends time writing and seeing students and clients.

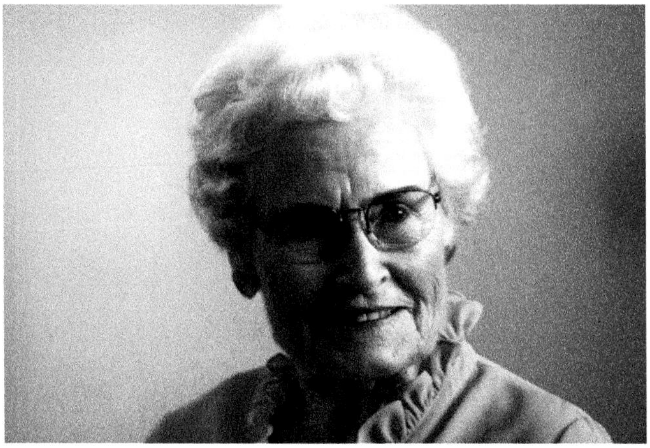

Edith Stauffer at 87

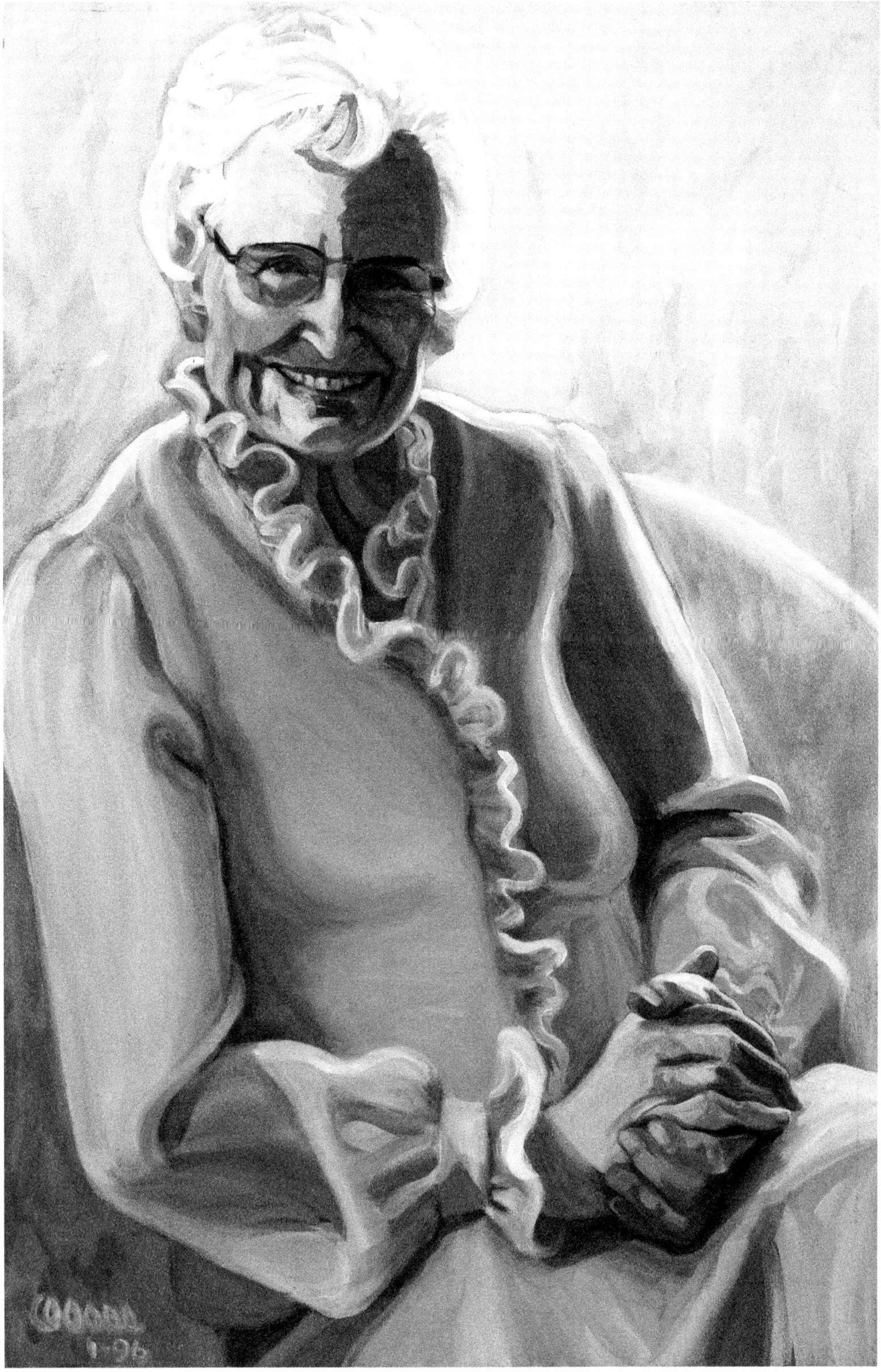

Painting of Edith Stauffer at 87

"Love, to me, is the only energy in the world.
Without love this world cannot exist at all."

Dominga Reyes at 83

PRESIDENT OF WORLD UNIVERSITY, BUDDHIST NUN

THE WORLD UNIVERSITY IS AN ACCREDited college that specializes in teaching about inner serenity and world peace. Each Sunday in its auditorium, which is decorated with symbols from all the major religions of the world, there is a nondenominational spiritual service.

Dominga was officiating the service on the day we met. A humble and tiny woman, she stood at the pulpit, and delivered her inspirational message. All of us in the congregation sat in rapt attention as we listened to this simple Buddhist nun. She said that in order to create peace in ourselves and peace on this earth, we must love, honor, and respect one another no matter what our age, race, or religion; that we must love, honor, and respect all living creatures; that we must love, honor, and respect our Mother Earth; that we are all interconnected and spring from the same source.

I wanted to depict Dominga in the painting as she was: a peaceful messenger of unity, urging the people of the earth to live in harmony with each other and with nature. I symbolized this by painting her in front of the earth, surrounded by a circle of golden light that is emblazoned with symbols from the major religions. In the corners of the painting are the four elements: air, fire, water, earth.

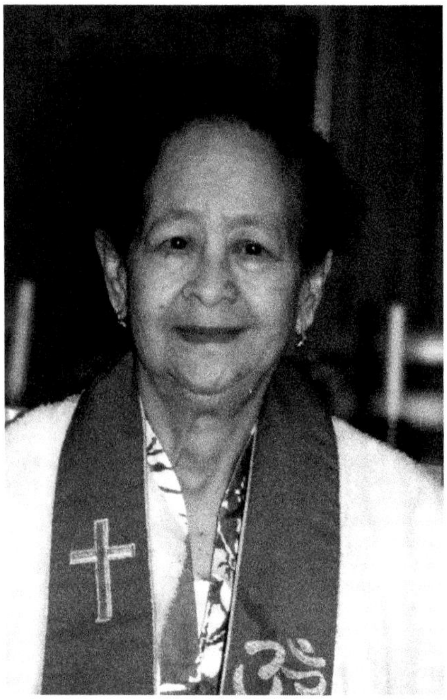

Dominga Reyes at 83

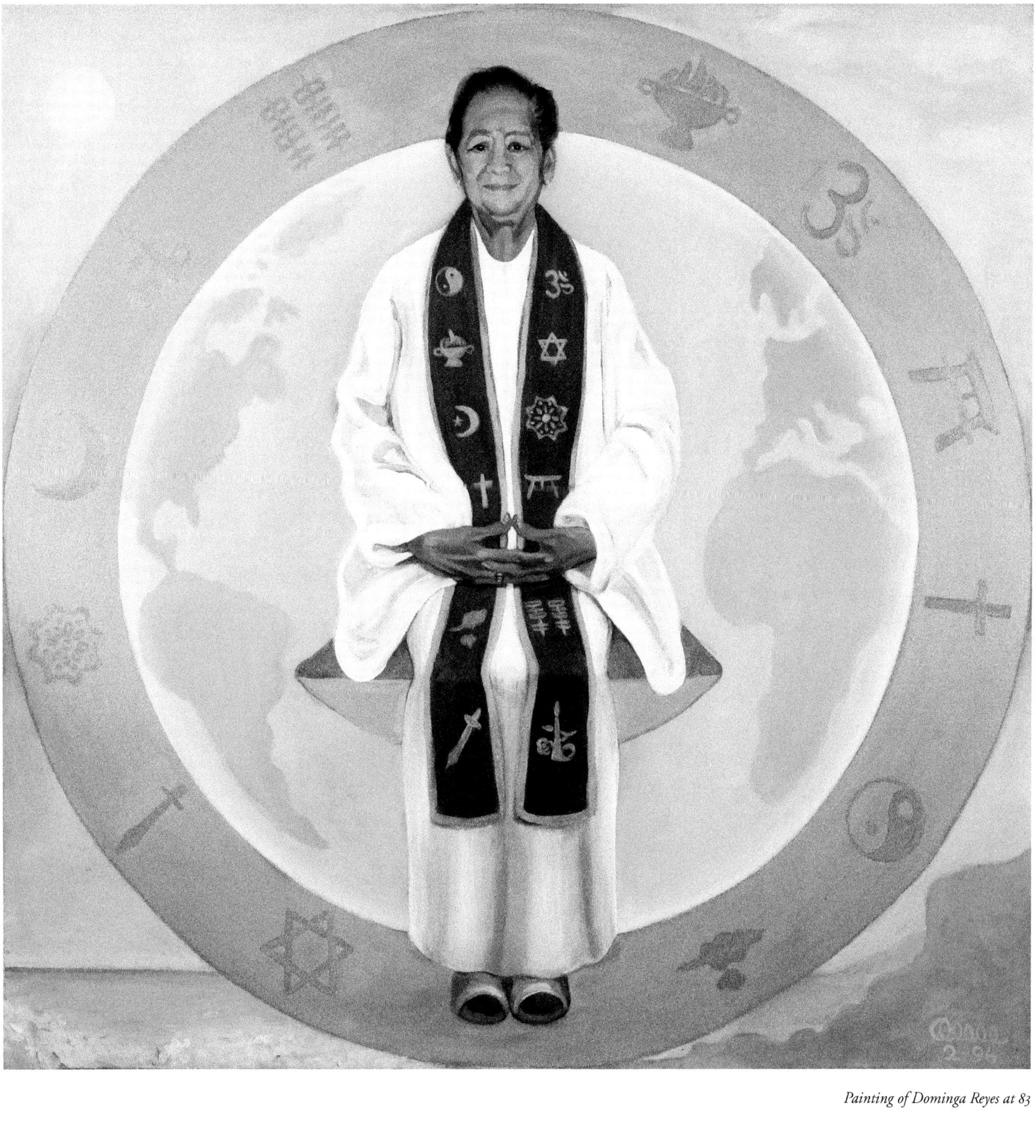

Painting of Dominga Reyes at 83

At this point in my life I really want to simplify things and get down to what is the most important: being useful in a way that connects to love and compassion."

Anna Halprin at 75

DANCER, DIRECTOR OF TAMALPA INSTITUTE, PERFORMANCE ARTIST

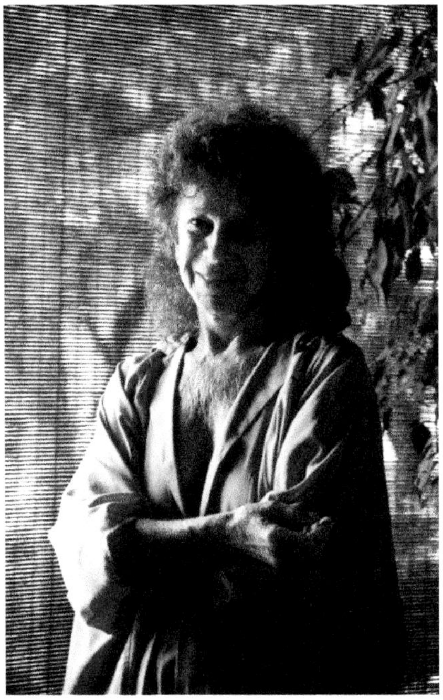

Anna Halprin at 75

RICHARD AND I HAD AN INSPIRING VISIT with Anna in her architecturally stunning, light-filled rustic home nestled in a grove of giant redwoods in Northern California. Within moments of our meeting, we were out in the forest, Anna was dancing with the trees, and I was photographing her. We ended the day in her cozy kitchen, sitting around the table, drinking tea, eating cookies, and talking about what makes her life worthwhile.

It was very affirming for me to meet a seventy-five-year-old woman who was physically fit and still living her passion by giving public dance performances, choreographing original dance pieces, and teaching and administrating a dance institute. Having survived life-threatening cancer many years ago, she finds great pleasure giving classes and workshops to cancer and AIDS patients using the expression of dance as a way of healing.

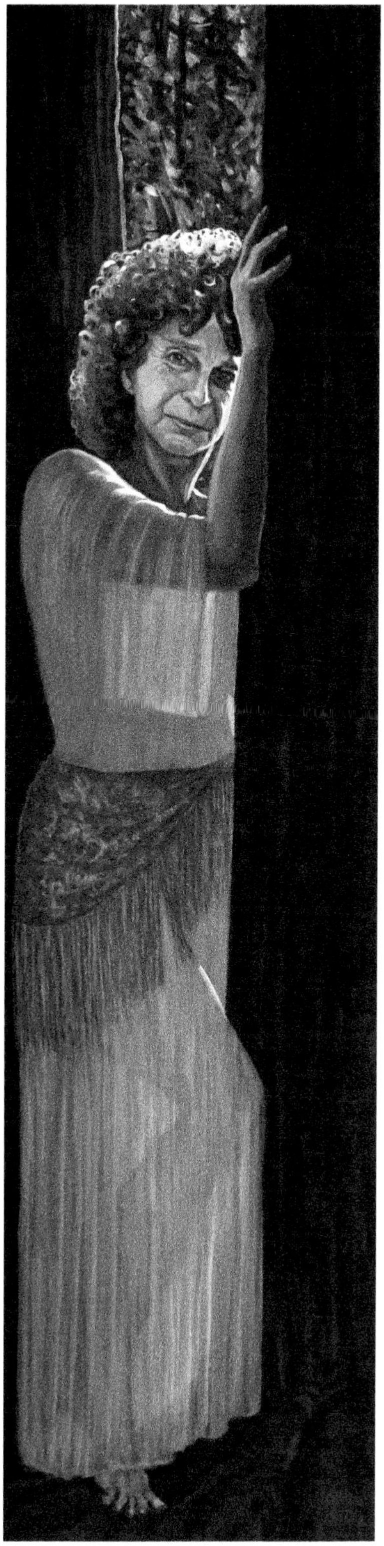

Painting of Anna Halprin at 75

"Working with different kinds of people enlarges my notions about diversity and challenges me to keep looking for what we all have in common."

"Appreciate each other. Thank each other.

Make no enemies. Have peace,

harmony, tranquility. Be humble."

Sosei Matsumoto at 83

Master of Japanese Tea Ceremony

One day I was perusing a senior newspaper and saw an article about Sosei Matsumoto, who is a master of the ancient art of the Japanese tea ceremony. It told how for over fifty years she has been one of America's most revered teachers of the 450-year-old Urasenke tradition of Chado, or way of tea. Chado teaches the Zen Buddhist principle that enlightenment can be achieved even in the most mundane task.

Entering Mrs. Matsumoto's serene and orderly traditional Japanese tearoom was a journey into another time and place. The woman standing before us, dressed in a beautiful silk kimono, was tiny, humble, and serene, yet she radiated quiet strength. We bowed to each other and she warmly invited us to partake in the tea ceremony. We sat on the floor facing her as she knelt on the tatami mat. Special tools, tea bowls, and powdered green tea were spread before her. Suspended by a chain from the ceiling, a kettle of hot water simmered over hot coals, which were sunk in a space below the floor. There was silent magic in the precision, balance, grace, and flow of her every movement as she prepared and served us tea.

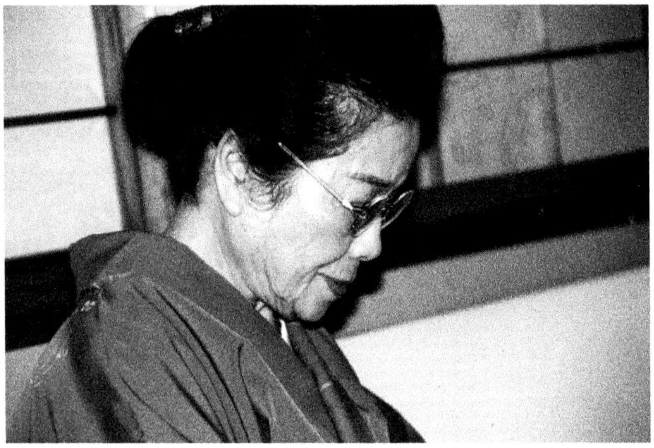

Sosei Matsumoto at 83

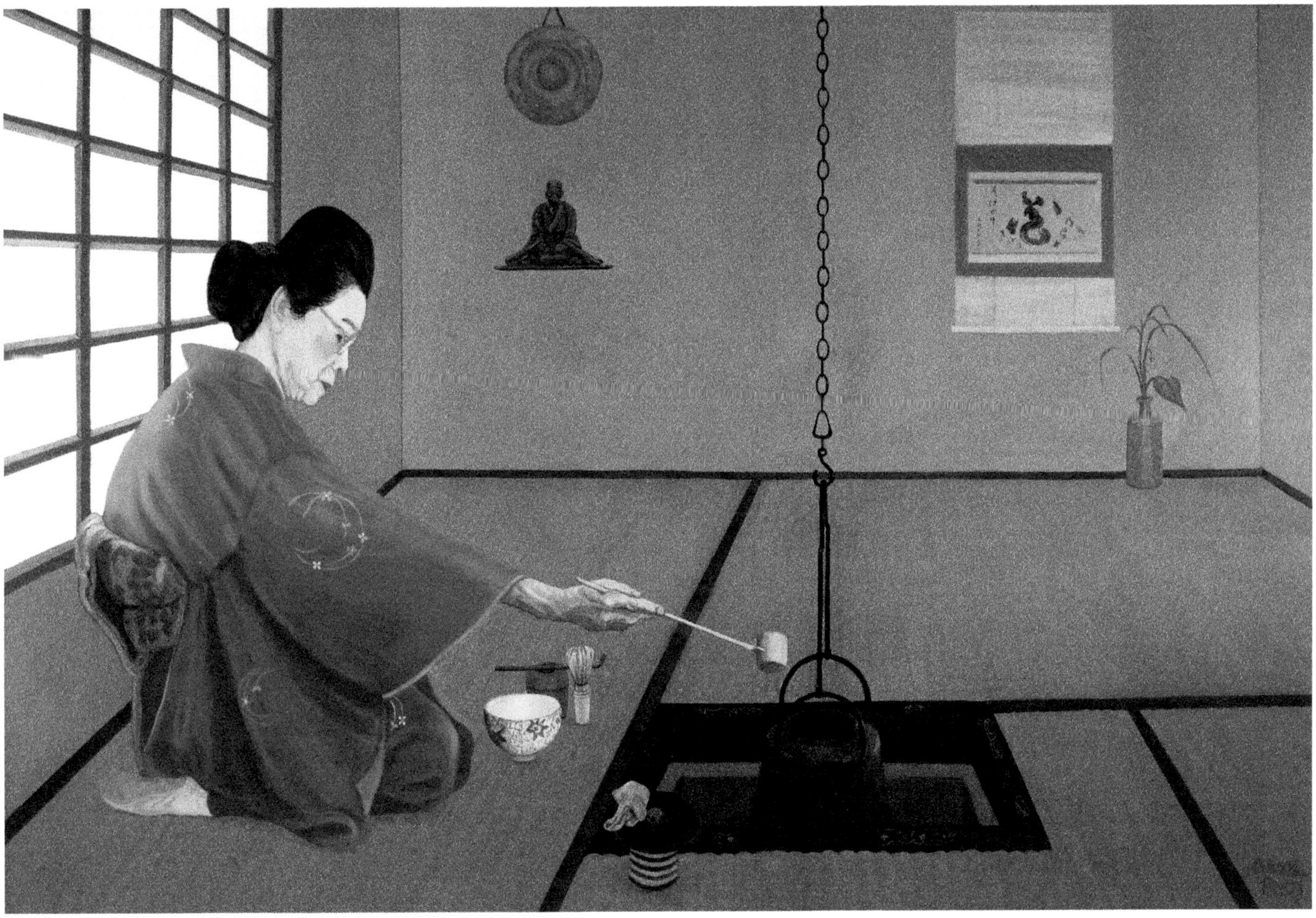

Painting of Sosei Matsumoto at 83

Fiona O'Connell at 81

POET, WRITER

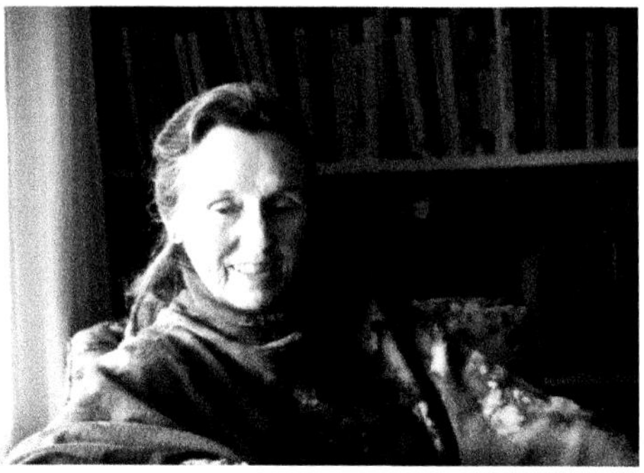

Fiona O'Connell at 81

FIONA WAS INTRODUCED TO ME BY A FRIEND. She is an ageless beauty who lives a simple hermit-like life with her partner, a young man in his forties. Every room in her warm and cozy home is covered from top to bottom with stuffed bookshelves. We spent hours nestled on her couch, talking about life. When I asked her what makes life worthwhile she said, "Just being alive—seeing light on the green trees, tasting food."

Expressing herself with words is her passion. Her gifts can be seen in this poem about aging.

"Makeup, high heels, sex object—
that is all peripheral to the main need, which
is to become an authentic creature who is not
a woman or a man, not a mechanical android,
but a person underneath the words."

What Is It Like to Be Old

By Fiona O'Connell

Before I'd begun to be old,
at seventy still giddy.
Not steady as the rocks
which chair Mona Lisa,
or the mirroring shield
that protects Perseus
from becoming stone,
one of my daughters asked
"What is it like to be old?"
"When I know I'll tell you."
I said, and waited to see.
Past eighty now,
more of time in my face
reaming the flesh of my years,
I think to answer her
but find words elusive.
"Age is a puzzler, Pat,
more a reflection of time
than consciousness dying.
It is not as it seems,
not simply appearance
receding as Goethe said.
That too, but a dance of days
performing an infinity,
stopping and starting before
resuming countlessness.
Not inching toward zero
but playing peek-a-boo
while I, quasi-butterfly
needing my nectar sip,
perform day to day,
breathe evenly,
sleep gratefully,
and work to articulate
what is notable about life.
Oldness is the sharp edge
of an absurd situation
teetering over
a poorly described void.
I take it to say: Eat well,
sleep well, feed the cat,
and the birds. Keep them apart,
and write. Write of
the amazement of moving on.

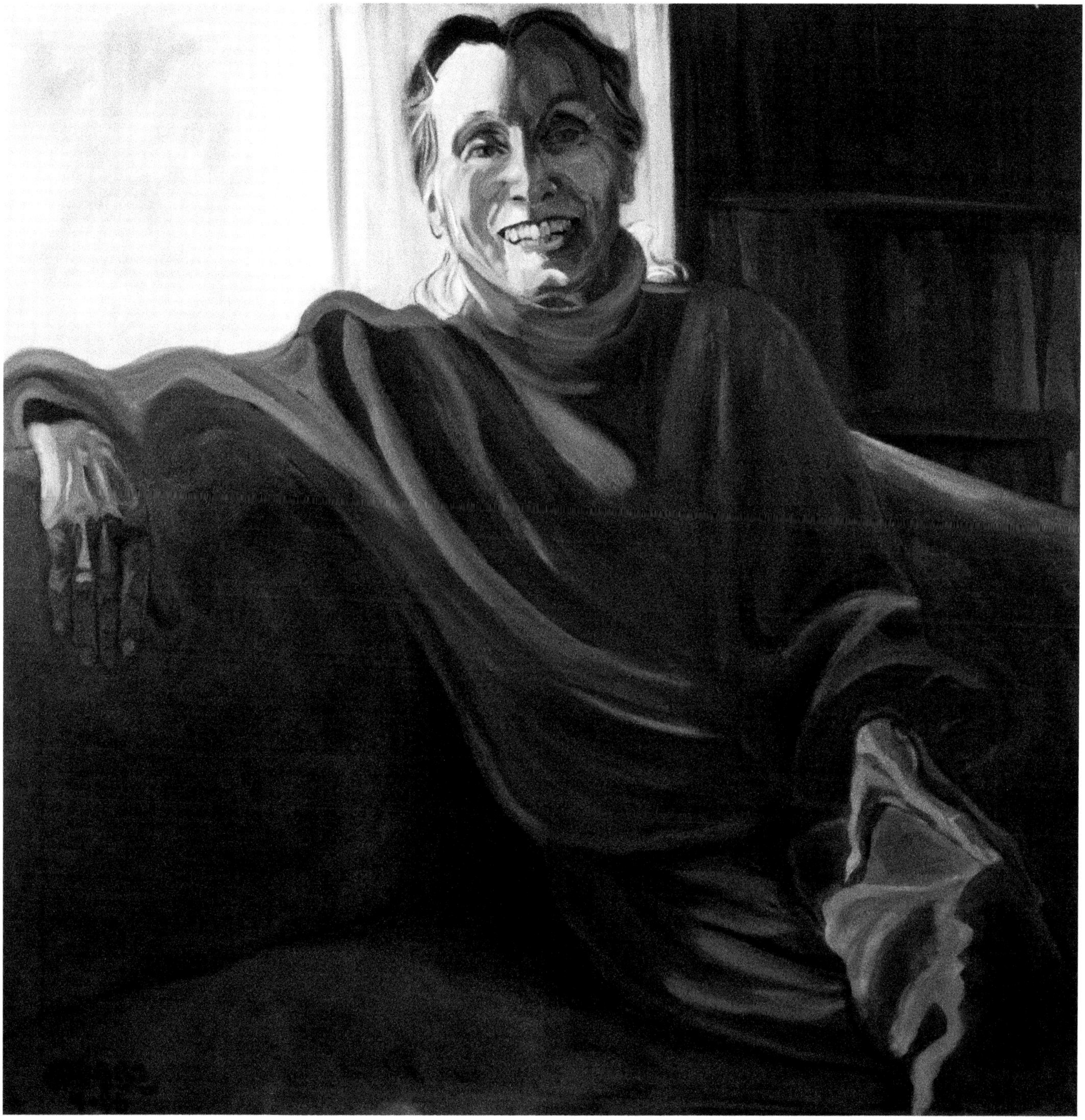

Painting of Fiona O'Connell at 81

"It doesn't matter if you have wrinkles on your face as long as you don't have them in your heart."

Julia Alvarez at 72

UN AMBASSADOR FROM THE DOMINICAN REPUBLIC

"Some people are old when they are young, and young when they are old."

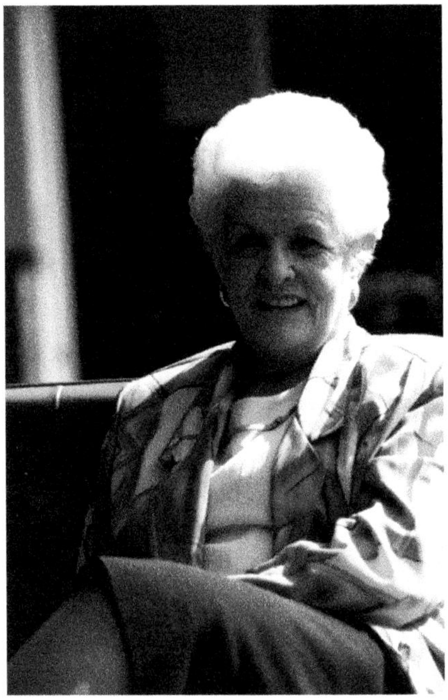

Julia Alvarez at 72

THE UNITED NATIONS BUILDING IN NEW York City is an exciting place to visit, especially when you are being guided by Julia Alvarez, the ambassador from the Dominican Republic. Julia is a strong advocate for the elderly in the United States and in her own country. She is a compact ball of energy and the kind of woman who won't take no for an answer. A few years ago her leg was badly injured and the doctor said she would never walk again. Yet there we were, running through the hallways and chambers of the UN building, trying to catch up with her.

We spent the entire day together, had lots of laughs, and enjoyed a beautiful lunch in the ambassador's dining room. We visited the empty UN Security Council Room, where Julia sat in the Secretary General's chair, banged the gavel, and solemnly called our meeting to order!

Julia has so much to say about living life in a positive way, and so much passion for life in spite of the many hardships she has experienced.

"A lot of people look toward the end of life as a sad period. For me, it has been wonderful. You learn that life is a passage from one stage to another. Try to enjoy every stage of life, because each one has precious moments."

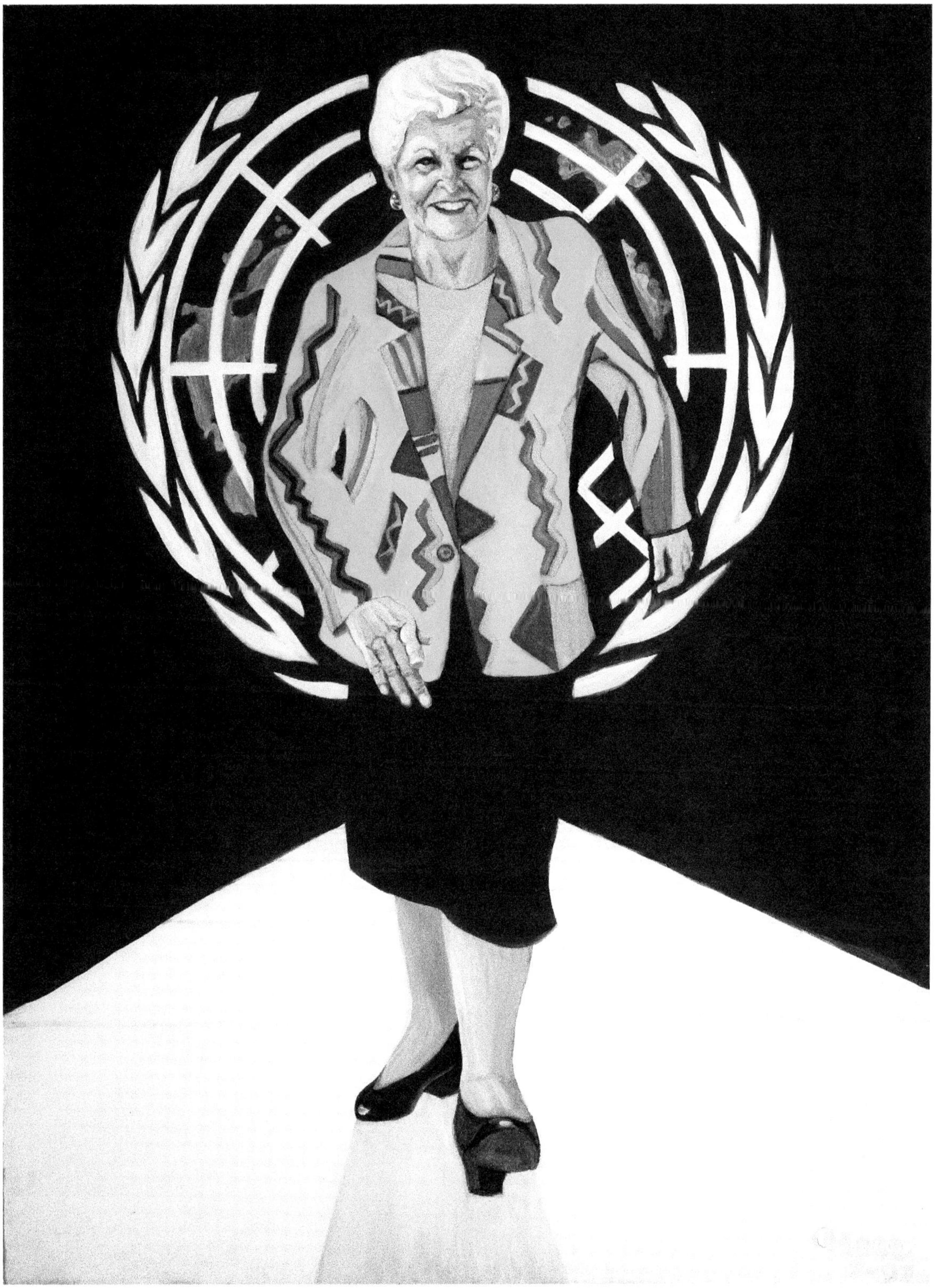

Painting of Julia Alvarez at 72

"I am involved in something important: helping to open people's minds."

Joy Mills at 76

Author, Lecturer, International Vice President of Krotona Institute of Theosophy

"Life is exciting—every day is a new opportunity."

Joy embodies the principles she teaches as she travels the world giving lectures and workshops as a representative of Krotona Institute of the Theosophical Society, an organization that promotes the spiritual uplifting of humanity. Krotona has a base in the town where we live. Joy resides here, and notices of her lectures are often posted in the newspaper. I am attracted to people who are focused on creating and promoting peace, so I called her.

Richard and I spent a lovely afternoon visiting in Joy's comfortable light-filled apartment. She told us that, if she died today, she had had a glorious life, and that if she was still alive in a few years, when she retired from so much traveling she would begin to do some writing. Her first name is perfect because she truly radiates happiness, humor, contentment, and quiet peace. Joy is a joy to be with.

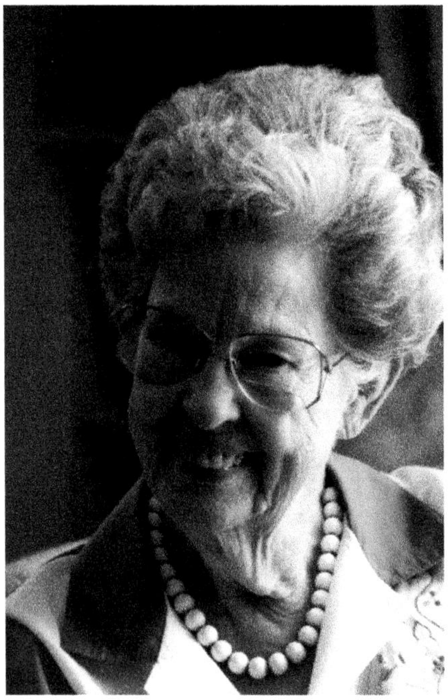

Joy Mills at 76

"If every individual really lived to the highest—not taking but giving, not wanting, not being greedy, caring for nature—the world would be a better place."

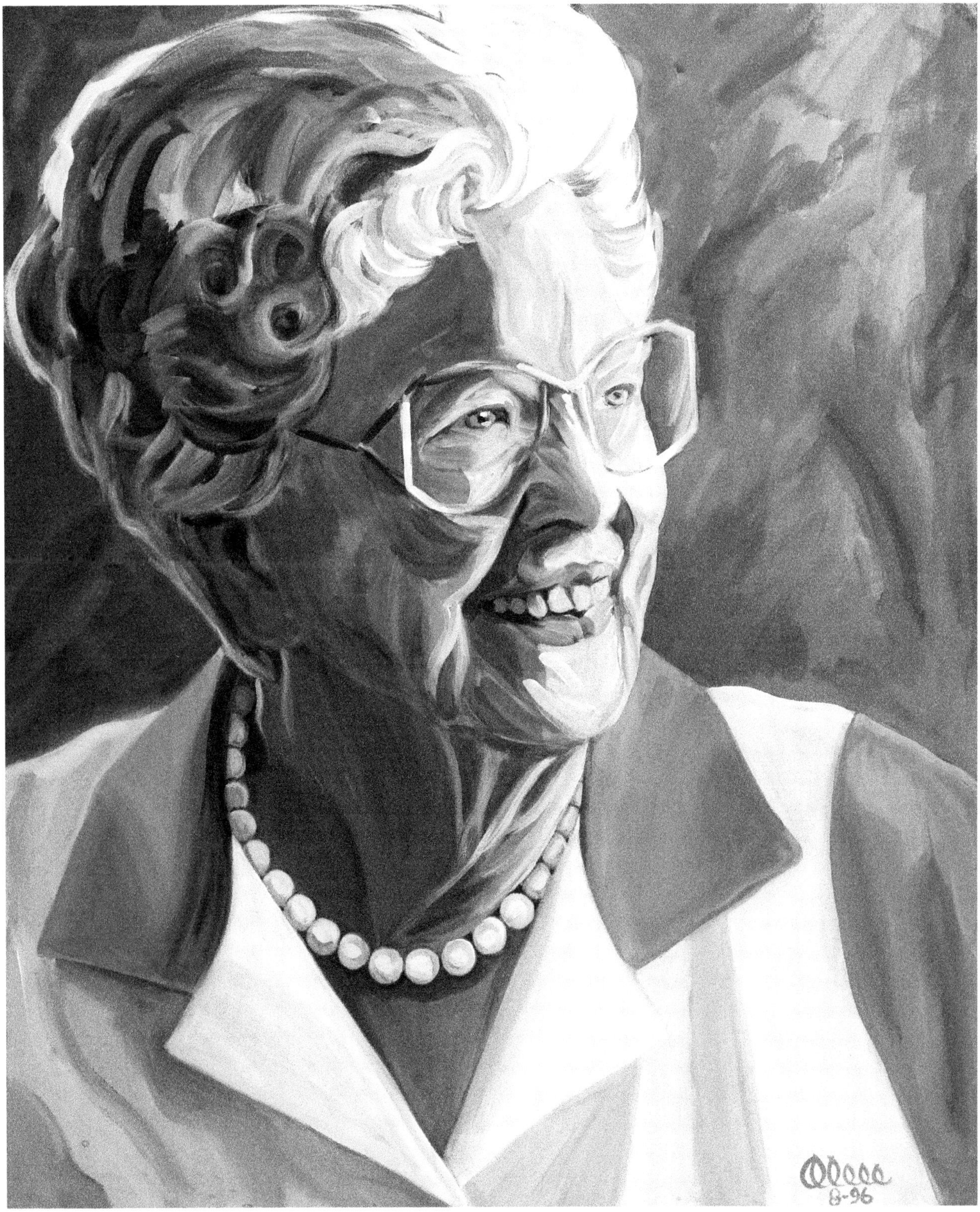

Painting of Joy Mills at 76

Sally Lillienthal at 77

PEACE ACTIVIST

RICHARD AND I WERE IN SAN FRANCISCO visiting my daughter, Angela, when I read a newspaper article about Sally Lillienthal. She is the founder and president of Ploughshares Fund—a grant-making foundation whose purpose is the elimination of nuclear war. The article described how, at seventy-seven years of age, she is still a dynamo who hasn't paused since her college days, pursuing concerns that have ranged from art and politics to civil and human rights. At this time in her life, Sally is focused on promoting world peace and curtailing nuclear proliferation. Realizing that she would be an inspiration to me as well as others, I decided to phone her.

We arranged to meet the next day at her art-filled home overlooking San Francisco Bay. It was an honor to interview and paint this woman who has put her time, energy, and resources on the line for peace and justice in the world.

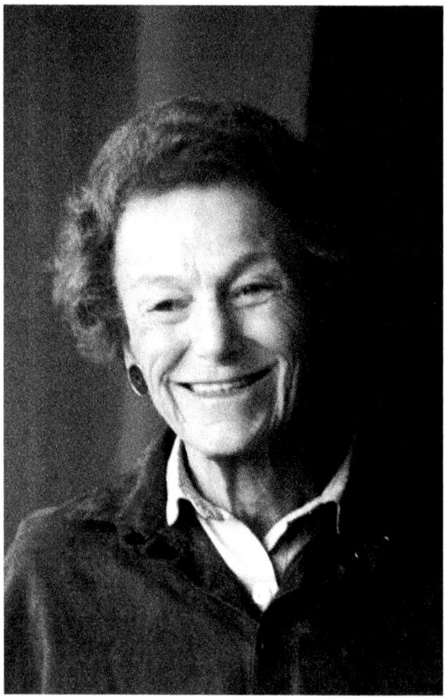

Sally Lillienthal at 77

"Be deeply interested in something outside yourself. Do something that matters and is nourishing."

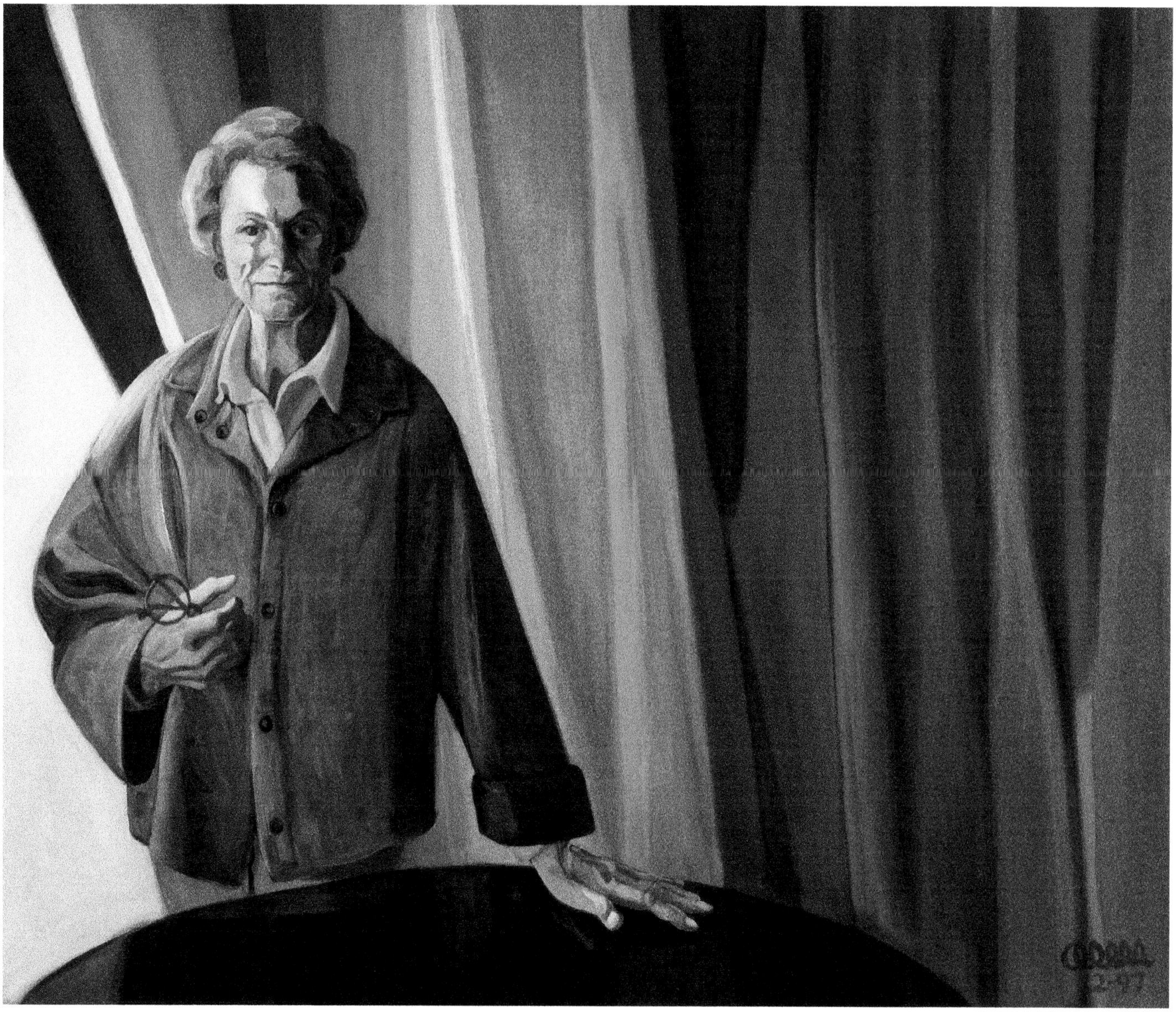

Painting of Sally Lillienthal at 77

"I don't let my limitations stop me

and I am thankful for that."

Mama Pat (Pat Patterson) at 73

SINGER, GOSPEL CHOIR DIRECTOR

"I have never been busier in my life."

FRIENDS OF OURS WHO LIVE IN SANTA Barbara, California, told us that if we wanted a dose of inspiration, we had to go to a gospel music performance by Mama Pat and her choir. The gospel choir is composed almost entirely of Caucasian men and women. Mama Pat's singing is heartfelt, and she is able to transmit her passion for gospel to her choir. When the music began, the whole audience was rocking back and forth, clapping hands and stomping feet to the soulful music, belted out with feeling by the choir members. When the choir makes guest appearances at African American churches, they become ambassadors of good will.

I was moved by the fact that even though Mama Pat suffers from many physical disabilities, she continues to follow her bliss and inspire others to spread goodwill through music.

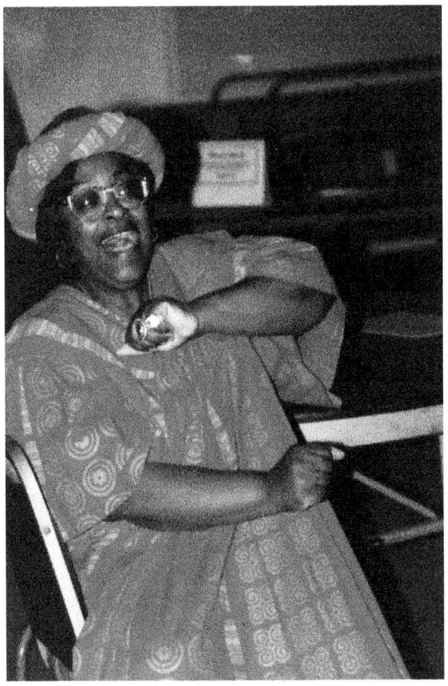

Mama Pat at 73

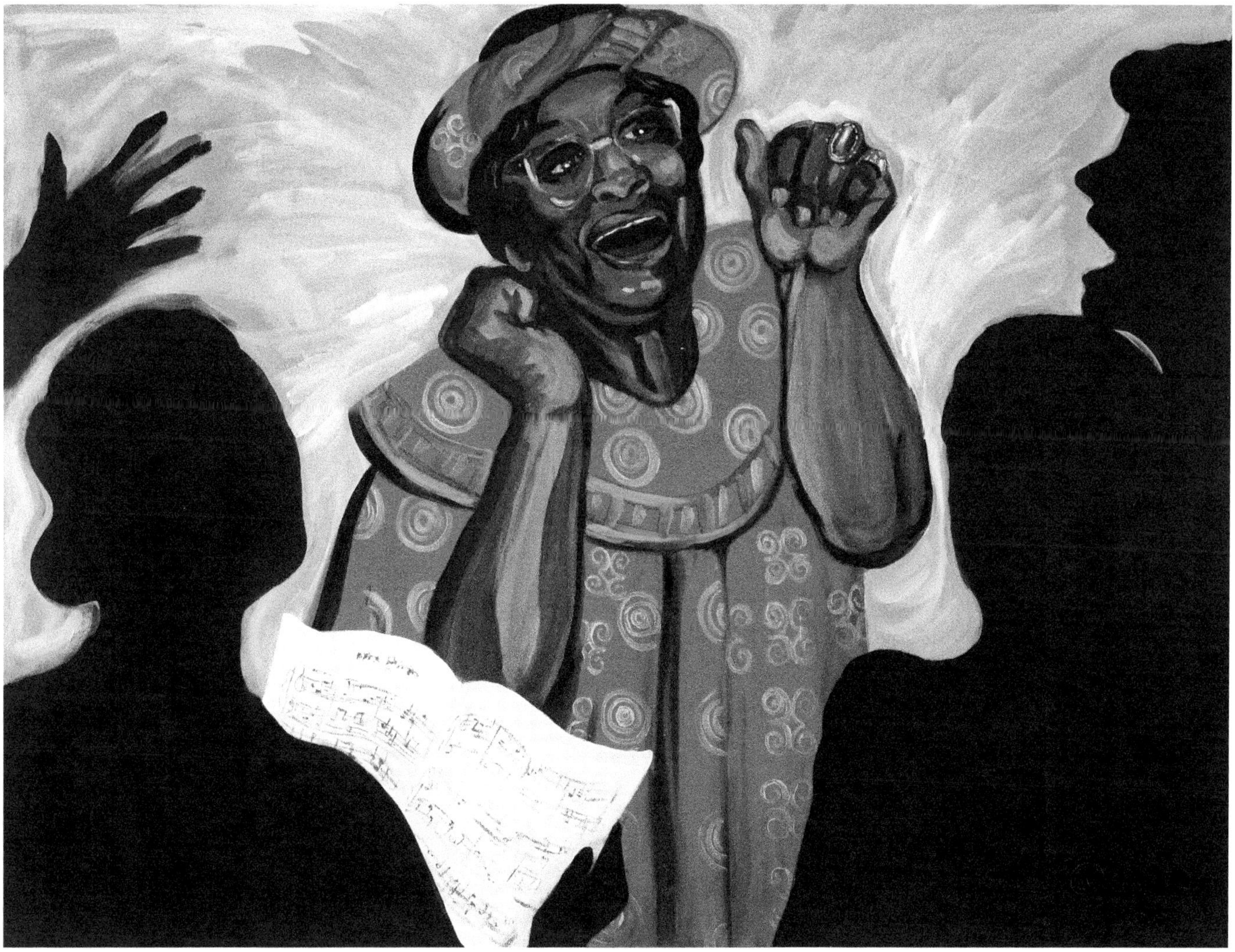

Painting of Mama Pat at 73

"Music is one of the greatest ways of communicating—
it crosses barriers, opens doors, and touches people."

"Music has always been in my life—

it is part of my spiritual heritage."

Frances Blaisdell at 84

MUSICIAN, MUSIC TEACHER

WE WERE INTRODUCED TO FRANCES BY one of her students. We met in her lovely Northern California home on a beautiful spring day. Seated on her patio, we enjoyed cookies and tea and warm conversation. Frances picked up her flute and gave us a beautiful interlude by Debussy. She played the lyrical melodies with so much feeling that we were transported into a magical world of sound and color.

Frances was a pioneer for women classical musicians, though she said that wasn't her intention. Rather, she was simply following her heart and her passion for playing classical music on the woodwinds. At a time when there was a great deal of prejudice against women who played anything other than piano and violin in the orchestra, Frances became the first female woodwind student at the prestigious Juilliard School of Music and the first woman woodwind player in the New York Philharmonic.

At eighty-four years old, Frances still is following her passion and playing her flute. She spends several days a week teaching woodwinds and inspiring students at Stanford University.

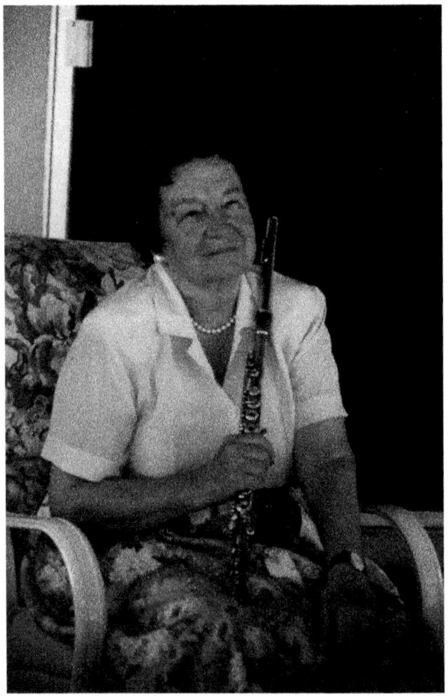

Frances Blaisdell at 84

"I would rather practice than eat."

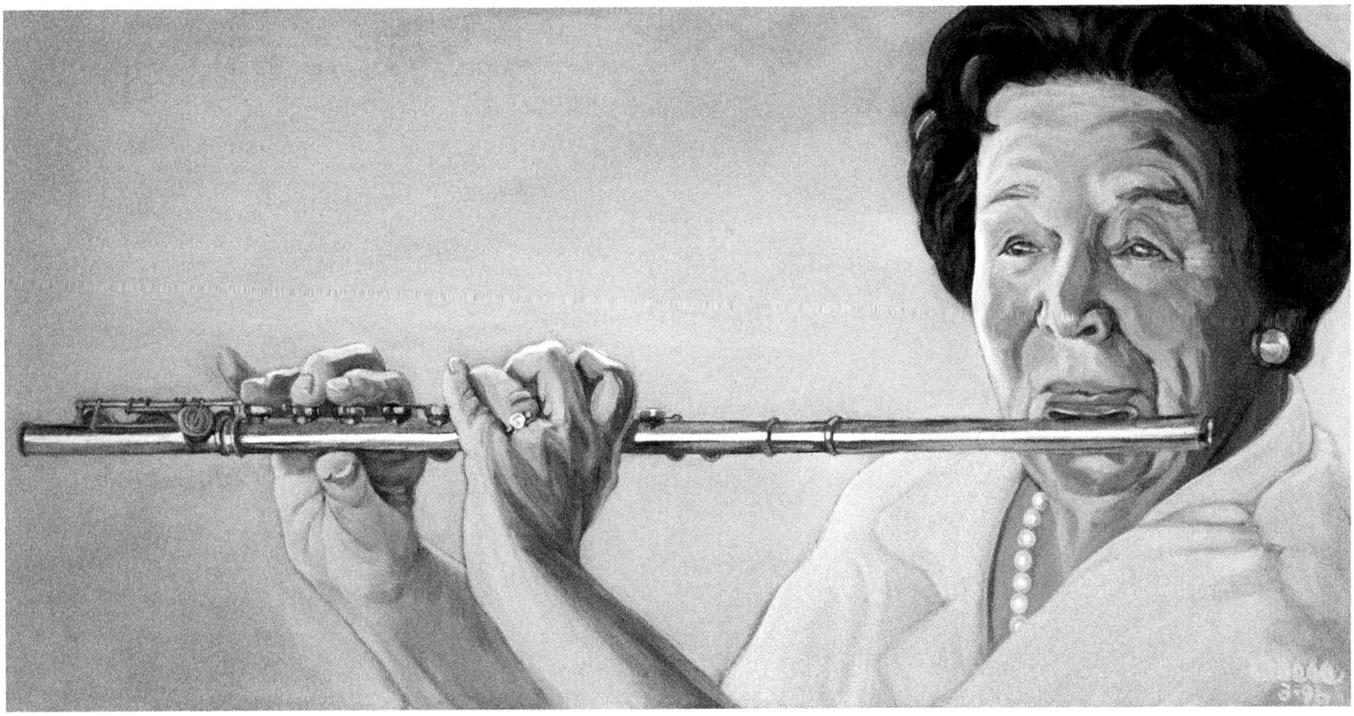

Painting of Frances Blaisdell at 84

"I don't focus on age.

We only have today."

"Remember all the blessings of the moment, don't forget your dreams, and be a loving person."

Margaret Cruz at 81

LAWYER, POLITICAL ACTIVIST, BREAST CANCER FOUNDATION FOUNDER

"Keep the faith."

AT THE DOORWAY OF THEIR SAN FRANCISCO home, we were greeted by Frank Cruz, Margaret's husband, whom she calls a "saint." As he ushered us into their living room, a vibrant and energetic woman welcomed us with a smile on her face. I instantly felt at home. Although I had only known her for a split second, it was as if we had been friends forever.

Margaret is a down-to-earth, fearless, religious, and loving person who says it like she sees it. She keeps company with the most humble people as well as U.S. presidents. Hanging on her office wall are many awards, photos of family and of herself with political dignitaries, as well as prints of Abraham Lincoln and the Virgin of Guadalupe. At age sixty-one, she received her law degree and practiced immigration law, doing lots of *pro bono* work. She is often invited to be a keynote speaker at graduations and other organization events.

Margaret is also a cancer survivor. After she was diagnosed and treated for breast cancer, she realized that Latina women had few resources and little information available in Spanish about the disease. To rectify the situation, she founded the Margaret Cruz Latina Breast Cancer Foundation and has received many grants, awards, and donations to further her work. Her life is devoted to service to her fellow human beings.

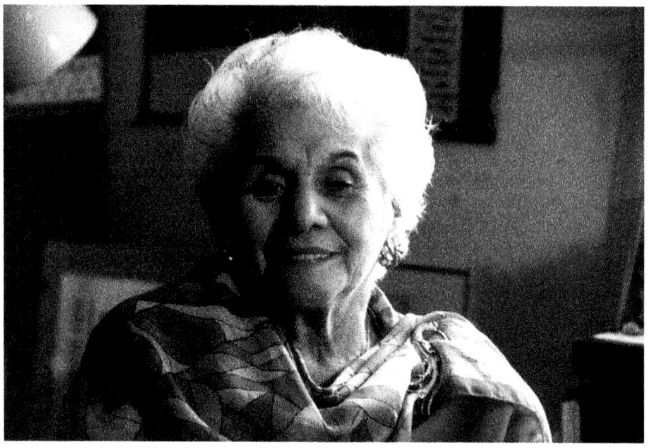

Margaret Cruz at 81

"Treat everybody alike—with some dignity, as human beings. They are a reflection of yourself."

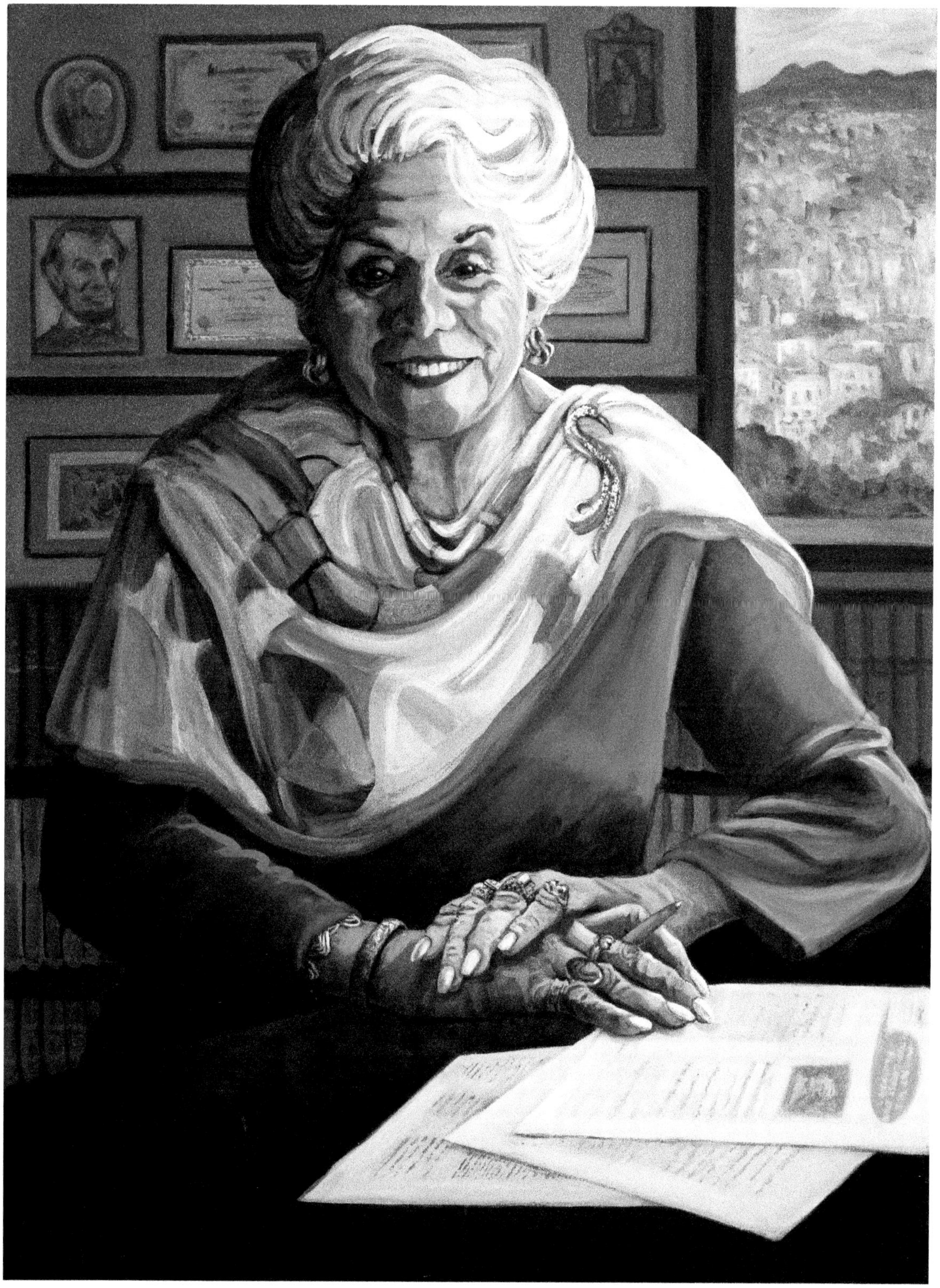

Painting of Margaret Cruz at 81

"Be old enough to know better,

but young enough to experiment and try things."

Rosalea Murphy at 84

RESTAURATEUR, COOKBOOK AUTHOR

"Live life to the hilt."

ROSALEA MURPHY IS A GREAT COOK, AND it is because of her delicious recipes and welcoming atmosphere that her Pink Adobe Restaurant in Santa Fe, New Mexico, is one of the most famous dining places in the Southwest. During a vacation, we were fortunate to meet with Rosalea in her restaurant. We were guided to her table in the corner, where she was waiting for us. From this table she presides over her domain. Many well-known artists, writers, and musicians have gathered at her table, sharing ideas and eating her tasty dishes. We were treated to a delicious lunch and had such a great time visiting, taking photographs, and conducting the interview, that we ended up staying for dinner.

I was impressed that at eighty-four years old, Rosalea was still actively involved in the day-to-day running of her restaurant, welcoming the many regular customers, creating new recipes, writing cookbooks, painting, and having fun. Her zest for life was obvious.

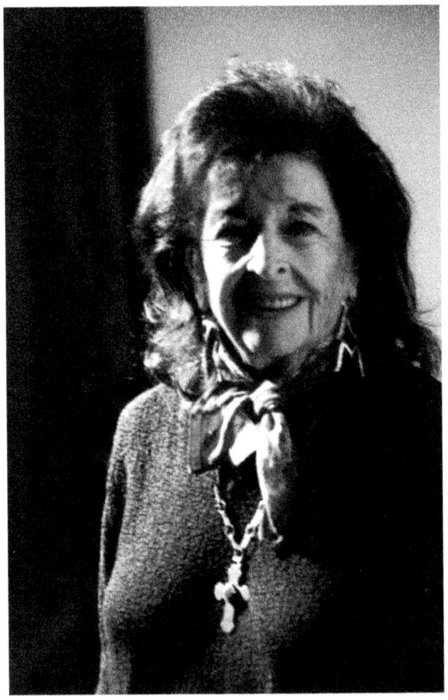

Rosalea Murphy at 84

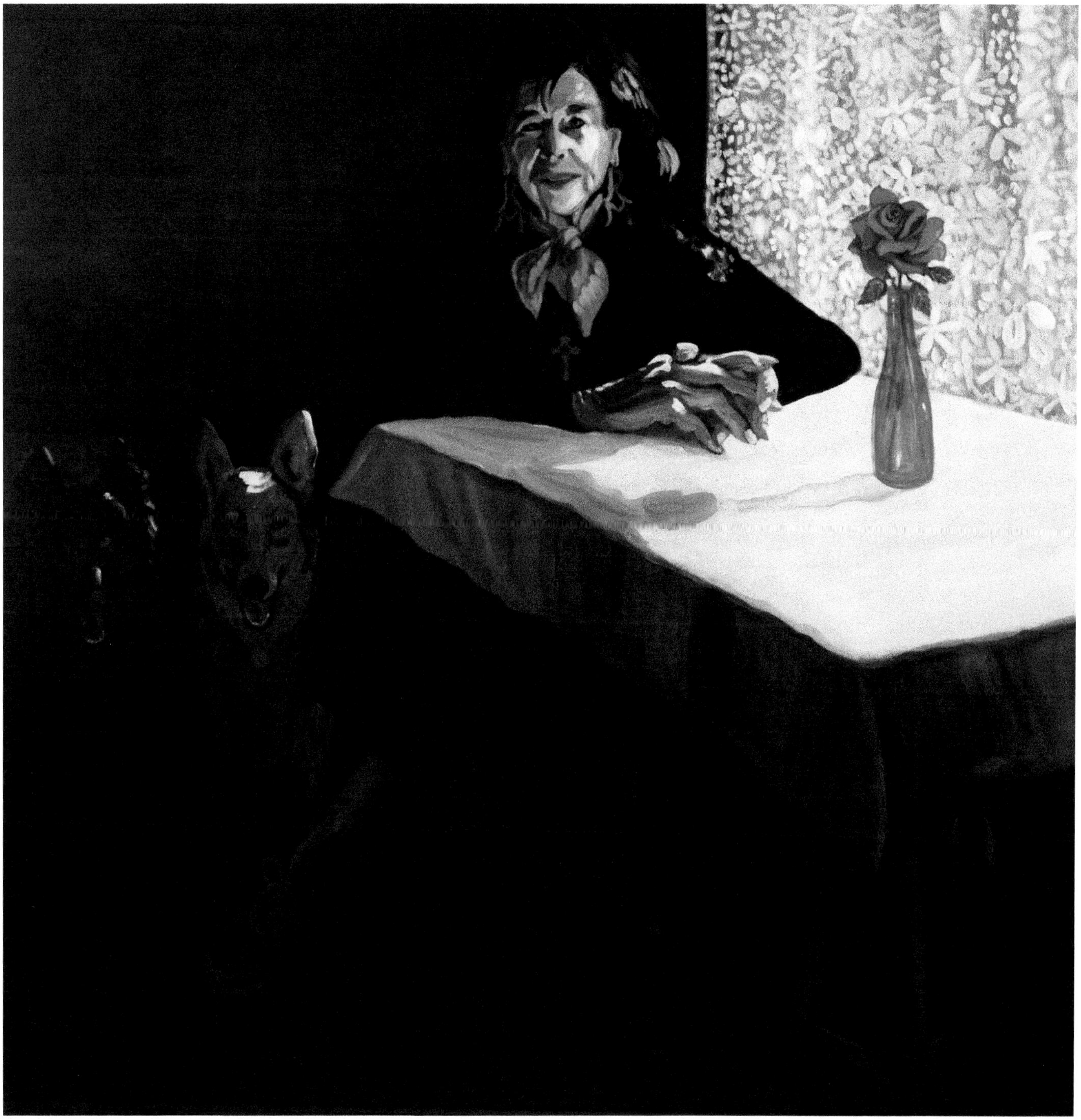

Painting of Rosalea Murphy at 84

"We must find out that we are not spirit-centered, not self-centered, not mind-centered, not body- or brain-centered, but virgin-soul centered."

Marie Hall at 93

AUTHOR, METAPHYSICIAN

MARIE WAS SUCH AN AGELESS, VIBRANT, and animated ball of energy that it was hard to believe that she was ninety-three years old. Her passion and commitment to her mission in life—to communicate about universal and transcendental truths—was very inspiring to me.

At one point while she was escorting us around her home, enthusiastically talking a mile a minute, her mind seemingly racing through the cosmos, she dramatically flung open double closet doors to show us some of the works she had authored. Revealed were scores of books piled in stacks that filled the entire space from floor to ceiling. *Introducing Macrocosmic Solar Redemptive Virgin Love Truth* is the title of one of her many books.

Her intellect was so out there that I painted her with the earth in the background.

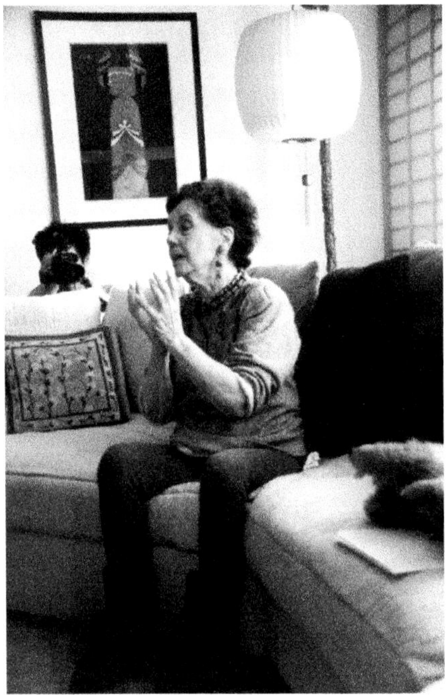

Marie Hall at 93

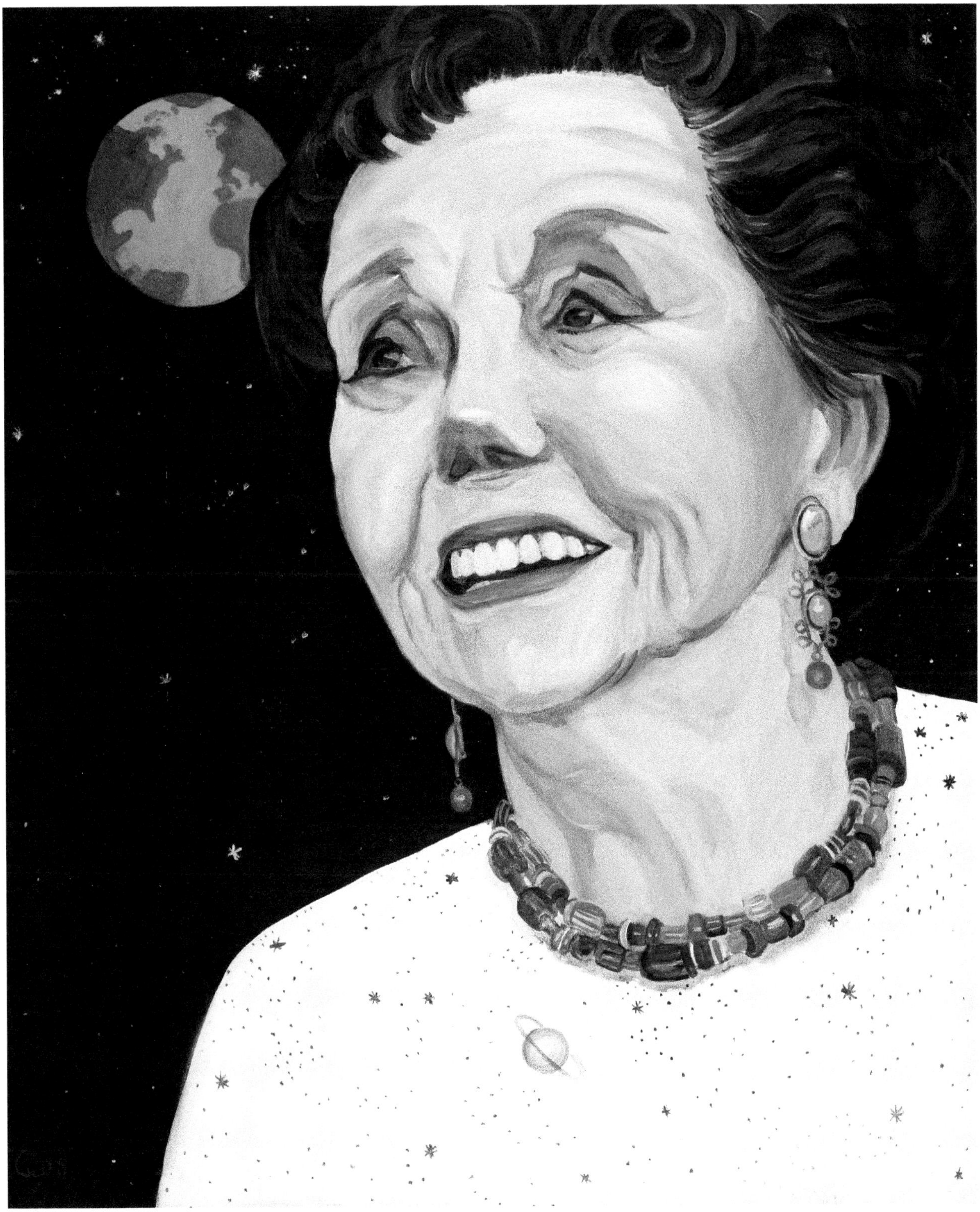

Painting of Marie Hall at 93

"It is privilege and honor, and I feel blessed to work on people. I love to touch."

Eve Venturi at 84

CHIROPRACTOR

"Be in love with what you do."

I WAS FINISHED WITH THE *Women of Age* series until I realized it would not be complete without including my dear friend Eve. We met several years ago when I was referred to her for a chiropractic adjustment. It was love at first sight and touch. We became immediate friends.

At eighty-four, Eve is still a practicing chiropractor who has the strength of a lioness and the gentleness of a lamb. When she works on my body, it is as if she has eyes on her fingertips and can "see" inside of me. Eve is always telling me how much she appreciates her life, friends, and family; how blessed she is to be a chiropractor; how much she loves her work; and what a privilege it is to touch with her hands and help people.

Anyone who is treated by Eve is not only touched with her hands, but also with her heart.

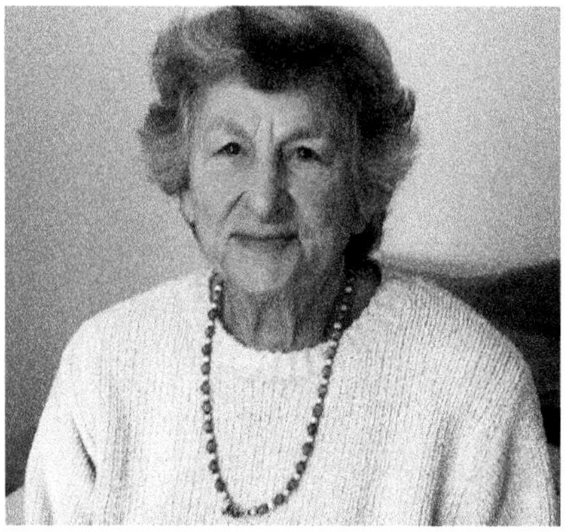

Eve Venturi at 84

"Be yourself—be happy that you are a woman."

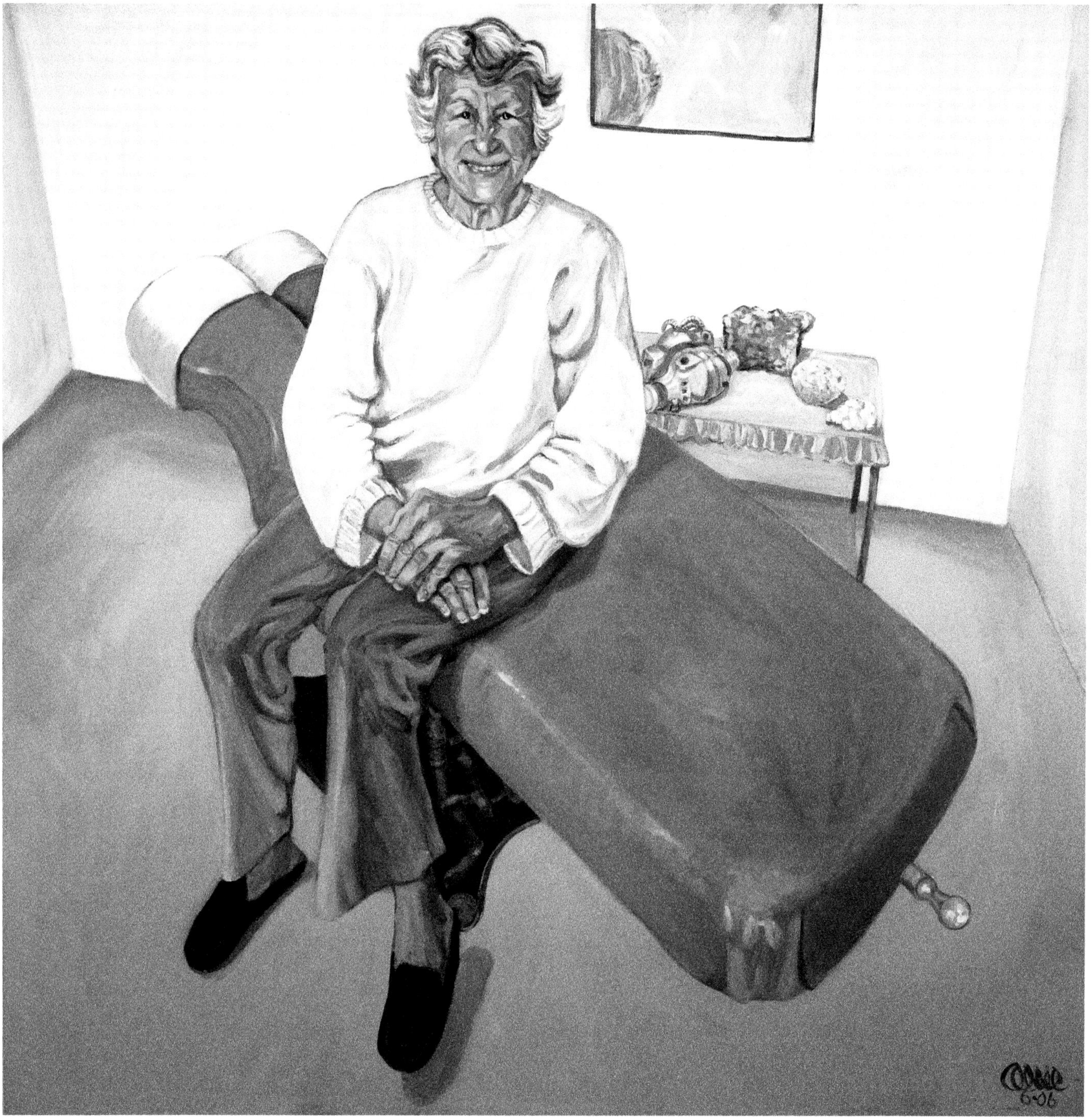

Painting of Eve Venturi at 84

"Envejecer es to destino.
Madurar es to decision."

"Aging is your destiny.
Maturing is your decision."

—WRITING ON A RETABLO FROM MEXICO

Naked Old Men

RICHARD

THERE IS A PASSAGE IN THE MAHABHARATA, ONE OF THE EPIC Indian philosophical poems, where the sage Yudhisthira is asked, "What is the most amazing thing in life?" He replies, "People see others dying around them, yet never remember that they too will die."

Somewhere in our psyches we unconsciously hold on to the delusion that everything will remain as it is now. We close our eyes to the fact that we will age, lose our health, and die one day. Once in a while, an event occurs that shocks us and breaks down that delusion of permanence—an undefended glance at our aging face in the mirror, a high school reunion, an illness, a death in the family. At these times we experience a tangible sense of how temporary life is. For a short while, everything becomes a bit more precious. Usually, the feeling soon evaporates, and we become caught up in the delusion of permanence again. But, never completely. Those experiences of our mortality leave a residue, and that residue can lead us to contract in fear, or open up to profound transformation. The Indian tale of Prince Siddhartha is an example.

Before Siddhartha was born, it was prophesied that he would be either a great king or a great holy man. His father, the king, wanted Siddhartha to take over the kingdom when he grew up, so he confined him to the castle grounds, making sure he was exposed only to the pleasant, comfortable surroundings of the court. This is how Siddhartha spent his childhood. When he grew to be a young man, Siddhartha prevailed upon his servant to take him for a chariot ride outside the castle gates. There he encountered a sick person, an old person, and a corpse. These experiences deeply disturbed the young prince. Eventually, they led him to renounce the crown and begin on the path that would lead him to become a great, enlightened teacher—the Buddha.

As we grow older, sickness, aging, and death become more real and take on greater meaning for us because they are more immediate. Grasping the truth of the vulnerability of our body to illness and accident, feeling the significance of the changes our body undergoes as we move through our life cycle, and realizing the imminence and finality of death can profoundly deepen our appreciation of life. But, we cannot grasp the true meaning of illness, aging, and death intellectually. We can only live out and suffer through them and allow the emotional impact to wash over us. It would be a mistake to wait until we, or those we care about, have become sick, old, or are dying. To struggle with these issues at any point in our life has the potential to awaken us to the incredible beauty and richness available during our short stay on this planet. More than that, sensing the transience of our life can, as it did with the Buddha, inspire us to more firmly tread the path of spirit.

This series of sculptures is in the ancient artistic genre of *memento mori*—"Remember that you must die"—a reminder of the passage of time and the shortness of life. This genre is characterized by the appearance of skulls and skeletons, the grim reaper, the hourglass, and the very old. The graphic images of aging, sickness, and death are meant to give a visceral message about impermanence—nothing lasts forever, so we must appreciate, appreciate, appreciate. Don't get caught up in the past or future, appreciate this very moment, and live it beautifully.

Memento Mori can come in forms other than art. Alice and I read the obituaries in our local newspaper. We pay special attention to the ages at death. It is a wakeup call for us to see how many people die who are younger than we are. Also, it is interesting to read a whole life encapsulated in a few paragraphs, and unsettling to know that one day we, too, will be in print.

When we were in Rome, Alice and I saw the ultimate example of *memento mori*. We visited the chapel in Cimitero dei Cappuccini, the cemetery of the Capuchin monks that is located under the church of Santa Maria della Concezione. There, on the walls and ceilings, artfully arranged in beautiful symmetric patterns, were the skulls and bones of monks who had died over a period of five centuries. On the side was a small sign that read, "As you are now, we once were. As we are now, so will you be." What a clear and impactful message.

The pieces in the *Naked Old Men* series serve as a reminder to me. I sculpted most of them for an exhibit around the time I was fifty years old. This half-century mark held a great deal of significance for me. It was a period when I was thinking a lot about old age and death. I was surrounded by a generation of aging relatives. My parents, my Aunt Kitty, my dad's brother and sisters, Alice's mom and family were all in their late seventies and mid-eighties. We were assuming a greater role as caretakers and witnessing firsthand the effects of age. Statistically, my life was two-thirds over. I was beginning to experience more of the aches and pains, diminished energy, memory lapses, etc., that usually accompany aging—and it was scaring me.

I was drawn to explore the ugliness and vulnerability that aging represented to me at the time. Many of these sculptures are caricatures emphasizing the grotesque quality of age. The collapsed figure in the chair, the confused Alzheimer's patient, the silent bedridden figure, all portray the powerlessness that terrorized me. They were my fears formed in clay.

The works in this series reflect my obsession during this period with the passage of time. I represented time's movement in a variety of ways—symbolically, as with *The Struggle* and *Fetal Man,* or by juxtaposing young and old, as with *Perfect Man* and *Old Man and Baby*, or by evolution from youth to old age, as with *Circle*.

The figures needed to be naked. Nakedness reveals vulnerability. Nakedness combined with the fragility of age was to me the extreme state of vulnerability.

The sculptures have a disquieting emotional quality. The specter of aging itself is a highly charged subject that can evoke deep and often repressed emotional response. The images in the form of these sculptures can bring those feelings to the surface.

I worked feverishly over a period of several months to complete the sculptures for the exhibit. While I have done other sculptures of older men since, I have never again felt that strong push to return to the subject. It seems that in completing this series of sculptures, something was brought to completion in me.

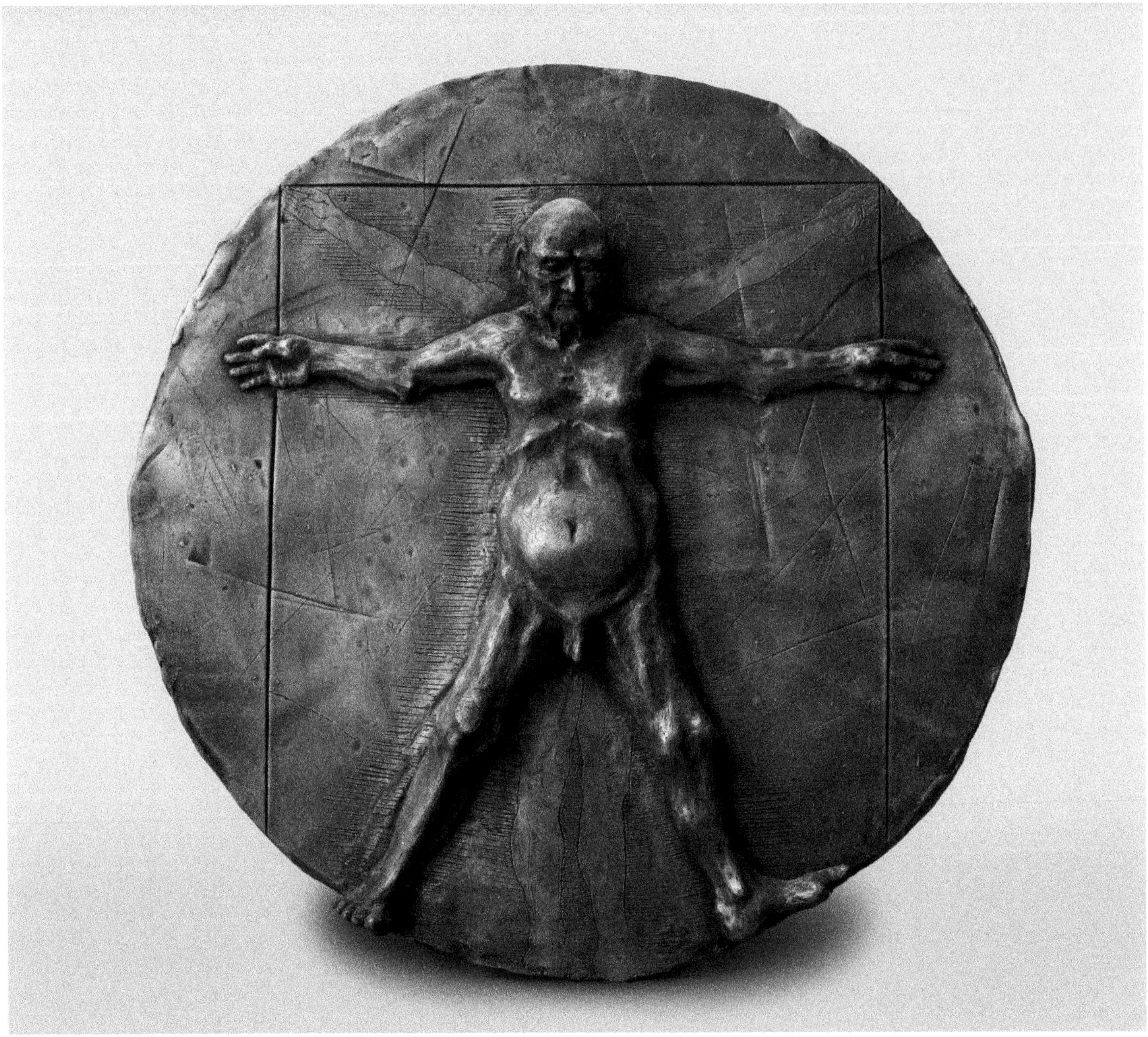

Perfect Man—40 Years Later. Based on the famous drawing by Leonardo da Vinci.

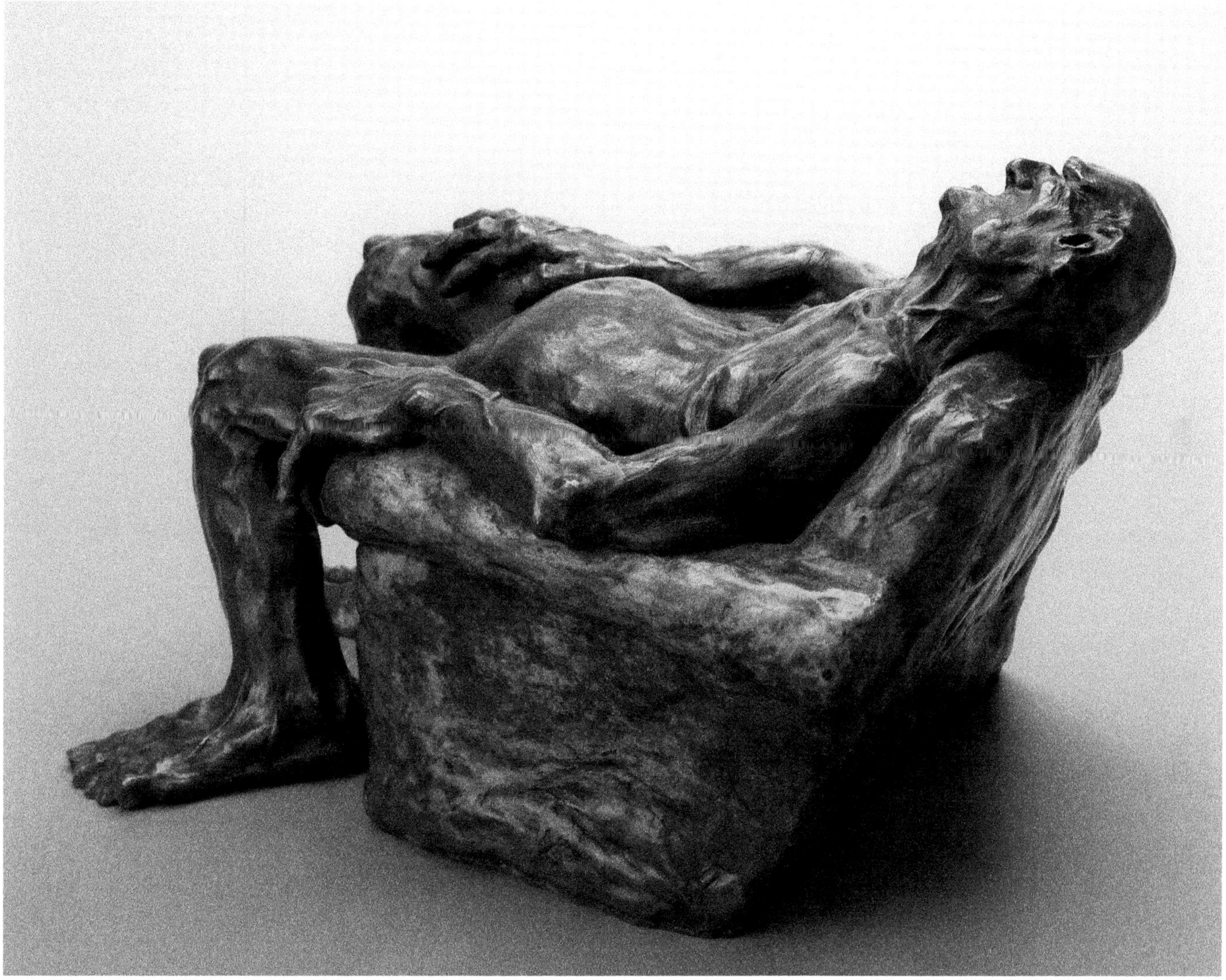

Old Man Watching TV. Television can sometimes be a great sleeping pill.

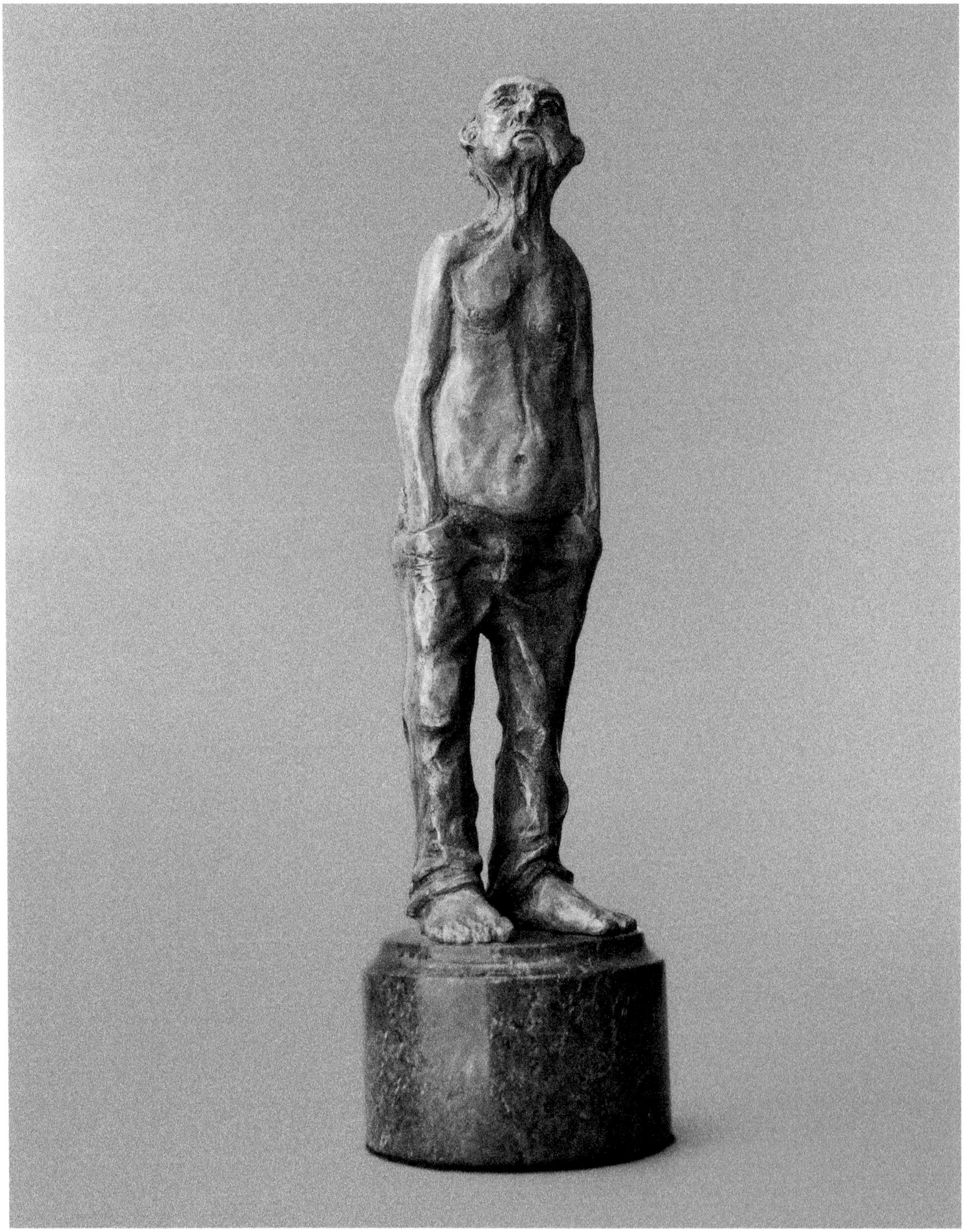

Alzheimer Man. This piece captures the lost quality of one of the patients in an Alzheimer unit that I visited.

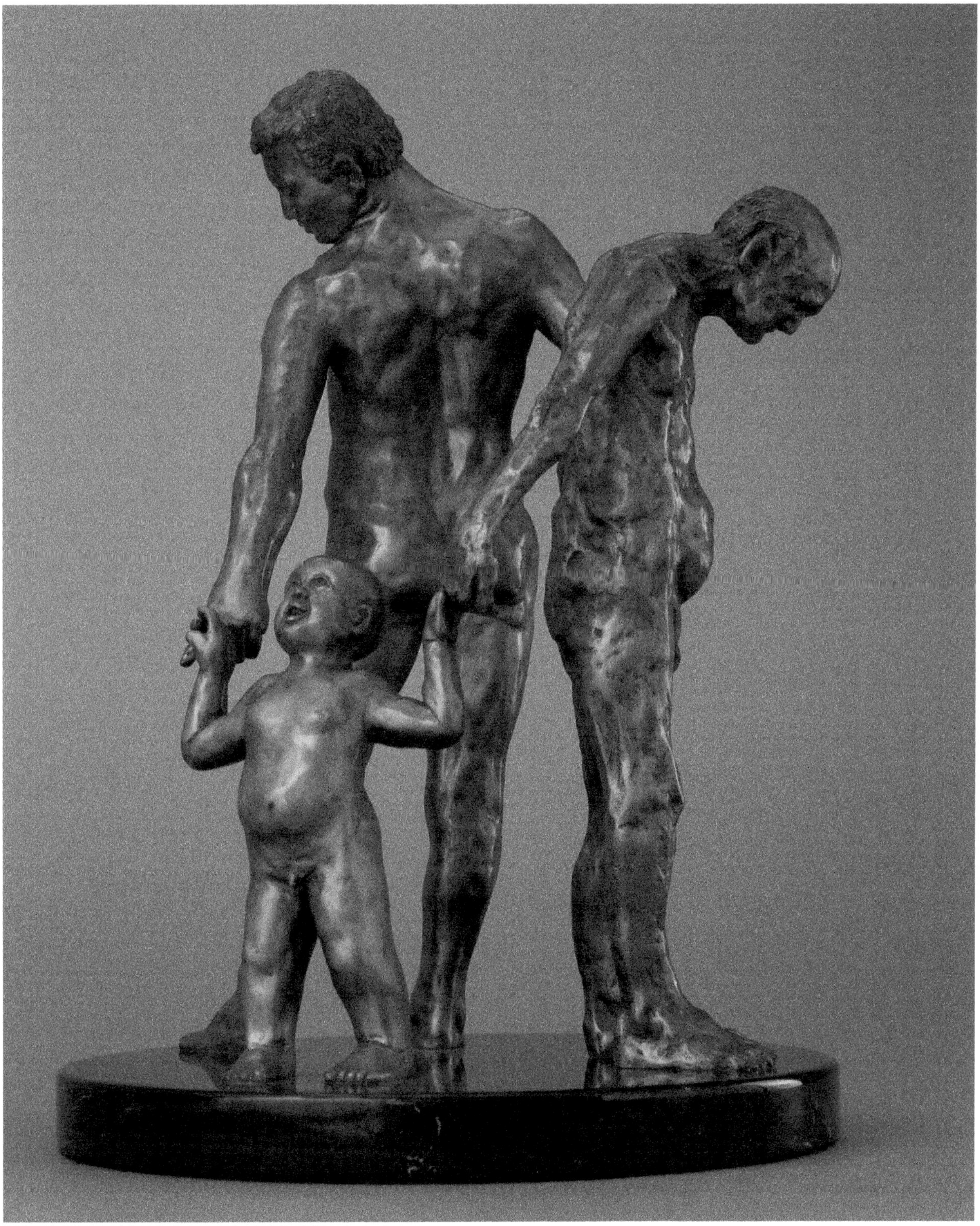

Circle. The life cycle from childhood to maturity to old age.

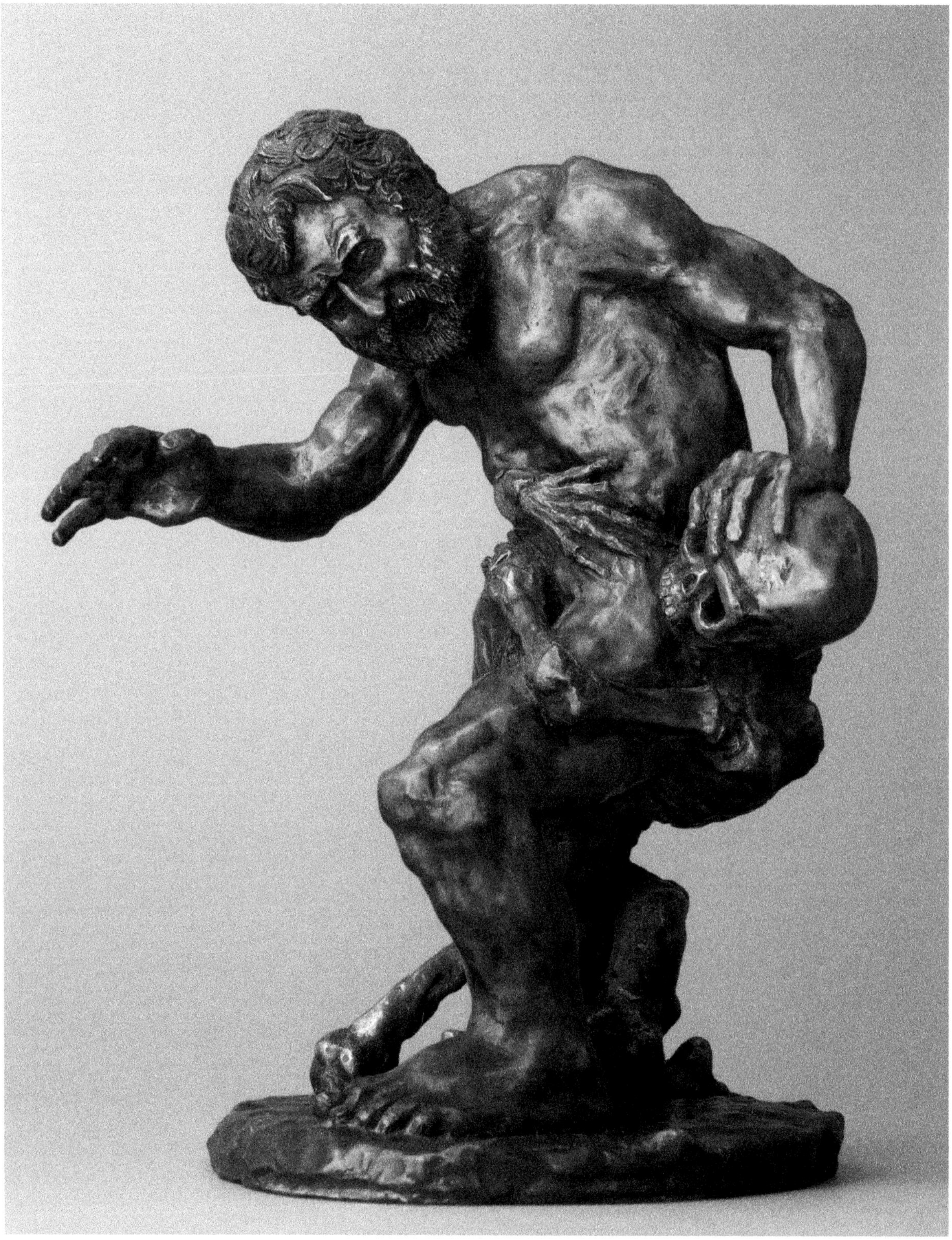

The Struggle. Man wrestling with death.

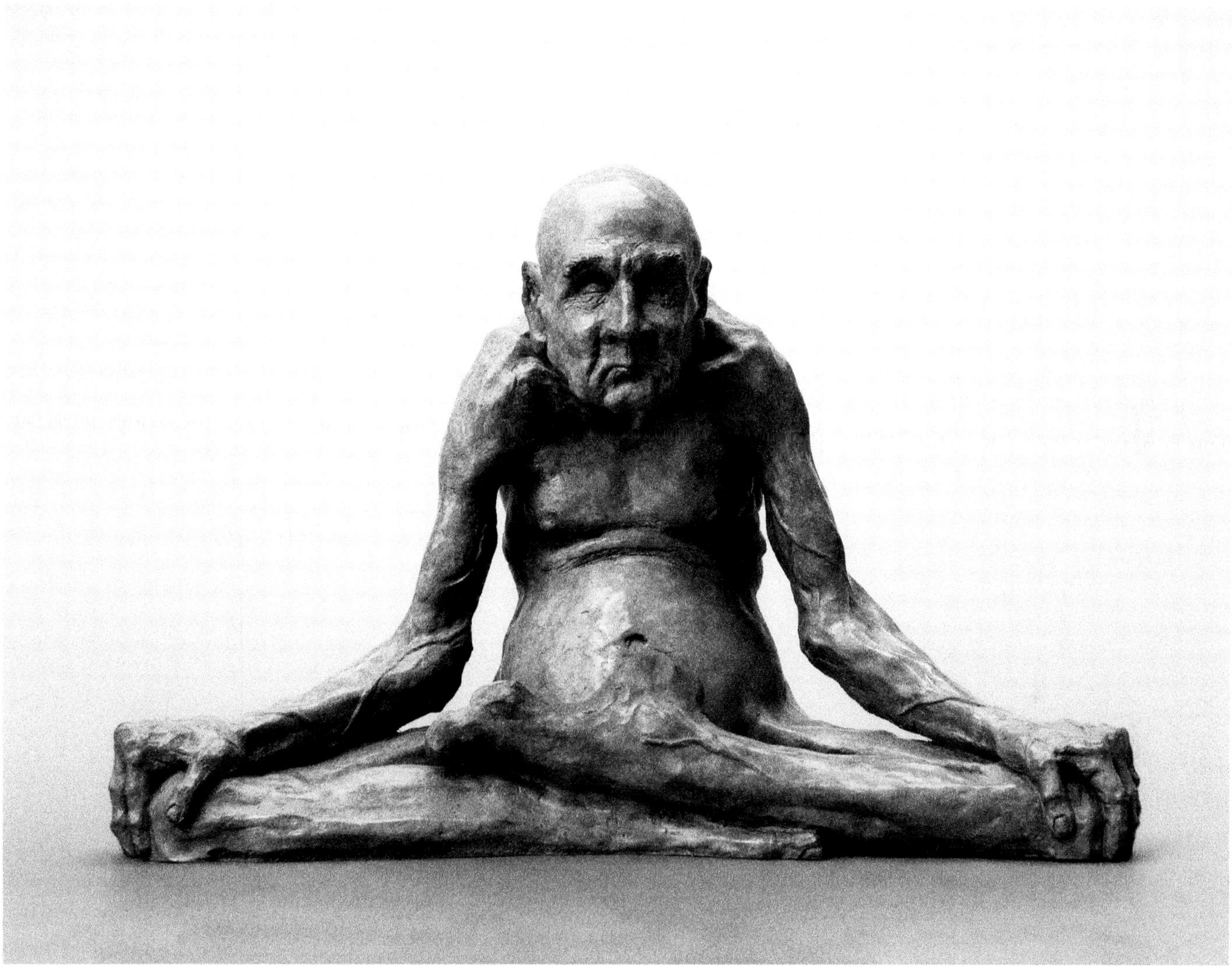

Yogi

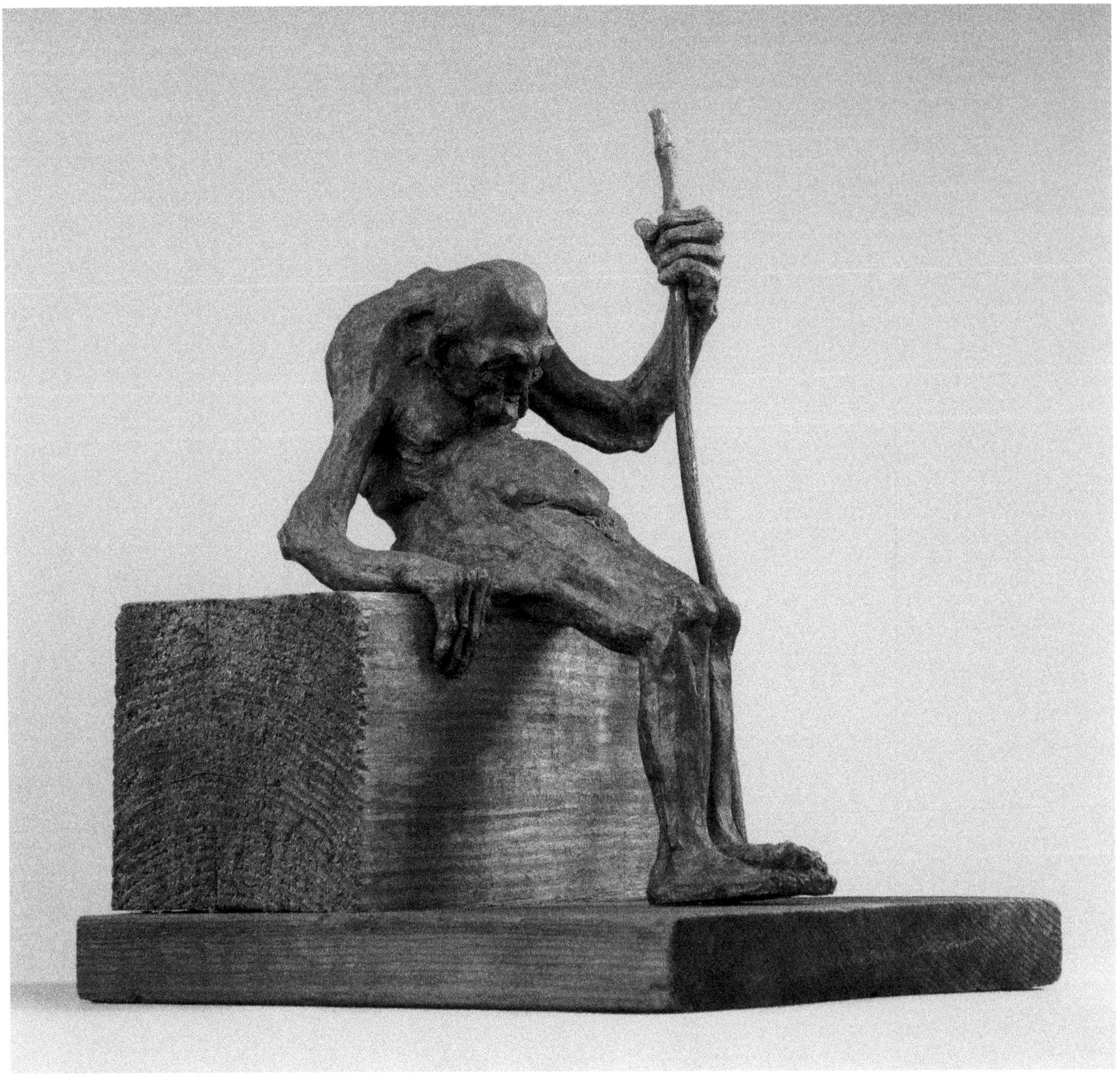

Old Man with Staff

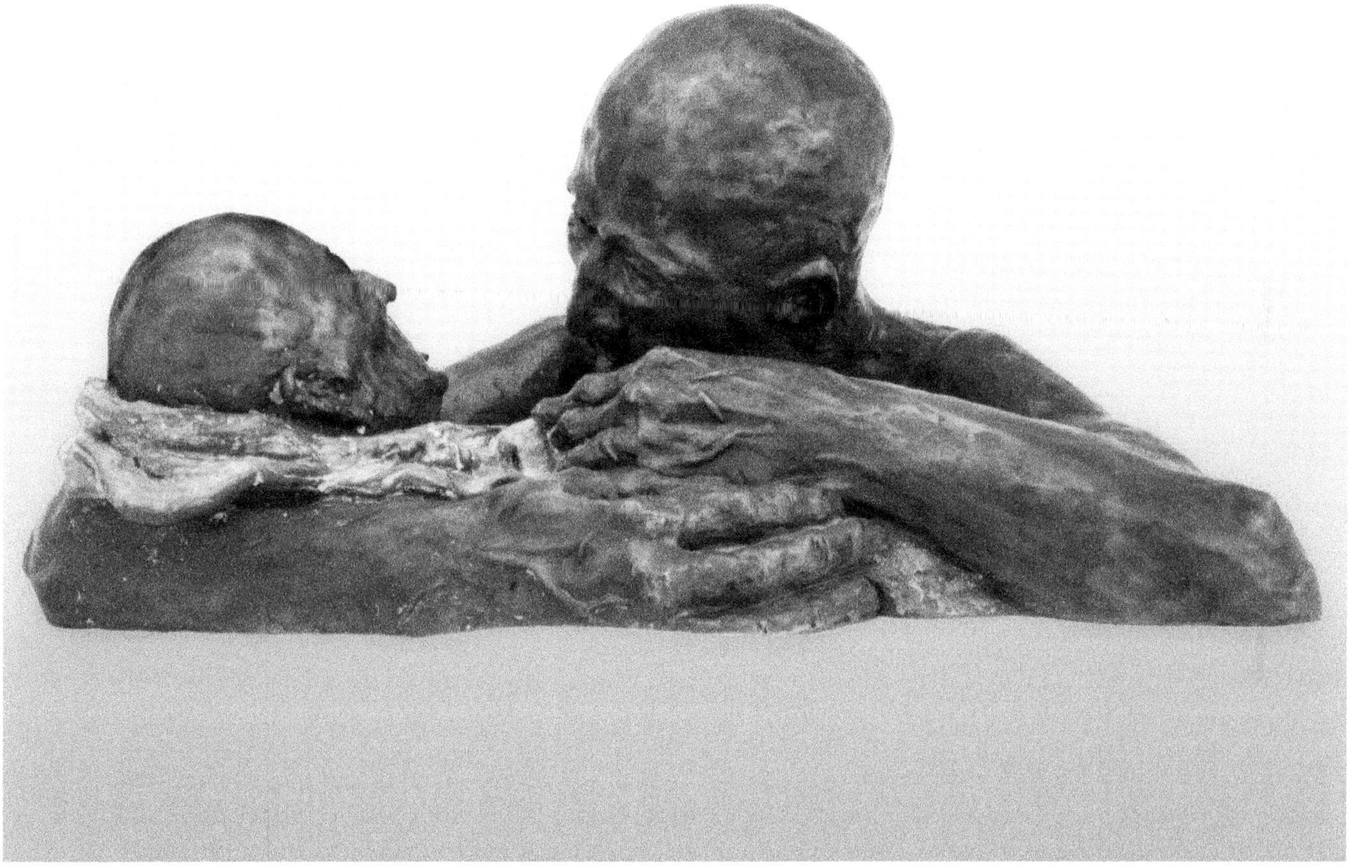

Old Man and Baby. The crying baby is himself.

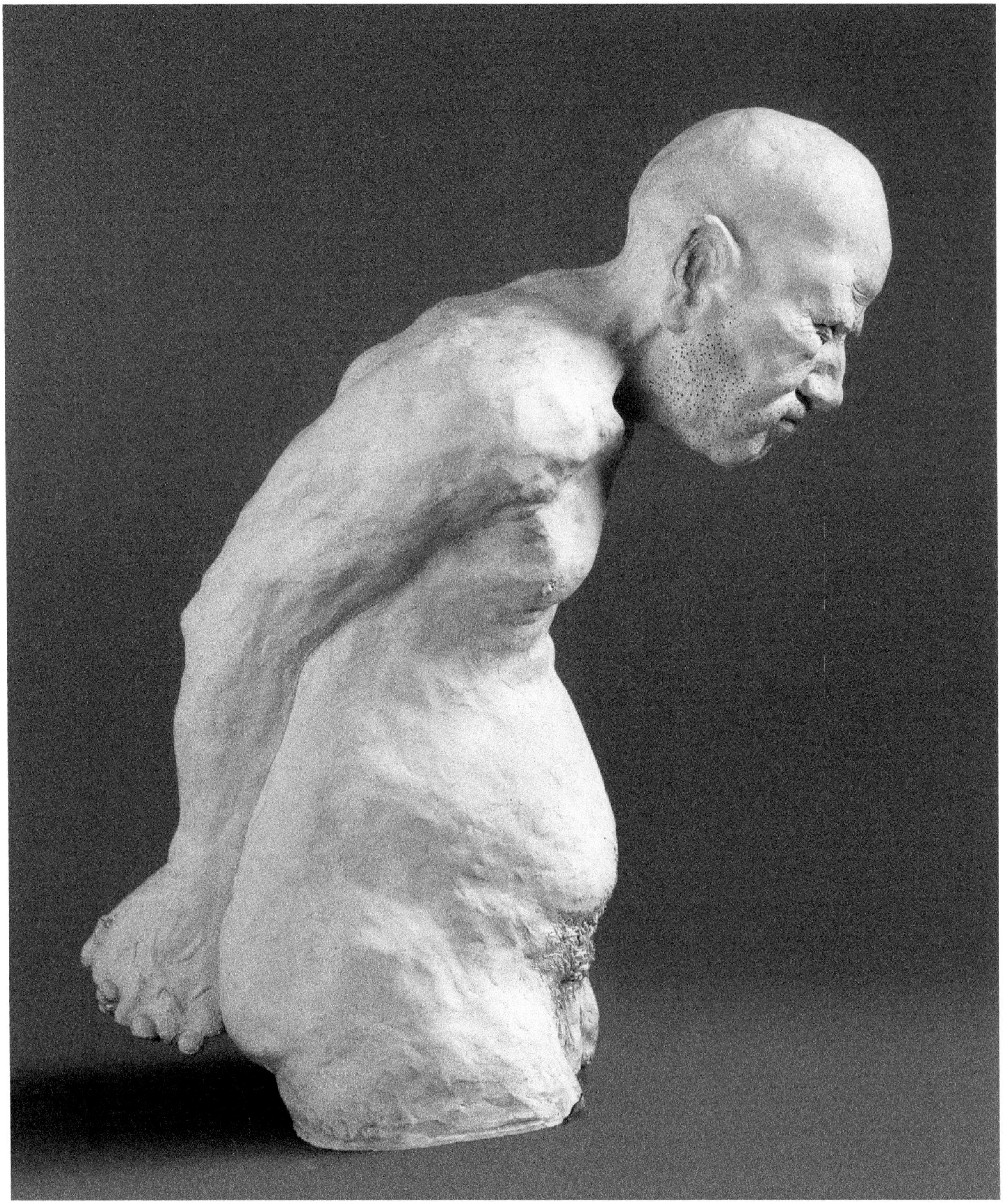

Man in Contemplation

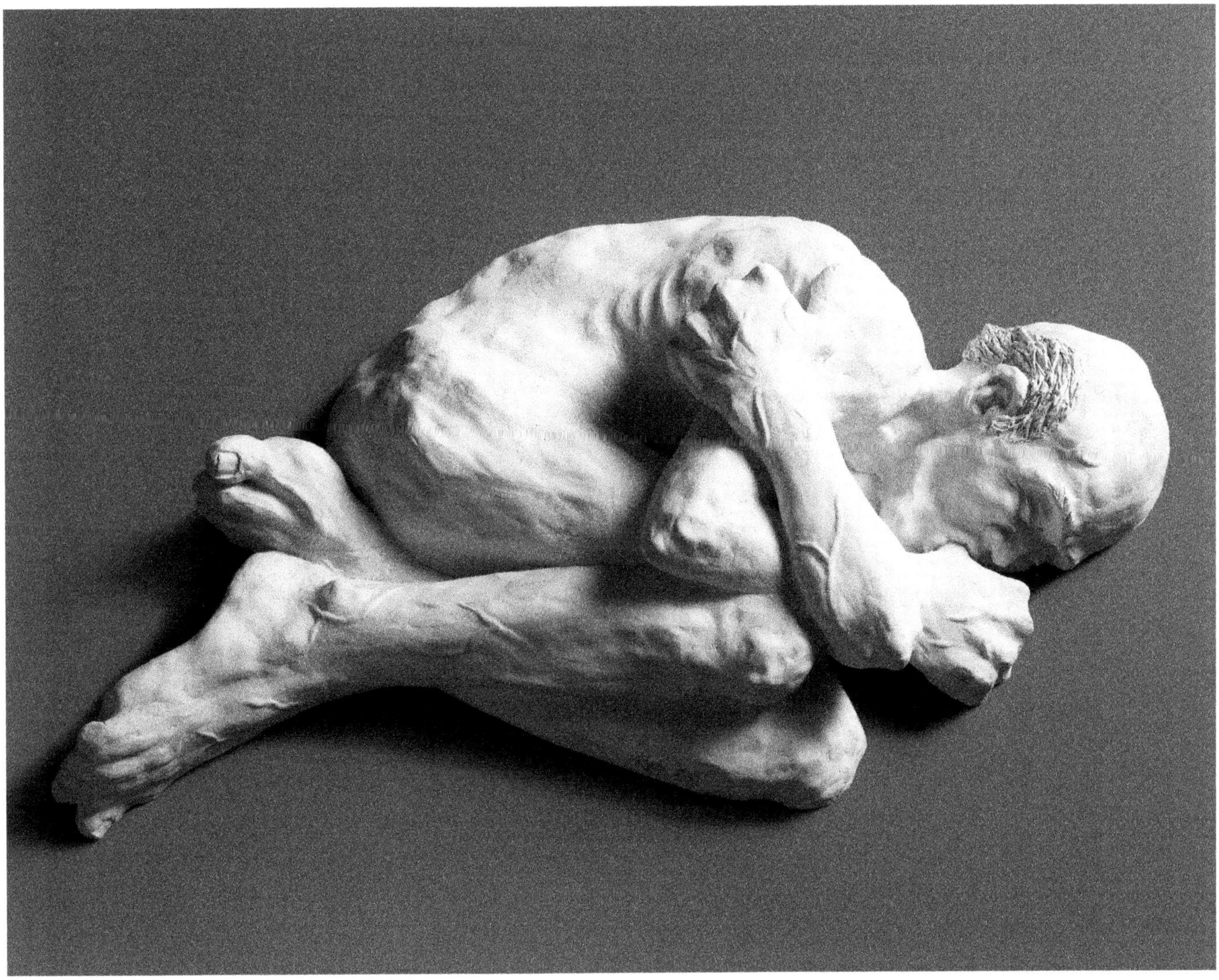

Fetal Man

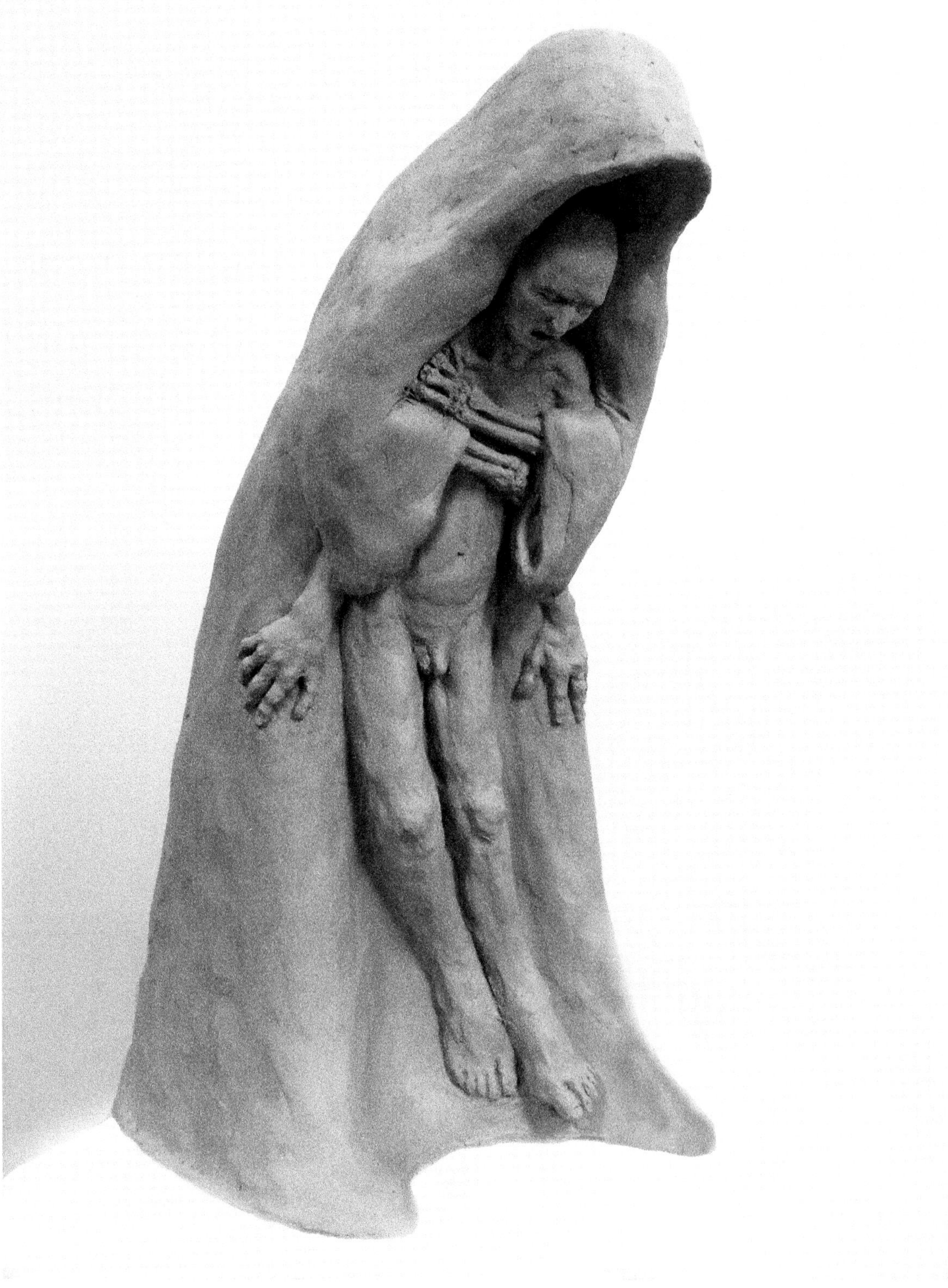

Embrace

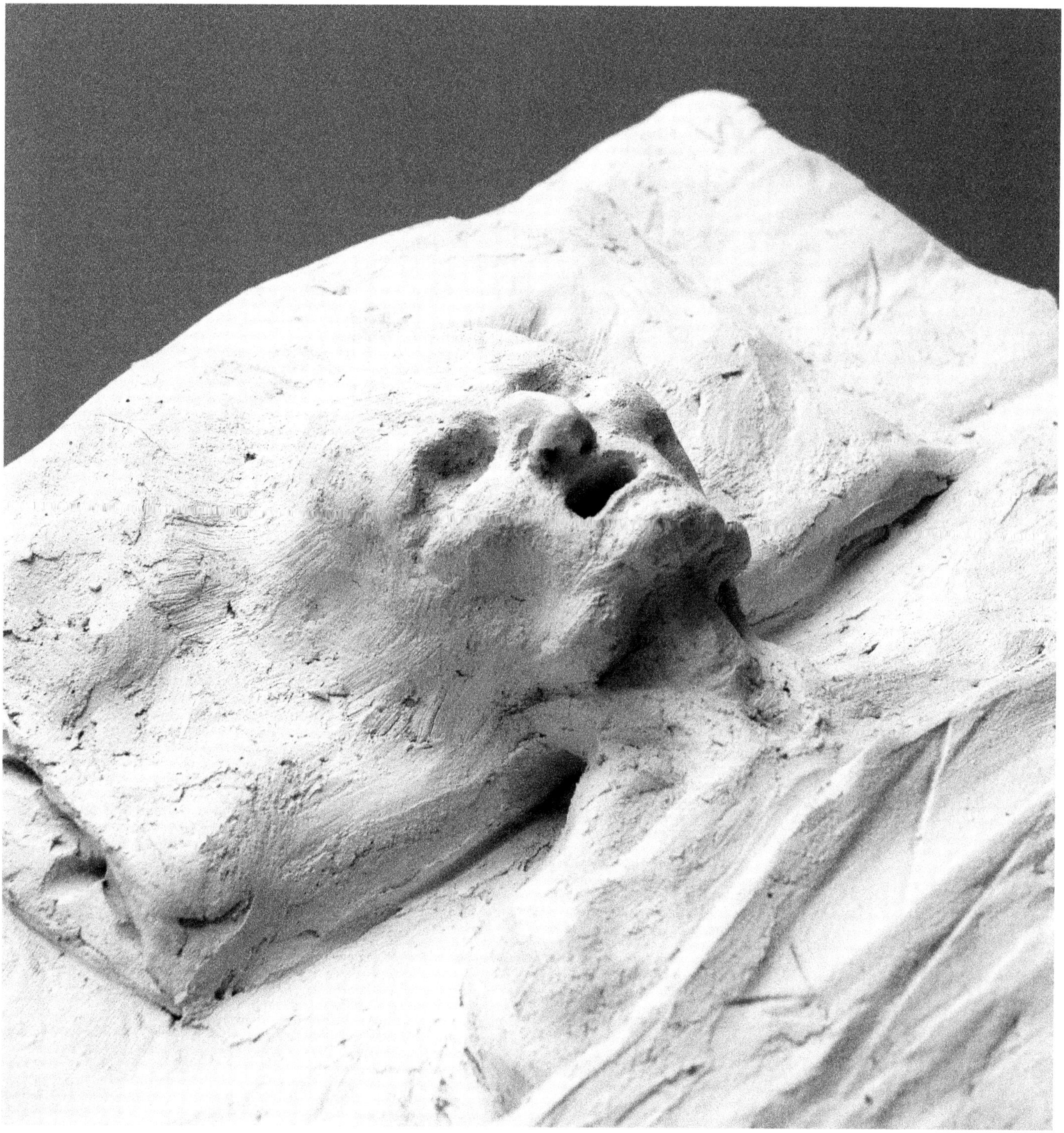

Death Bed

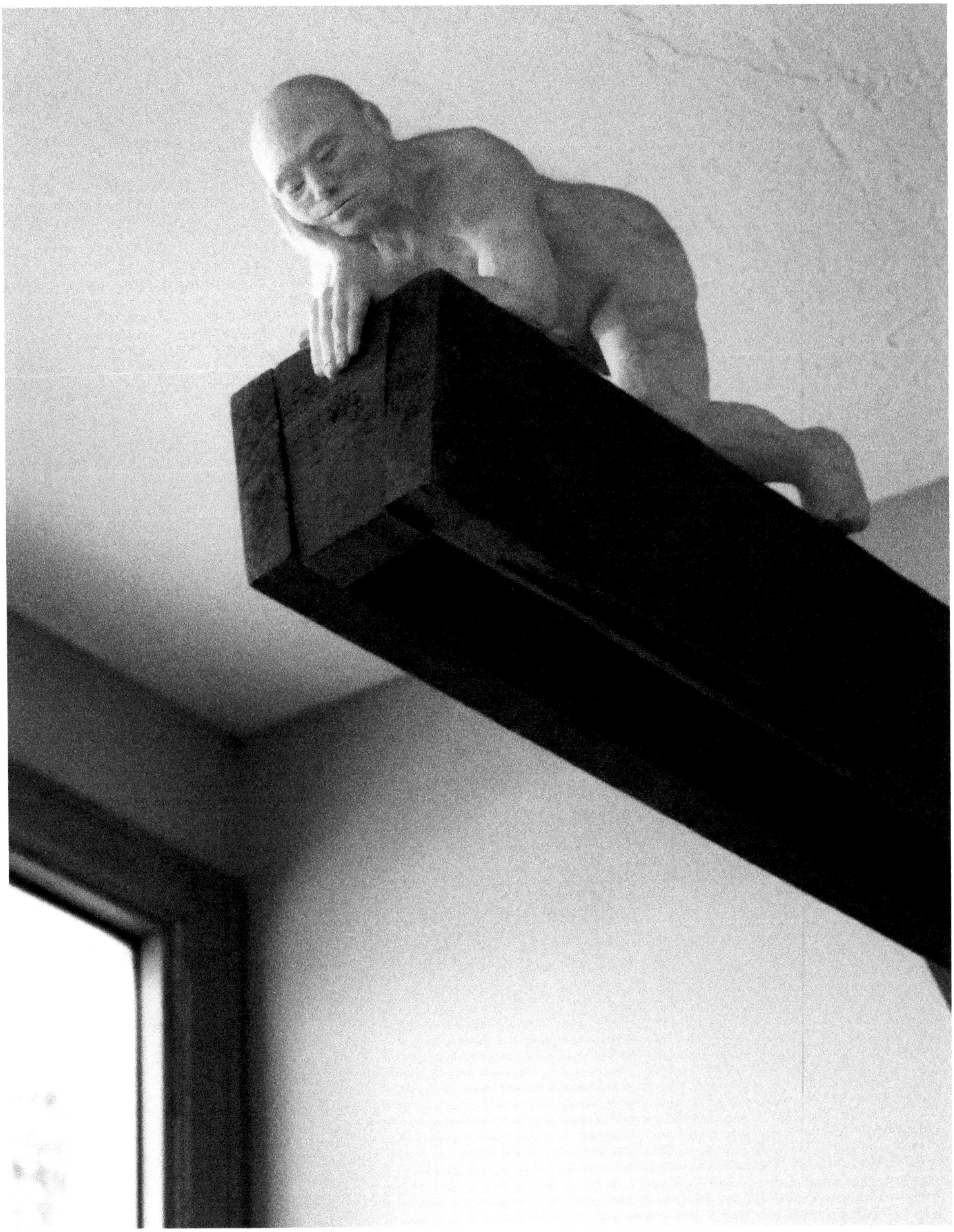

The Watcher

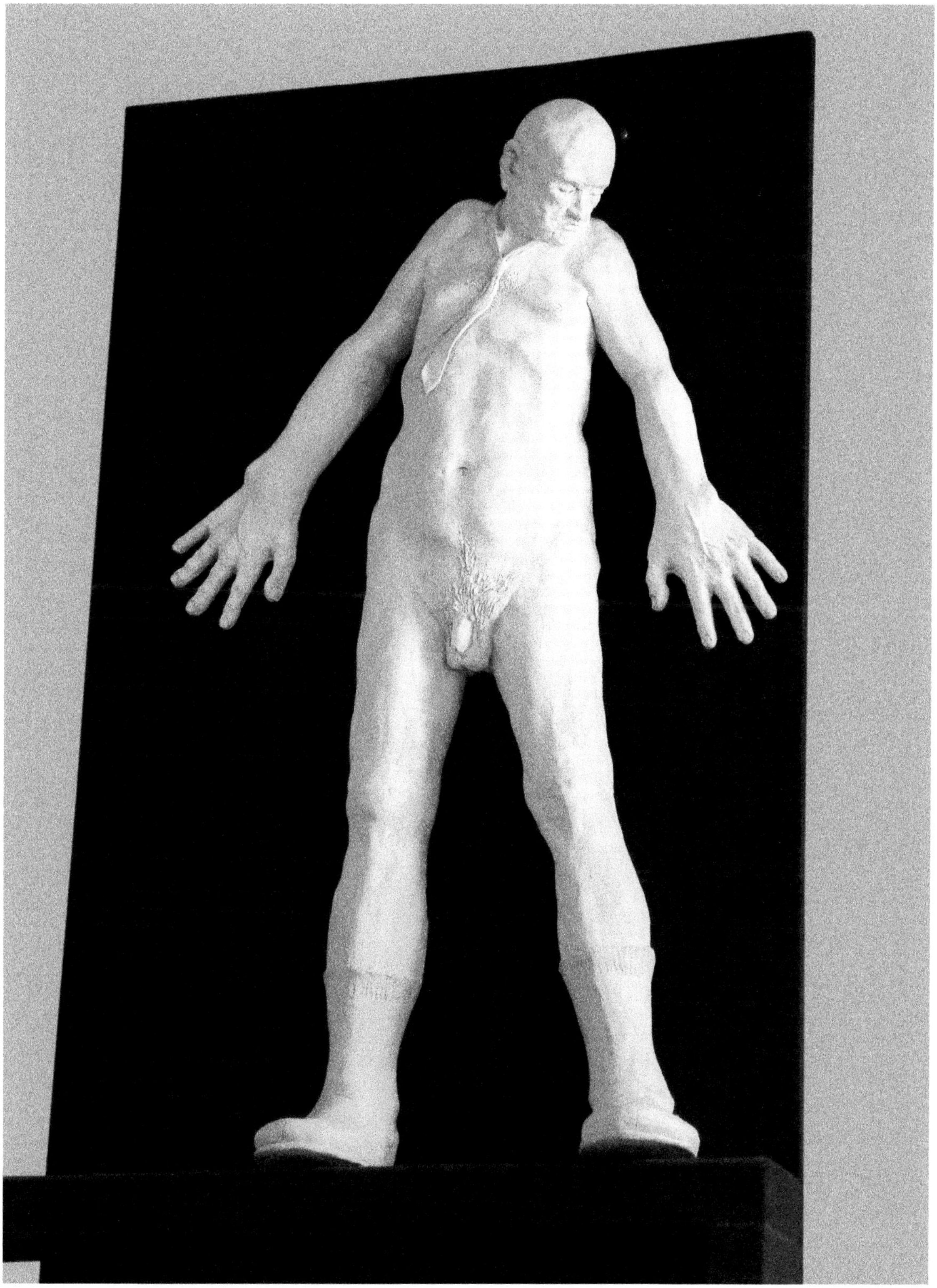

Altophobia

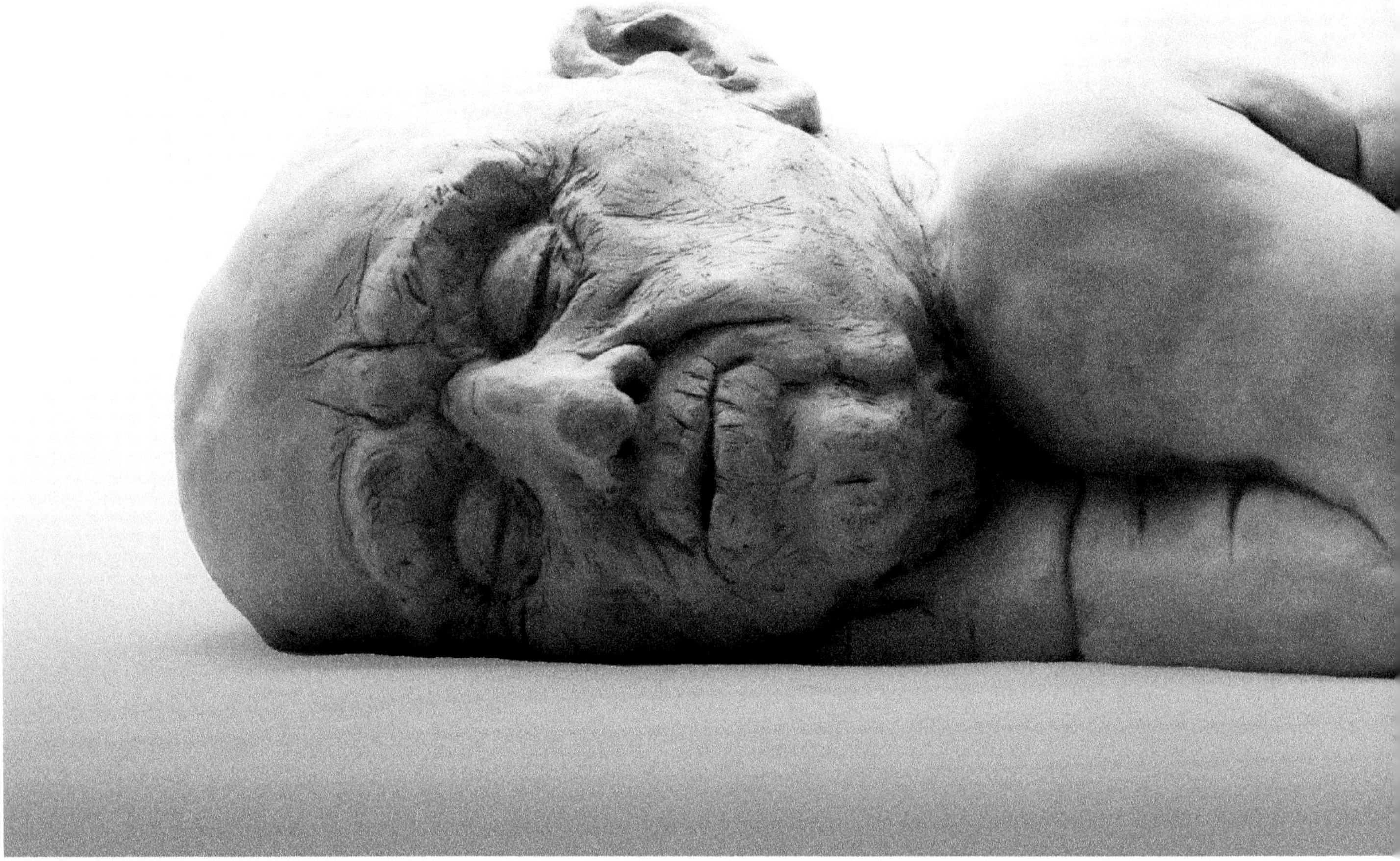

Old Baby

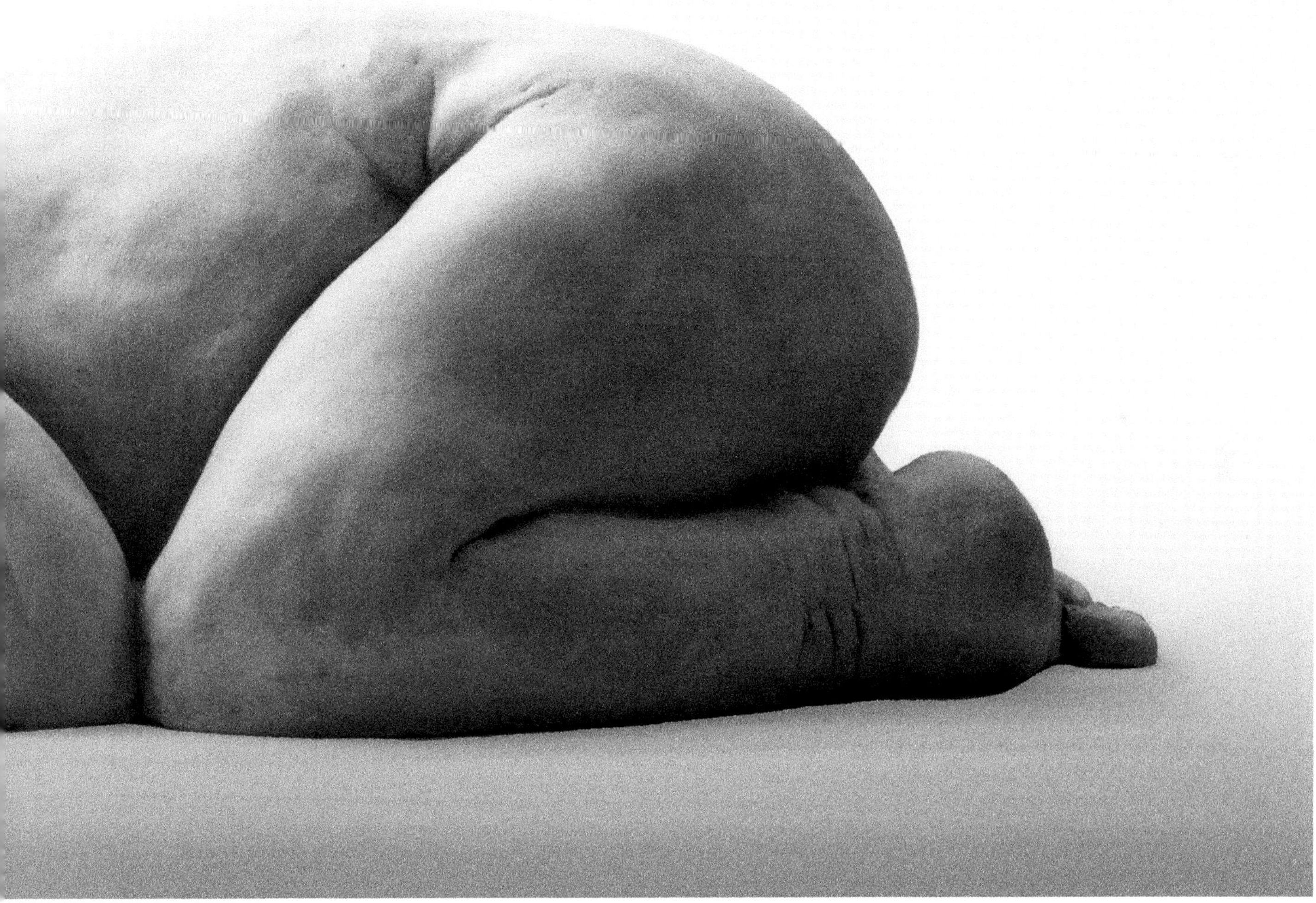

"It's not how you look,

it's how you see."

—BUMPER STICKER

Naked Truth

ALICE

AFTER I FINISHED THE *WOMEN OF AGE* SERIES, I REALIZED THAT I was not complete with my search for acceptance of my aging body. By the example of the women I had met and painted, I was learning that I could indeed live a fruitful and creative life in my older years and that my lines and wrinkles were just nature taking its course—by-products of getting older. But I was still very judgmental about my body. The mirror had become my enemy, and I knew it would become a more merciless opponent with each passing year. If I was to be a happy person, I needed to look at my image with acceptance rather than judgment. So rather than employing a cosmetic surgeon's knife or a psychiatrist's couch, I decided to again use paint brush and canvas to find myself.

Since I was fifty-eight at the time, I chose to embark upon a quest to meet women my age and older who were accepting of their aging bodies—and who were comfortable enough to allow me to paint them nude. I found that this was no easy task. Nine out of ten women I approached wouldn't even consider the idea. They felt as judgmental about their bodies as I did of mine.

Fortunately, there are older female role models who inhabit their bodies with ease and comfort. They look at their own bodies with acceptance, and are not embarrassed to be seen by others. I was lucky enough to meet and paint some of these women. They have taught me that feminine beauty comes in all sizes, shapes, colors, and ages—that it is unnecessary to be young, thin, and unlined to be beautiful, sensual, and attractive. They have served as an inspiration and wonderful mirror for me, and I am forever grateful to them.

In order for me to come to this understanding, I went through a revolution in the way I saw aging bodies—others and my own. At first glance, a naked, aged body, with its bulges, wrinkles and varicose veins is not a pretty sight, especially compared with the firm, smooth body of a young person. My first impulse was to turn away in disgust. However, I spent months in front of canvas in loving communion with the bodies of my subjects. For hours on end I was able to become familiar with, and caress the wrinkled flesh with my paintbrush. This resulted in an indelible change in the way I perceived an old body. I saw through eyes of love and acceptance.

How judgmental my concept of beauty was when I was younger. I had bought into the typical media ideal of feminine beauty—a skinny adolescent girl with long legs. Now I recognize that every age has its own beauty. Is summer more beautiful than fall? Is fall more beautiful than winter? No, each season and each age has its own variety of beauty. The beauty differs not in terms of better or worse, but in terms of diversity.

After much pain and suffering and self-reflection on my part, coupled with the experience of painting these generous women, I have come to realize that I am happier being in my body just as I am. It is much more fruitful and enjoyable for me to live my life free from as much self judgment as possible. Now, at my age, I feel lucky to be alive and still have a body, and I don't intend to spend one more minute of my life feeling bad about its shape and age. I have let go of the impossible goal of pursuing the fountain of youth, and have laid claim to my authentic aging self—gray hair and all.

The truth is that this body of mine—sagging and wrinkled as it is—is my vehicle of creation, transportation and communication, abode of my senses of taste, sight, smell, hearing and touch and home to my mind and spirit. I love it and am so grateful to reside in it.

I hope that those of you who view this collection will also look at your reflection in the mirror and be inspired to accept the reality of your form, no matter what its age and shape, accept the changes that are taking place and be grateful for the miracle that you are alive.

True at 59

TRUE WAS THE FIRST painting I did in this series. We were walking on an almost-deserted, rocky beach in Northern California when I asked her if she wanted to be a subject in the *Naked Truth* series. Suddenly, without warning, she ripped off her clothes and began leaping from rock to rock with wild abandon—totally naked, totally free with her body. When she stood still for a moment, laughing out loud, I quickly photographed her standing on a rock.

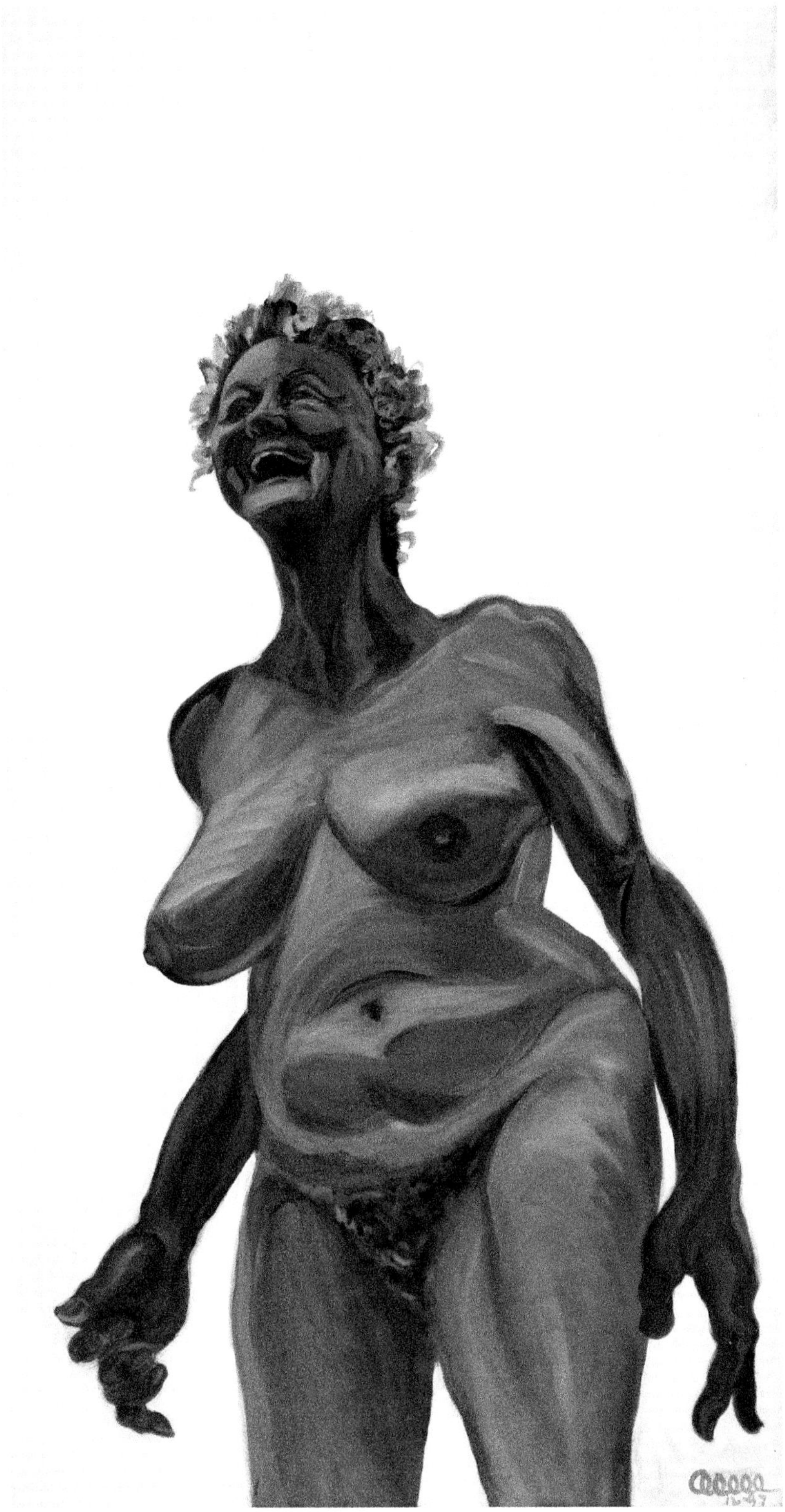

True at 59

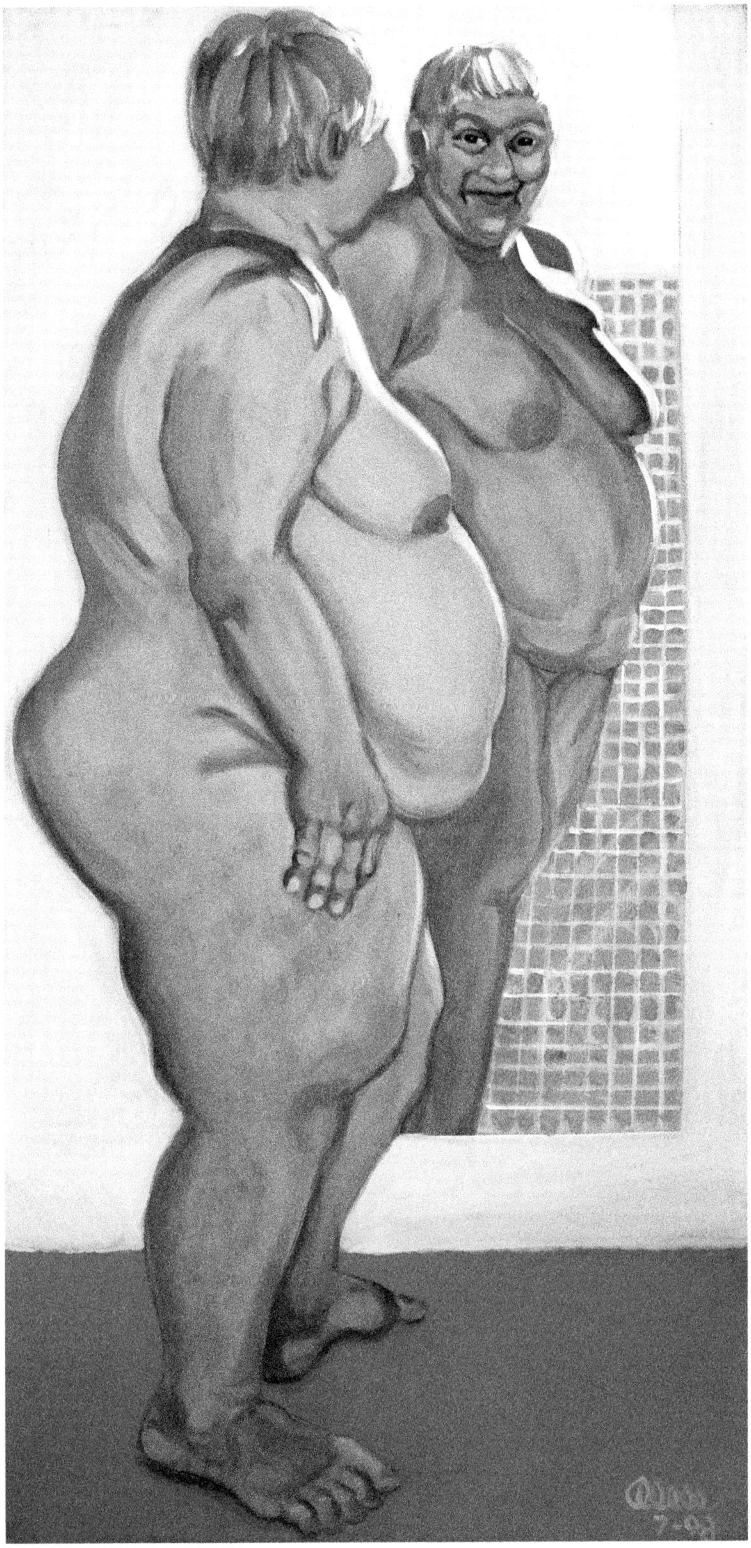

Elizabeth at 70

Elizabeth at 70

MINUTES AFTER ELIZABETH and I met for the first time, she completely disrobed and was ready to pose. Her body is far from what we have been programmed to believe is beautiful, yet, judging from her freedom and contented smile, she seems to occupy it with total acceptance and no self-consciousness.

Virginia at 83

VIRGINIA WAS VISITING from out of town and came to our studio with her family. She was so moved by the paintings of the naked women that she agreed to model. I asked her why she would want to do such a crazy thing and she told me, "I am doing it for my grandchildren." I always smile when I imagine a scenario of an unsuspecting person walking into the home of Virginia's grandchildren, and seeing, hanging over the fireplace, a six-foot painting in a gilded frame of their nude eighty-three-year-old grandmother!

Virginia posed for the painting in the beautiful Victorian setting of her son's mobile home. I just loved the way she looked as she comfortably languished in the velvet chair holding a rose in her hand. I really got into painting the background, symbolically depicting the passage of time with a doll in a doll bed, old photographs, a fading rose, and a painting of the sunset.

This painting also became the centerfold in a national women's magazine.

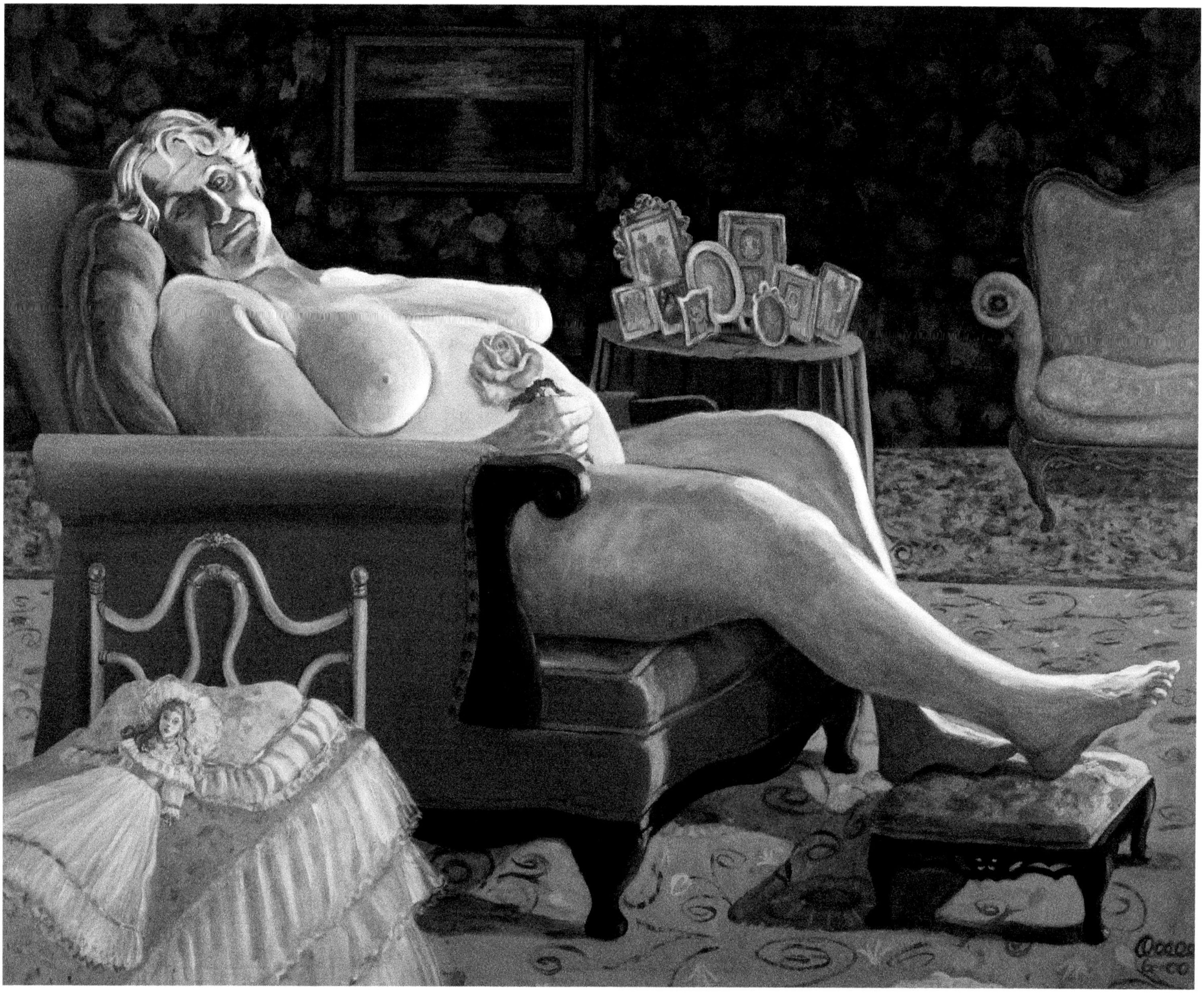

Virginia at 83

Jonsey at 64

Jonsey was vacationing from out of town and came with her son to visit our studio. Some of the *Naked Truth* paintings were hanging on the wall. The project was still a work in progress. Jonsey looked at the paintings and said something like, "These are great. I love them!" So, I asked, "Want to pose for one?" She replied, "Today is my sixty-fourth birthday, I am happily and newly divorced, have a new boyfriend, and yes, I will do it!"

After her son got over the initial shock of his sixty-four-year-old mother naked and posing for a painting, he laughed and said it was great that his mother felt so free.

Within an hour of her arrival, Jonsey and I were ready to begin—she naked and me with camera. As we wandered around from outside to inside, she told me that she amazed herself by agreeing to model—that for the first time in years she was experiencing so much personal freedom. She had truly given herself a birthday present by posing in her birthday suit! I loved her courage and her instant decision to "go for it."

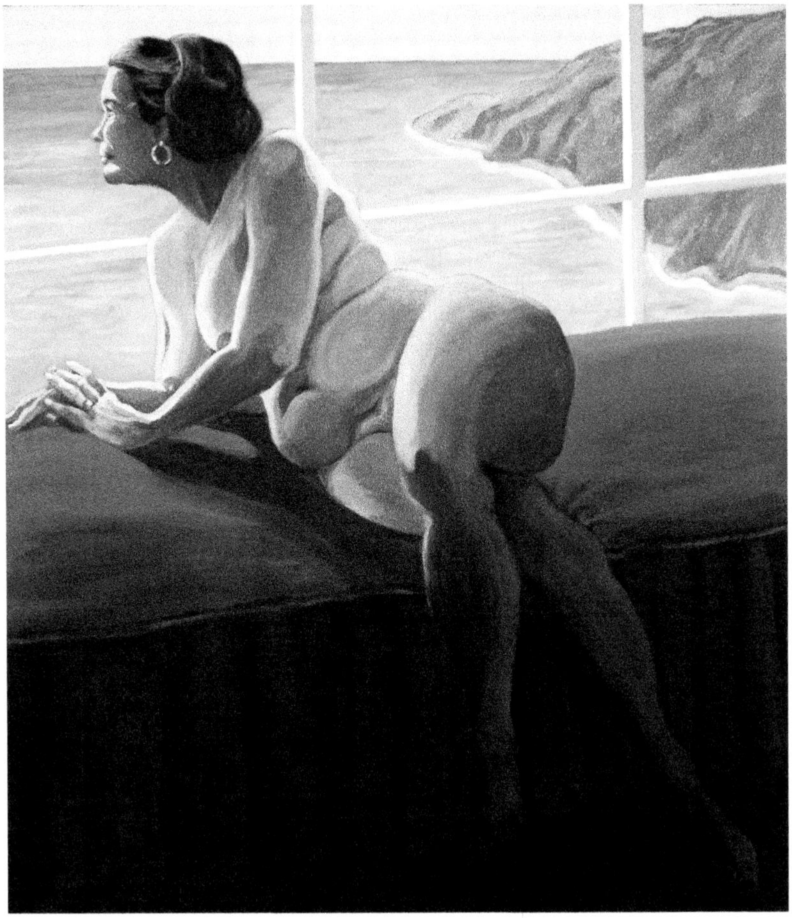

Jonsey at 64

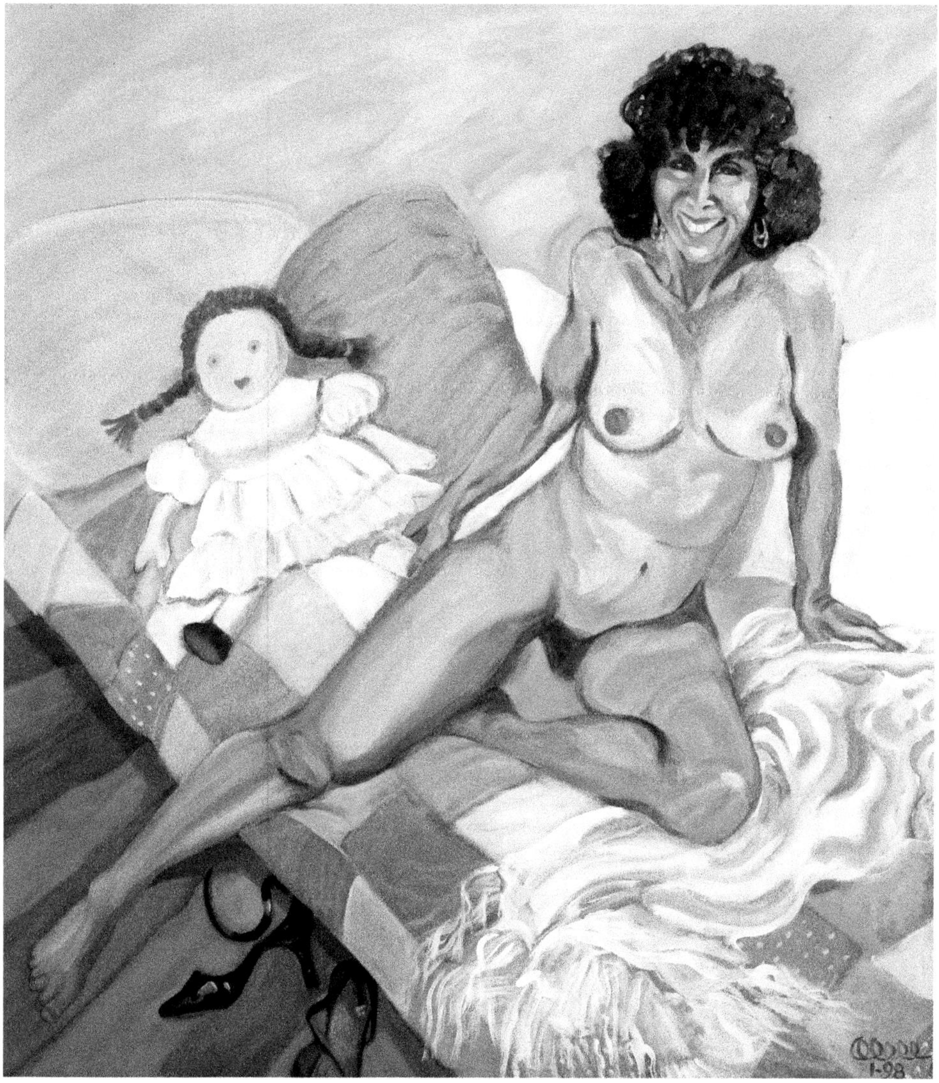

Glori at 69

WHEN I PHOTOGRAPH subjects for a painting, I never pose anyone, preferring to let them choose their own position. It is much more natural and they are relaxed and are free to be themselves. Glori is very comfortable with her sexuality and has no qualms about displaying it, so when she "cheesecaked out" and posed in an enticing way, it seemed perfectly normal.

Glori at 69

Phyllis at 68

AFTER READING AN ARTICLE in the newspaper about the *Women of Age* collection, Phyllis phoned to tell me about a wonderful elderly friend she thought would be a great subject. At that time I was directing my energies to the *Naked Truth* series and I told her about it. She hesitantly confided that she only had one breast and doubted I would be interested in painting someone with a mastectomy. I told her I would be honored to paint her and was moved that she had the courage to give her cancer a face by showing her body to the world.

The next day I was at her house. Phyllis, beautiful and bald, dressed in a long tunic, opened the door and invited me in. We had an instant connection. After visiting for a while, it was time to take photographs. Phyllis disrobed. She stood regally with not an ounce of shame. There was not one hair on her entire body. Her naked form was voluptuous and soft. She had only one breast while scars engraved the place where the other had been. The only jewelry she wore was a beautiful gold necklace.

The experience of spending hours painting Phyllis' image on canvas brought home to me the stark reality of how vulnerable we all are. Our lives are in such a delicate balance. Sickness and death can stalk us at any moment.

A few months after the painting was completed, Phyllis' cancer worked its way to her other breast and she underwent a second mastectomy. A few months later she slipped into a coma and peacefully left this world.

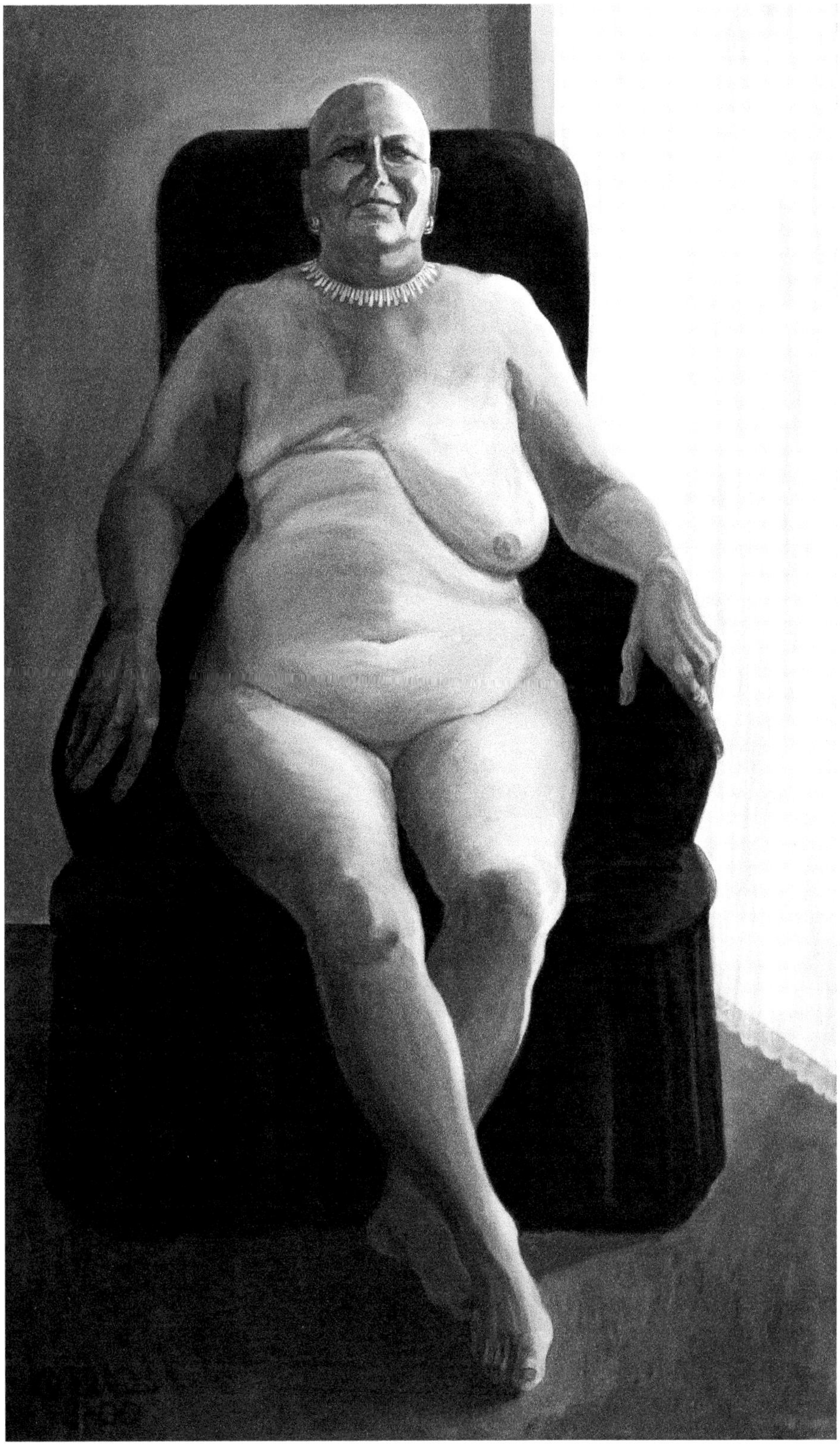

Phyllis at 68

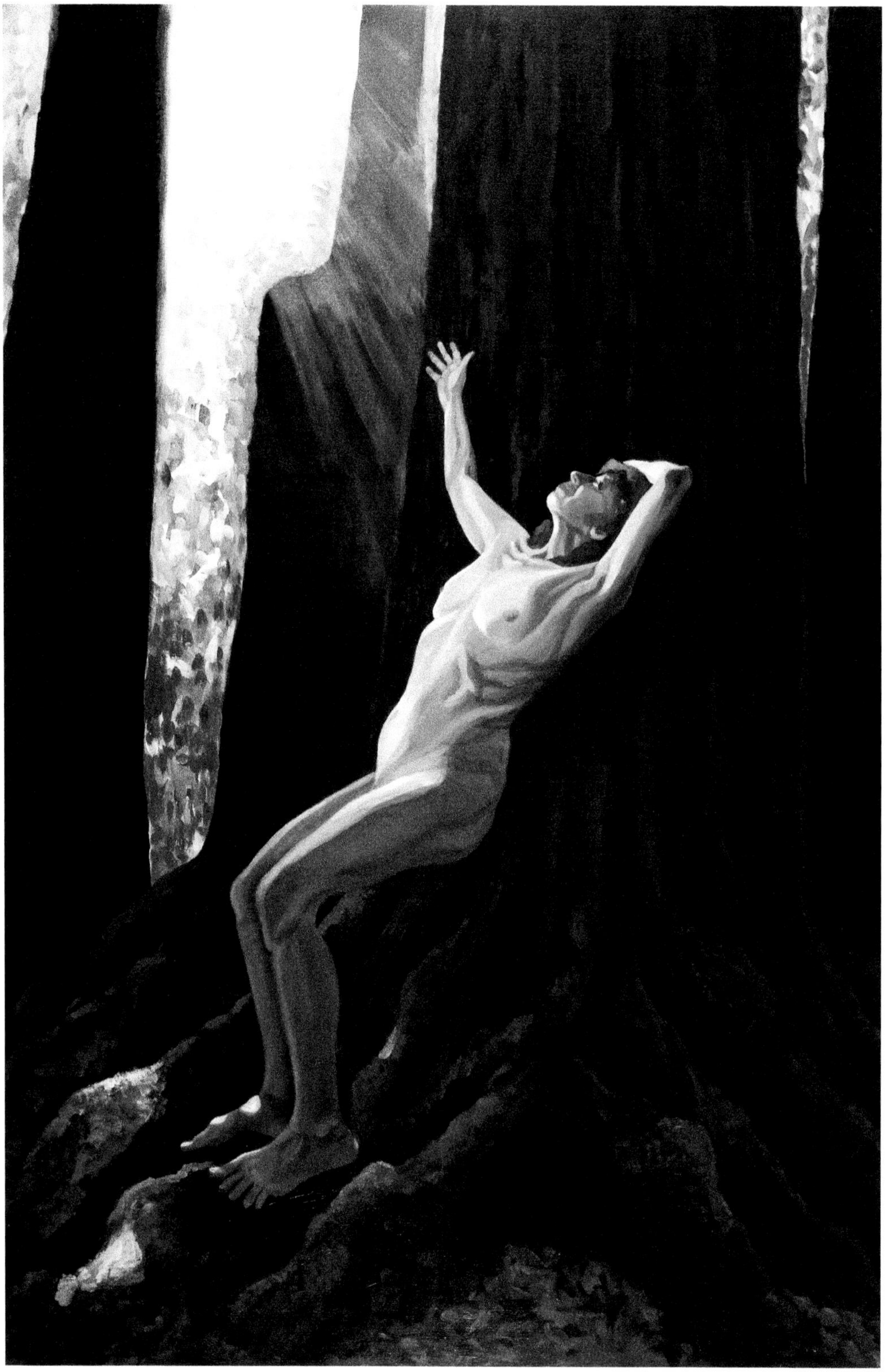

Lanna at 75

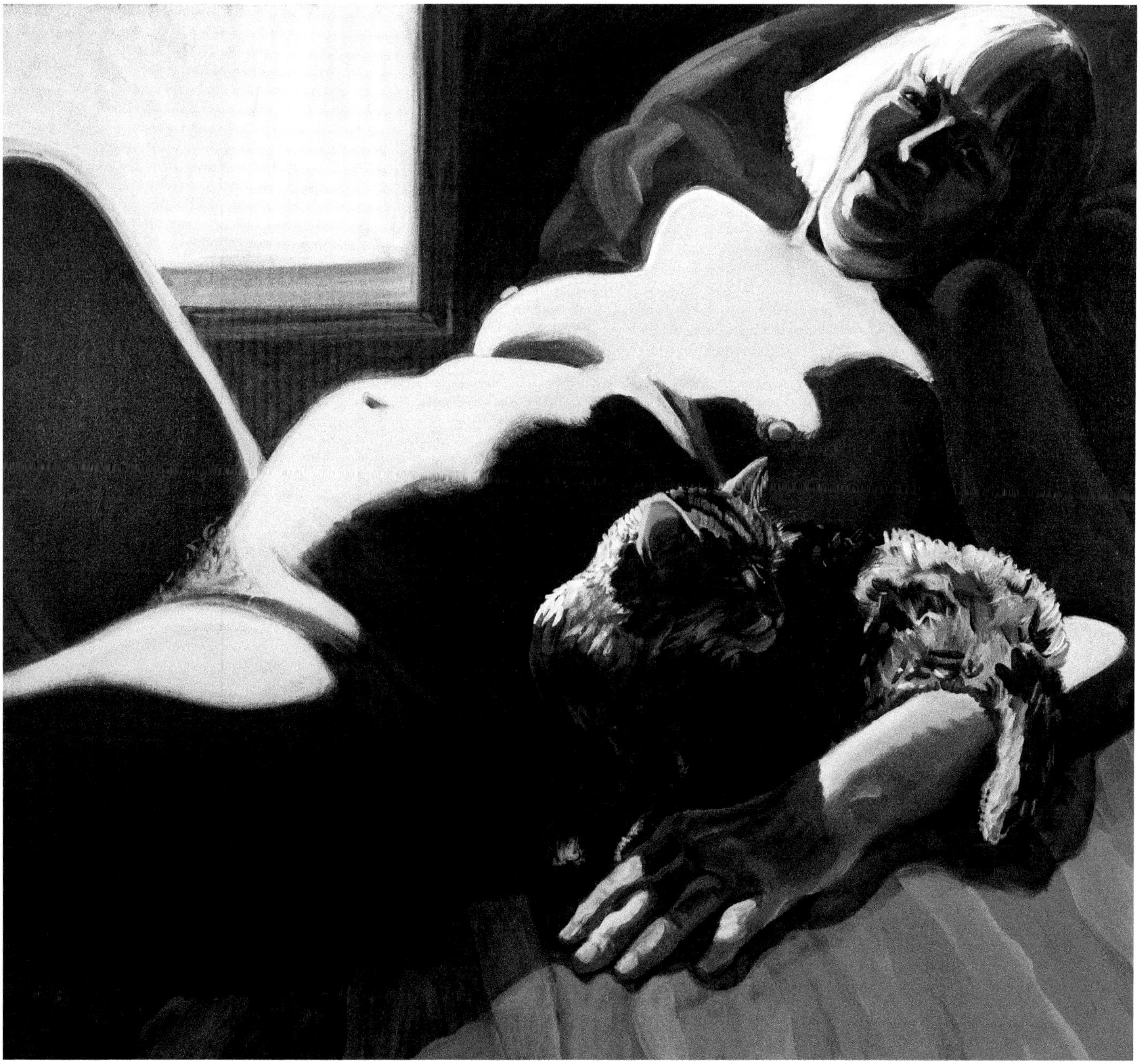

Cypruss at 73

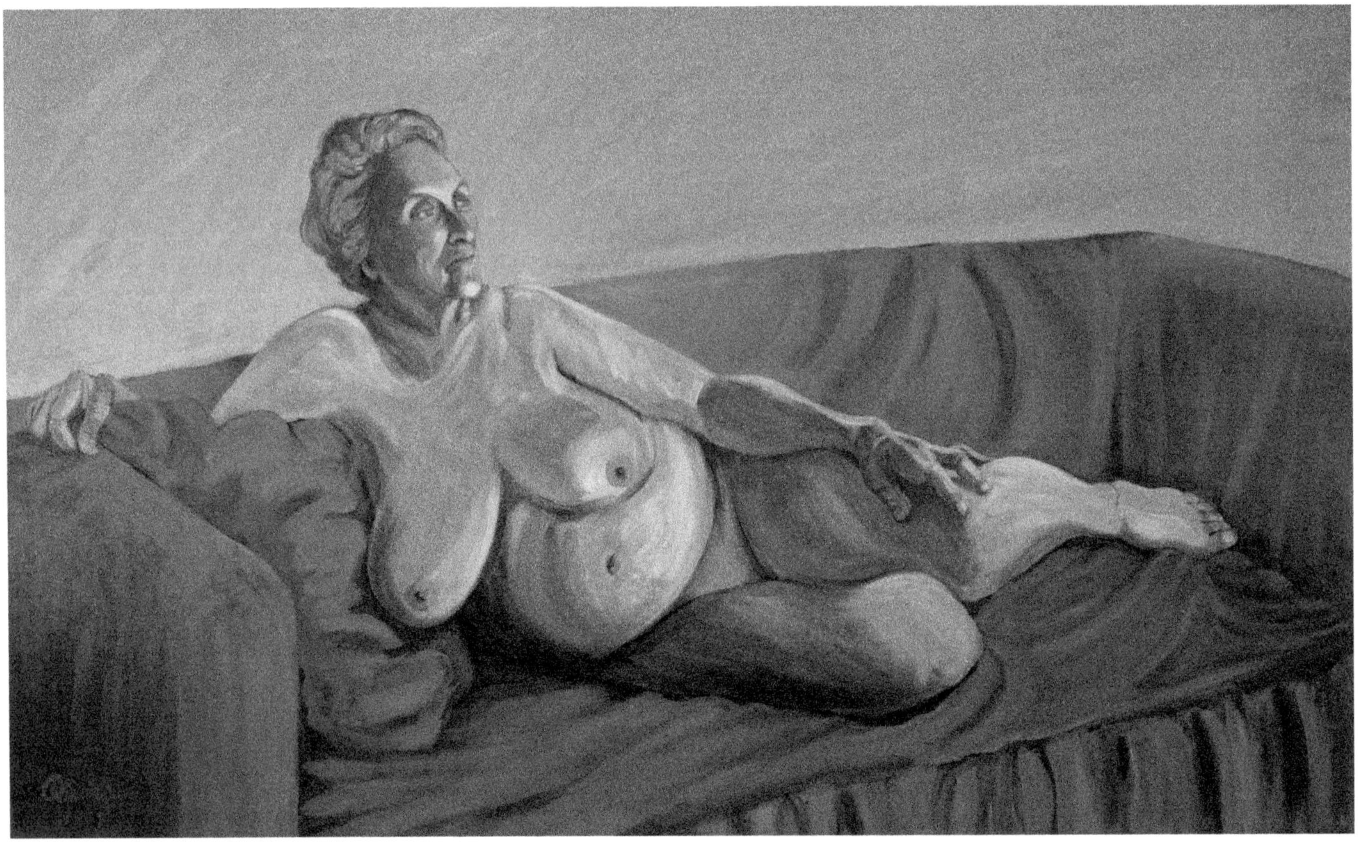

Sylvia at 87

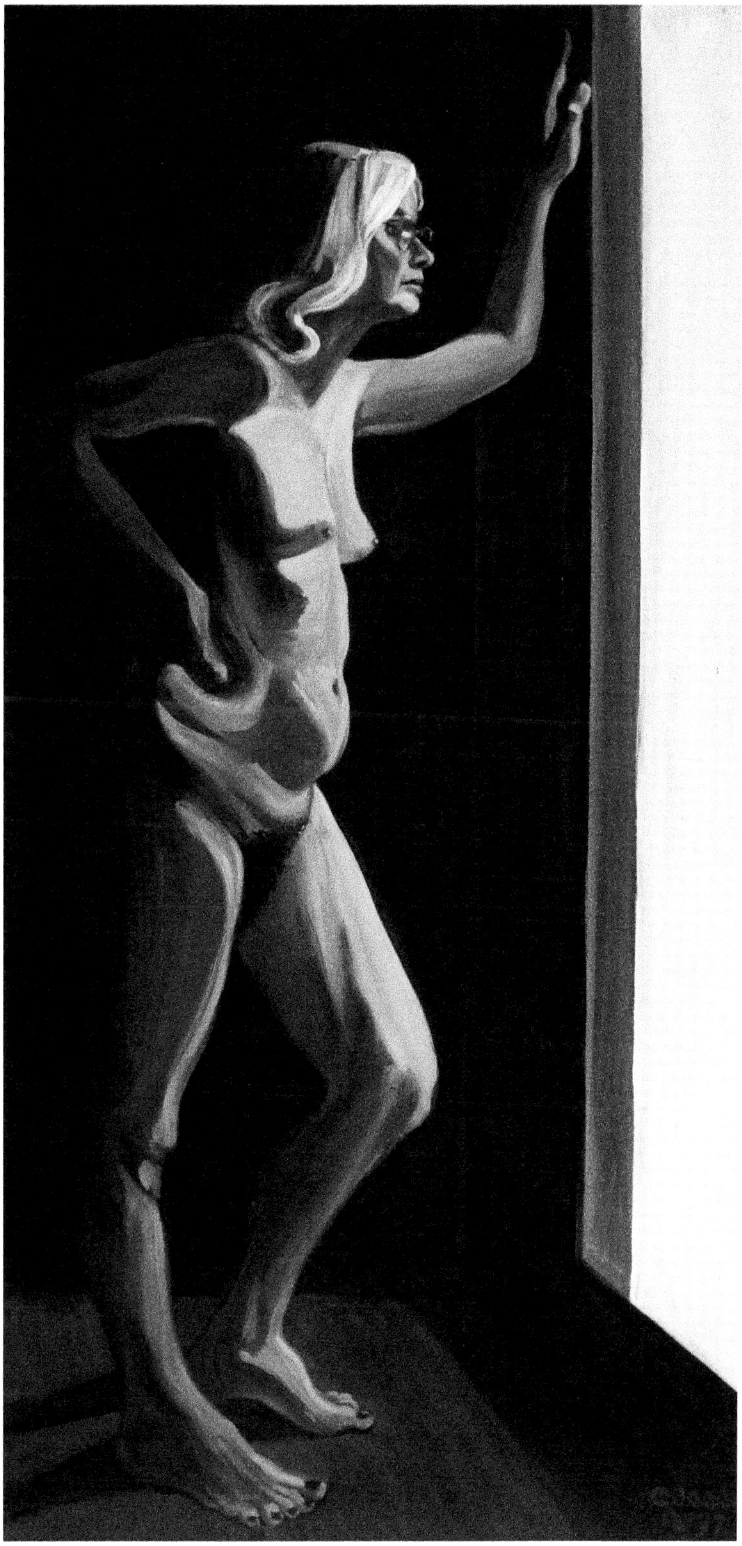

Darlene at 60

My Naked Truth

I have always been a rather modest person, so it makes me very happy to see how far I have come in accepting my form as it is. For sure, I have spent way too much of my life comparing my body to something else—anything but what I was given. How could I—an aging woman with graying curly hair, large drooping breasts, and short legs—ever be a young woman with straight hair, small breasts, and long legs? Lord knows, I tried!

When I began the *Naked Truth* series, I certainly was not as brave as the women I was painting. Toward the end, I did manage to include this self-portrait of myself half naked with one breast exposed. (If I did this painting today, the canvas would be several inches longer).

I was actually painting myself clothed when I decided it was necessary for me to be part of the series. So I set up the mirror in front of my easel, took off my top, painted out the blouse and painted in my breast. One breast was about all my modesty could handle. A few years later I thought I had reached a point where I could paint myself fully naked. I set up dramatic lighting and staged a picture of my nude self, sitting at the easel painting. The shadows hid half of my body. I took digital photographs and went to the computer to download the images. In an instant the photos were erased from my camera and deleted from the computer. To this day I haven't figured out how the computer glitch happened, but I am very glad that it did. I was relieved that I didn't have to paint that nude portrait! It was so contrived, and I wasn't ready.

Months later I was ready. I was sitting in my studio, quietly staring out the window, when suddenly a vision came to me of a painting I must do. In my mind's eye I saw an image of myself—naked—on a stark black background, unadorned and

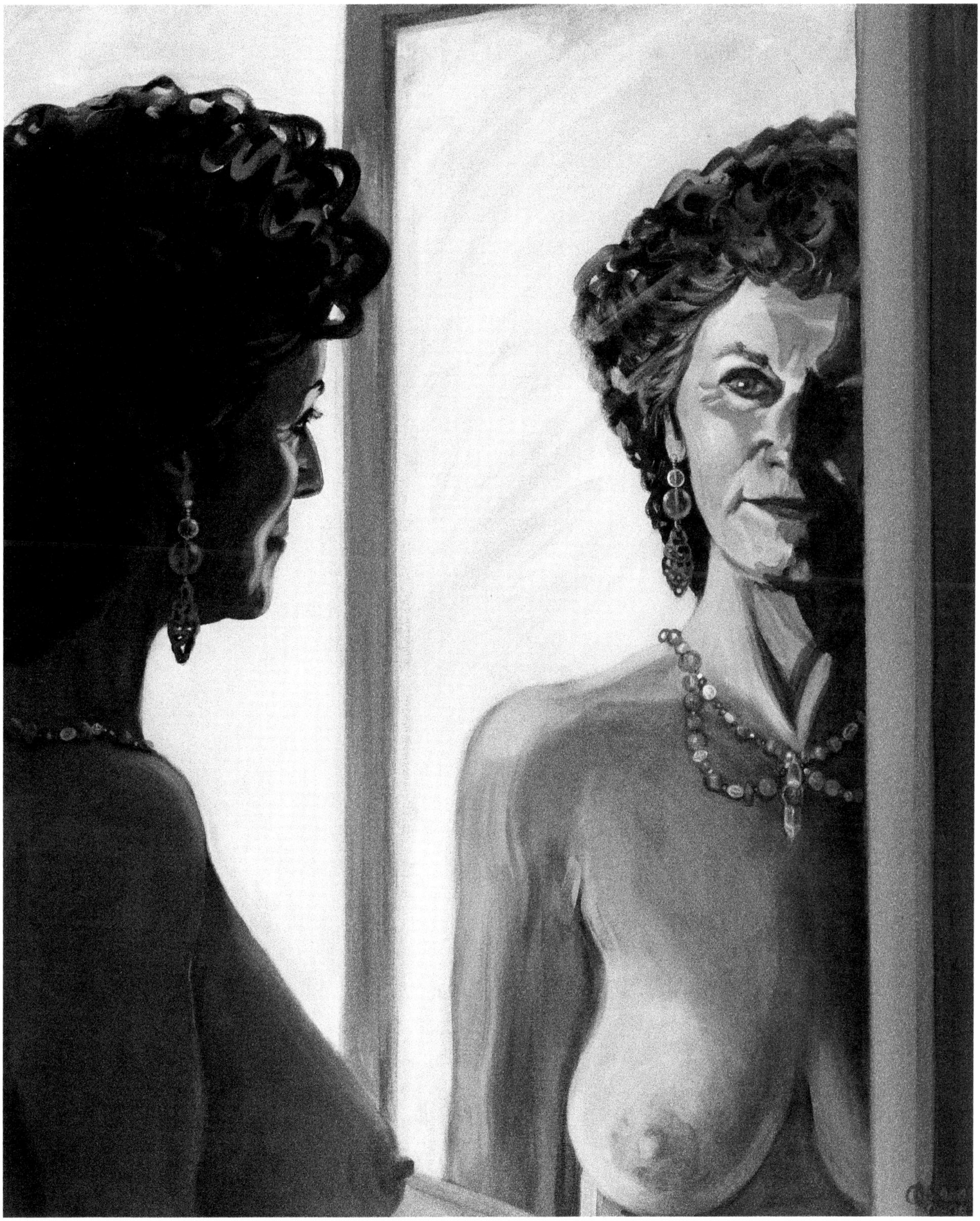

Alice at 58

standing, facing straight out, hair up, arms by my side, no makeup, no jewelry (except for the wedding necklace I never remove).

Within the next ten minutes a beautiful, blank 3x6-foot canvas was sitting on my easel, waiting to receive the image of my body in paint. As I began, it was almost as though the painting was painting itself. A likeness began appearing on the canvas of my then-sixty-five-year-old body with one breast bigger than the other, freckles, wrinkles, veins, and all the other so-called "flaws." I was amazed that I didn't have one moment of judgment about myself. I was just having a great time moving the paint around the canvas.

A few hours after completing the painting, I was to deliver a talk about my work to a large audience. I decided to give the painting its first public viewing by standing it at the entrance of the auditorium. As the people filed in, there were mixed reactions—from shock to awe. Several people commented about the unevenness of my breasts. They were surprised that I painted them that way, and that I didn't do plastic surgery with the brush and even them up. It is a personal relief that I had no desire to do that. I was more interested in being truthful about the reality of my body.

This doesn't mean that I have suddenly become a nudist. The modest person I am still resides in me. I have just become more accepting of the physical changes taking place in my aging body. Watching the deterioration is a constant reminder of the passage of time and preciousness of being alive. I am able to be a calm and fascinated witness to those changes, rather than a reluctant opponent.

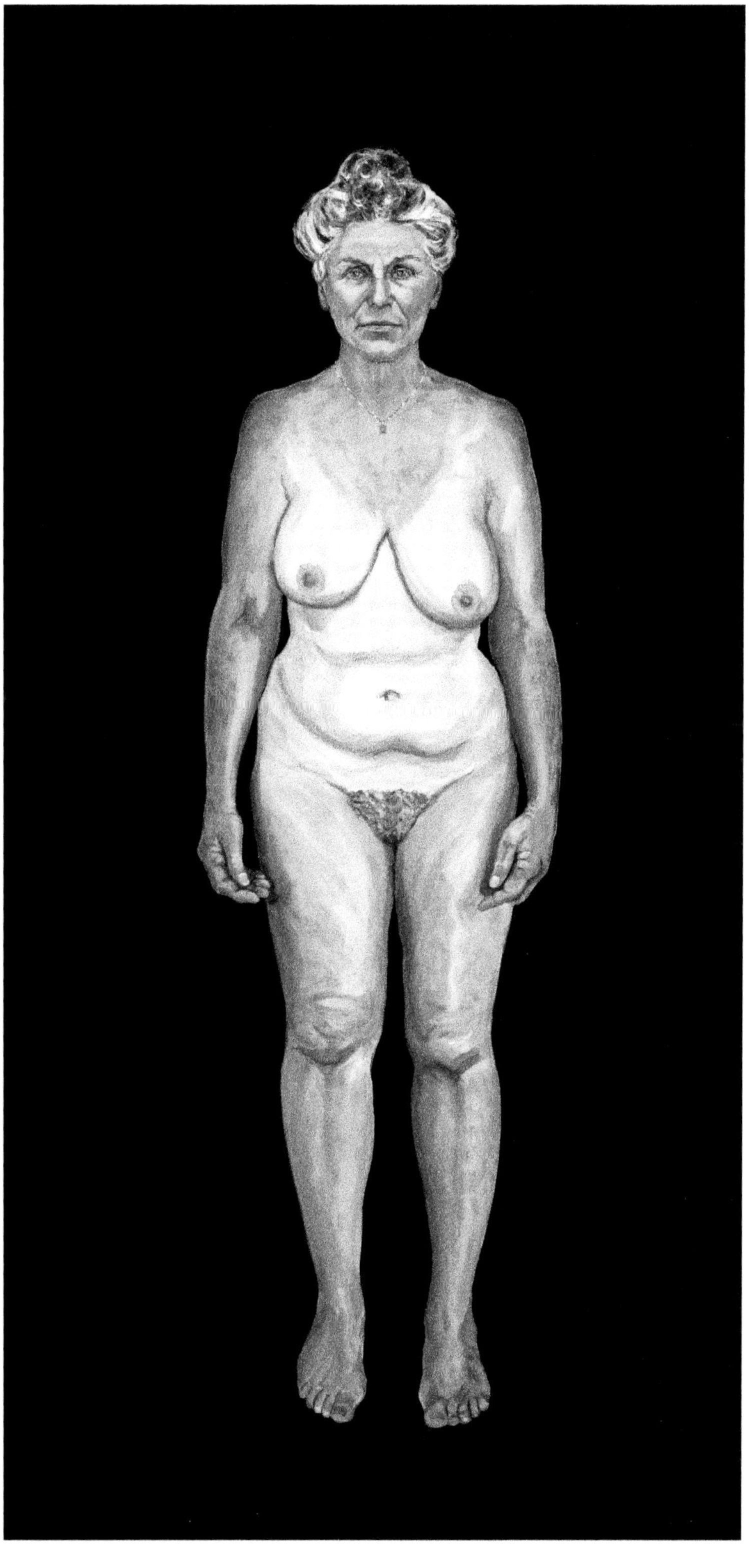

Alice at 65

"Y'know, it's a wonderful thing, as time goes by, to be with someone who looks into your face when you have gotten old, and still sees what you think you look like."

—From the movie *The Bachelor*

Lovers

RICHARD

"For one human being to love another: that is perhaps the most difficult of all our tasks, the ultimate, the last test and proof, the work for which all other is but preparation."

—Rainer Maria Rilke, *Letters to a Young Poet*

PICTURE A COUPLE IN A ROMANTIC SCENE—A DARKENED ROOM with candles and soft music, hands touching while staring dreamily into each other's eyes. More than likely, this couple would be young—in their twenties or early thirties. Love, sensuality, and romance are almost invariably linked with youthfulness.

The sculptures in the *Lovers* series depict couples in intimate loving embrace. What's incongruous about these pieces is that the couples are old. Some people report being shocked when first viewing the figures. Their judgments about older people and sensuality are stimulated. (As if once a couple reaches a certain stage in life, passion and physical intimacy are supposed to drop away.) At one time I had considered provoking this shock by portraying older couples in explicitly sexual poses. I realized, however, that this was not what I was after. I wanted to capture the tenderness that results when, after many years, a couple has grown to know, accept, and appreciate one another. What I wanted to convey was gentle, comfortable love. The age of the couples was an indication of the enduring quality of that love.

Alice, in *Naked Truth*, asks us to accept ourselves as we are—flaws and all. In *Lovers* I extend this by asking us to accept the other, the beloved—flaws and all. The "flaws" here are the physical manifestations of aging. The couples portrayed in my sculptures are wrinkled and sagging, yet, through pose and gesture they reveal that they clearly cherish each other. This is one of the things that moves people the most about these pieces—the subjects express love for each other despite the ravages of time. This touches a deep yearning in all of us, the desire to be loved and accepted throughout our life span, in spite of our physical imperfections, and in spite of our other shortcomings.

This vision of steadfast acceptance and dogged commitment by a partner is especially meaningful in later life. The challenges of the illness and fragility of the older years can be overwhelming. To have a helpmate who is eager and willing to share the burden is a great blessing. I am fortunate to have such a staunch ally in Alice. There is not an ounce of doubt in my mind that if I am in need, Alice will be there in a second to lend her strength and encouragement. She knows I will be there for her. Knowing I am not alone is a great comfort in my life. This easy give-and-take Alice and I share was not always there. We were both tested and tempered by our mistakes in previous relationships and failed marriages.

Older people have the potential to achieve a quality of love that is rare in younger people. It arises from having the perspective of years of life experience, and being able to separate through that experience what is important and meaningful from what is not. At this level of love, physical appearance takes on an insignificant role. At this level, love becomes truly blind—it blinds us to the physical imperfections (aging features) of our beloved. But more than blinding us to their shortcomings, aged love can also allow us to see our partner more clearly. With loving eyes, we are able to perceive all of who they are. We see them in their unadorned humanness—their vulnerability, their strength, their stupidity, their wisdom—without judgment or blame. This depth of vision even makes an exquisite work of art of our partner's imperfections.

I am not blind to the ongoing effect of age on Alice's face and body, yet to me, she could not be more beautiful. In fact, a facelift, dyed hair, liposuction, or wrinkle-removing injections would only take away from the natural essence that I find so beautiful in her. I stroke her age spotted hands, kiss the loose flesh on her arms, run my fingers through her grey hair. This is her body. This is the body I love. Without a shadow of a doubt, I know I will find Alice beautiful no matter how old she becomes, just as I know she will feel the same about me, with my balding head and expanding belly.

After a quarter century of marriage, romance is still alive and well. We also share a profound friendship/love, as comfortable as an old shoe, where support is given freely, and volumes are communicated with a single glance or touch of a hand.

Years of living together has expanded the way we can be with each other. We are no longer limited to the roles of "romantic lover," or even "husband and wife." Our relationship now encompasses "sister/brother," "mother/son," "father/daughter," and, of course, "friend/friend." With this wide range of possibilities, our personalities, both in and out of the relationship, have blossomed.

Aged love can grow more delicious with the years because time becomes more precious. Alice and I understand that each passing day is one day less that we have together. This makes our shared moments all the more treasured. Right there is the rub with aged love. The sweeter, more delightful, and harmonious the love, the greater will be the pain of loss when one partner's life ends. The best of loves have this bittersweet quality. All we can do is savor the moment as we live it and remember it will pass. The sense of uncertainty about how long we have together prompts us to be as loving as possible. If one of us can say or do something that will let the other know they are loved, we will. And we refuse to hold on to anger and resentments for even a minute. Releasing negative feelings makes more room for love.

An unexpected bonus from this feeling of the preciousness of our time together is the quality of our sexuality. Our lovemaking has become a bodily expression of our love for each other ... a communion. Our intimate moments are revered—partly because there are fewer of them, and partly because with years of practice we have become expert in pleasing one another, and partly because we know we haven't a lot of time left, and this might be the last opportunity we have to make love.

We recently renewed our wedding vows—which we do from time to time. As we were thinking about our original vows, we realized there was no need to retake them since we have already been doing a good job following them. So we came up with a new one, which has a great deal of meaning for us: "May we always remember that today may be the last day we have together." We contemplate this vow a lot, and it does give a taste of the possibility of life without one another. However, the reality of dealing with our beloved partner's death is impossible for us to conceive. We cannot go there, it's too sad. (We are both crying as we write this.)

The characters in each of the pieces of the *Lovers* series are alike—the men are bald, the women wear their hair in a bun. They are modeled after no one in particular—just images from my imagination. But they are actually a very personal expression. They are symbolic of the love Alice and I share. We are fortunate to be blessed with a deep, abiding love for each other. Each pose in the *Lovers* series expresses aspects of that love. Alice and I find ourselves instinctively falling into these poses without thinking. It is just how we relate physically with each other.

I believe that what inspires people most about this series of sculptures is that they carry the genuine energy of love—our love.

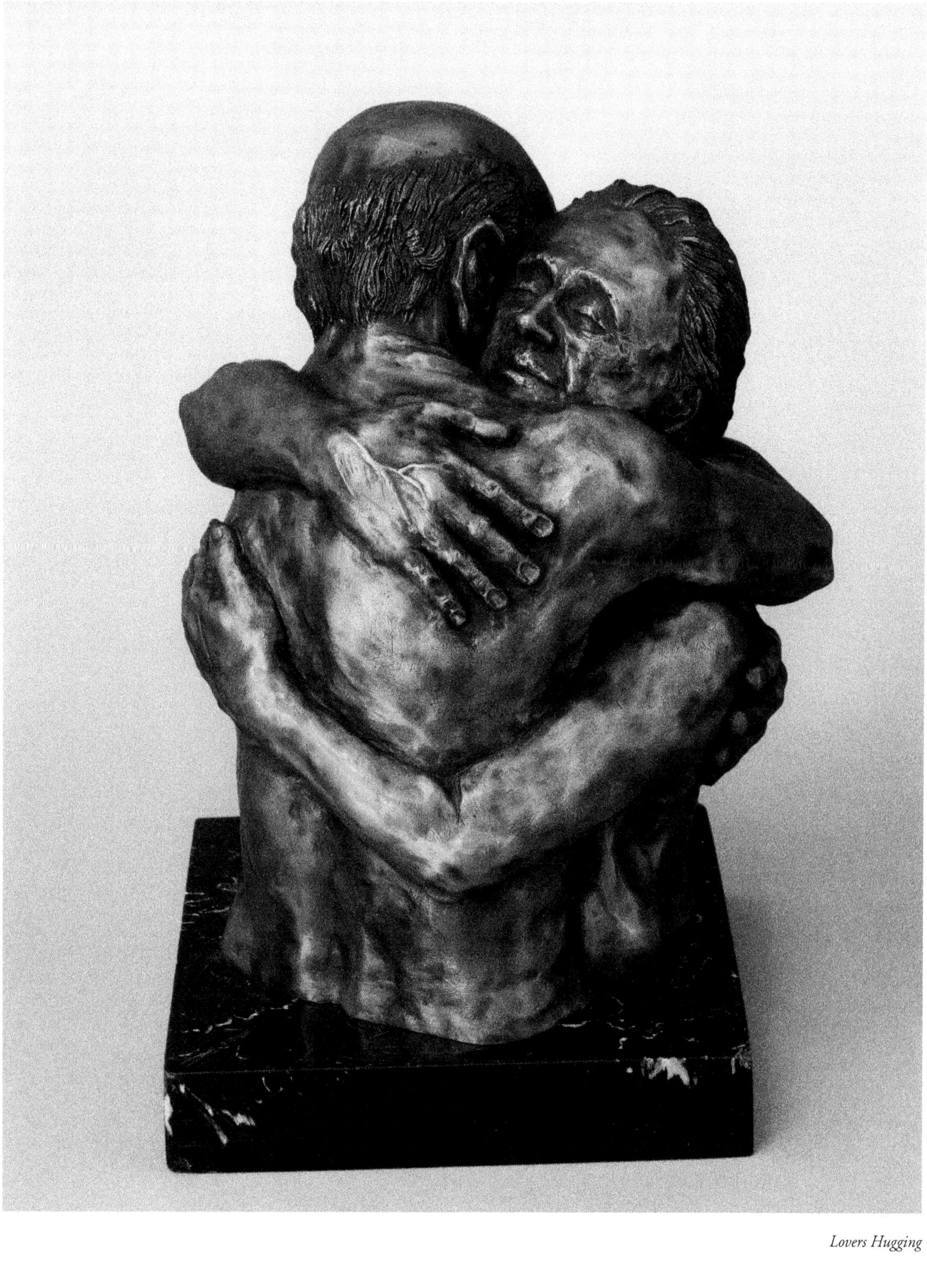

Lovers Hugging

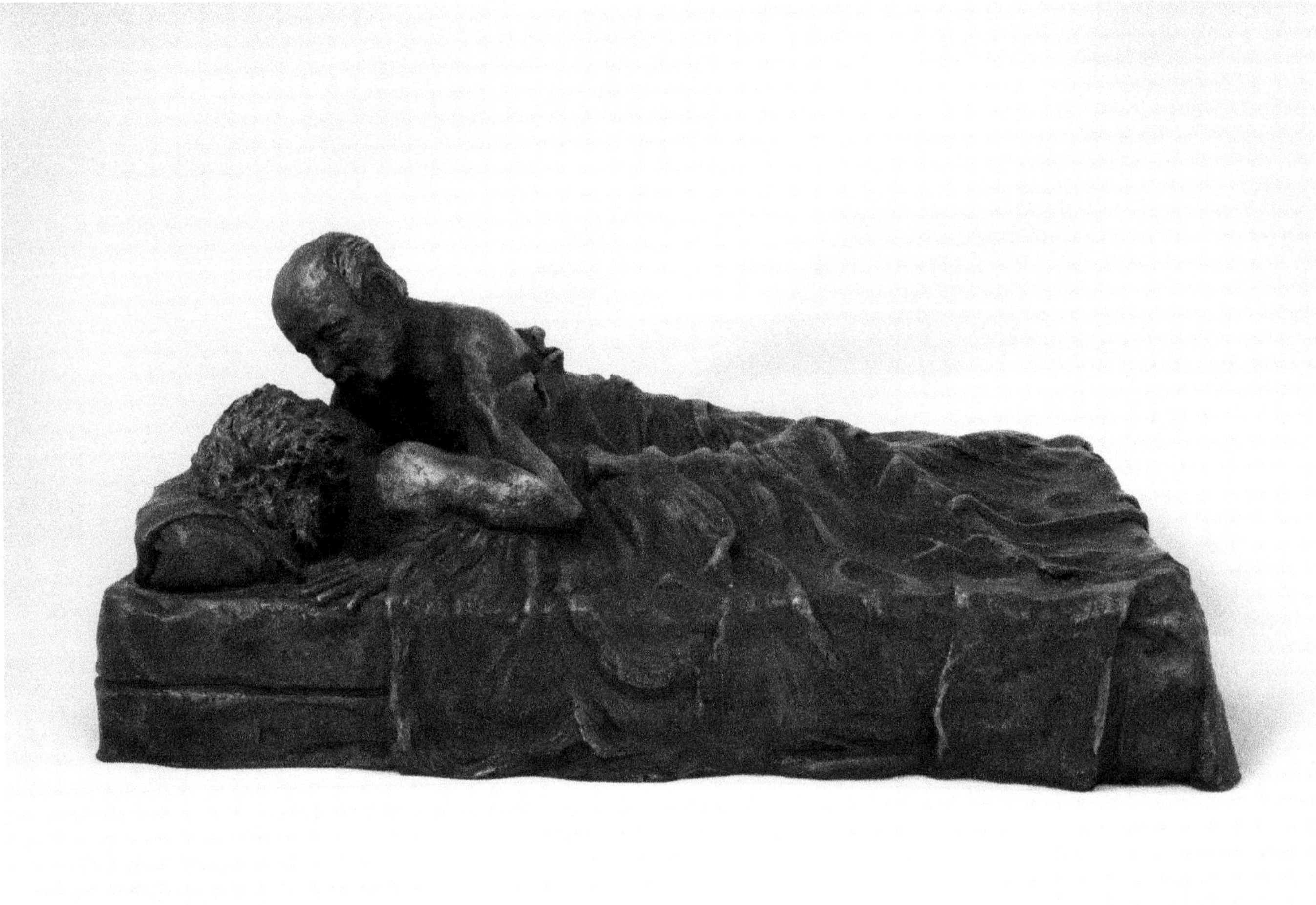

Lovers in Bed

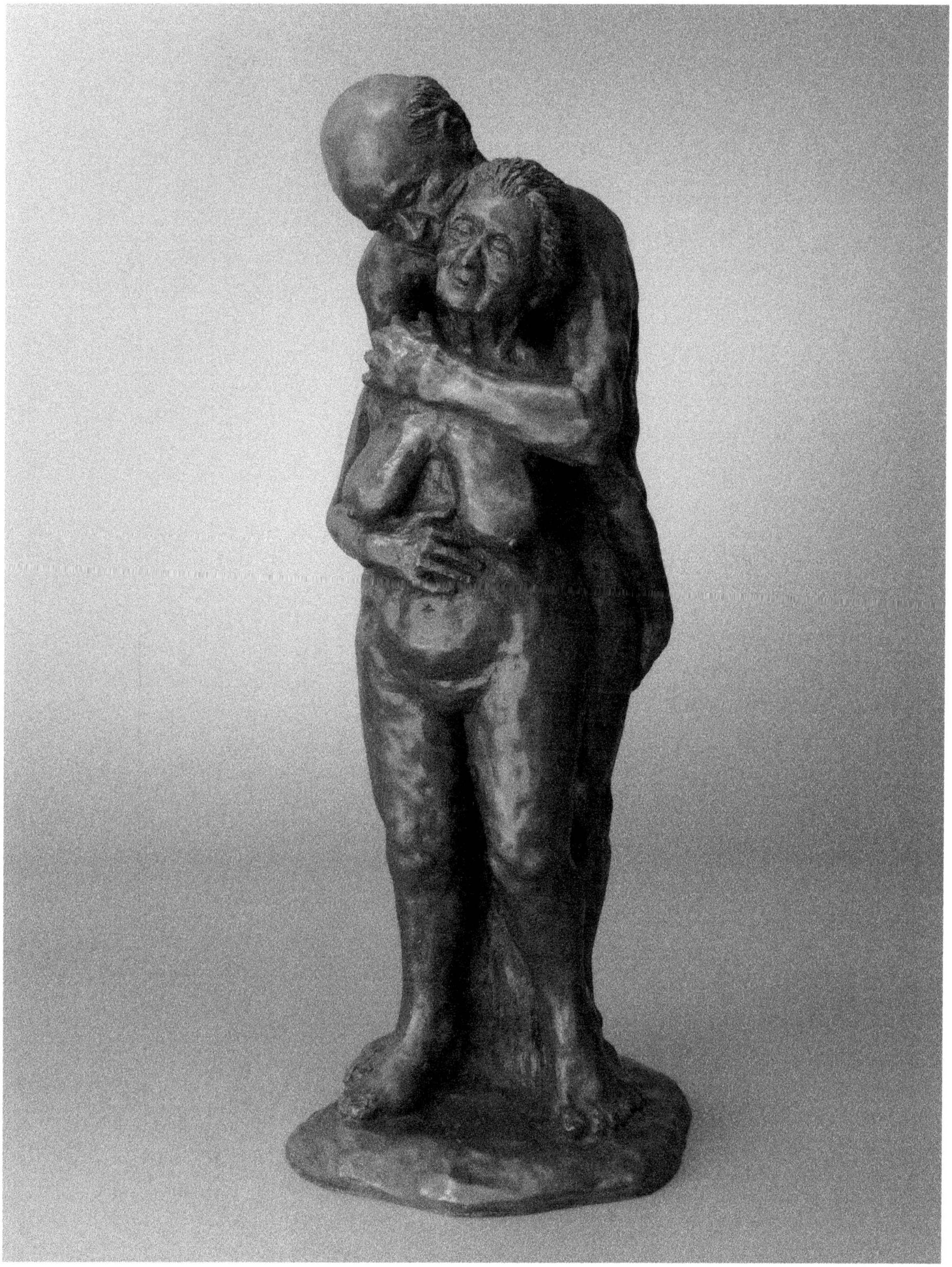

Lovers Embracing

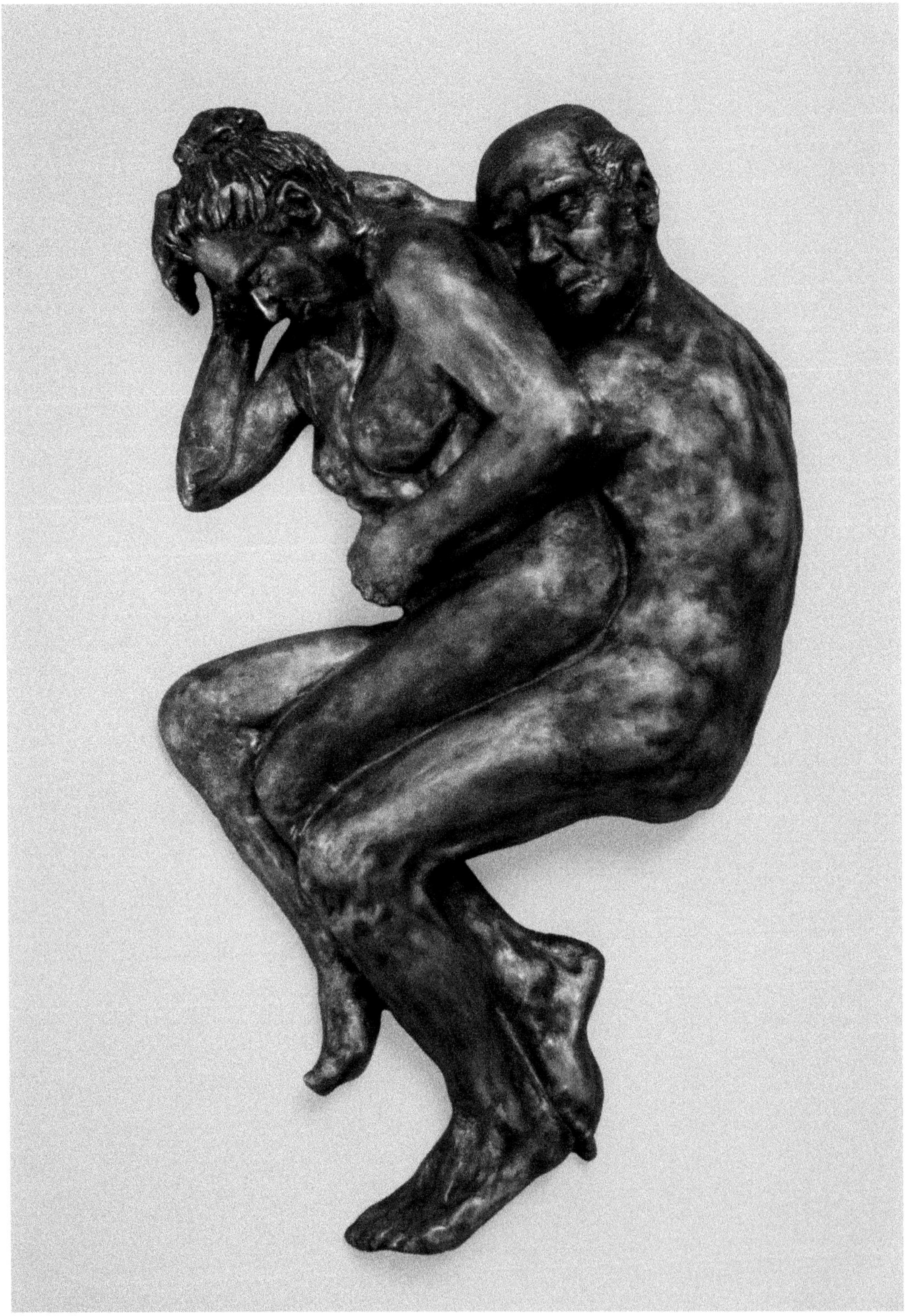

Lovers Spooning

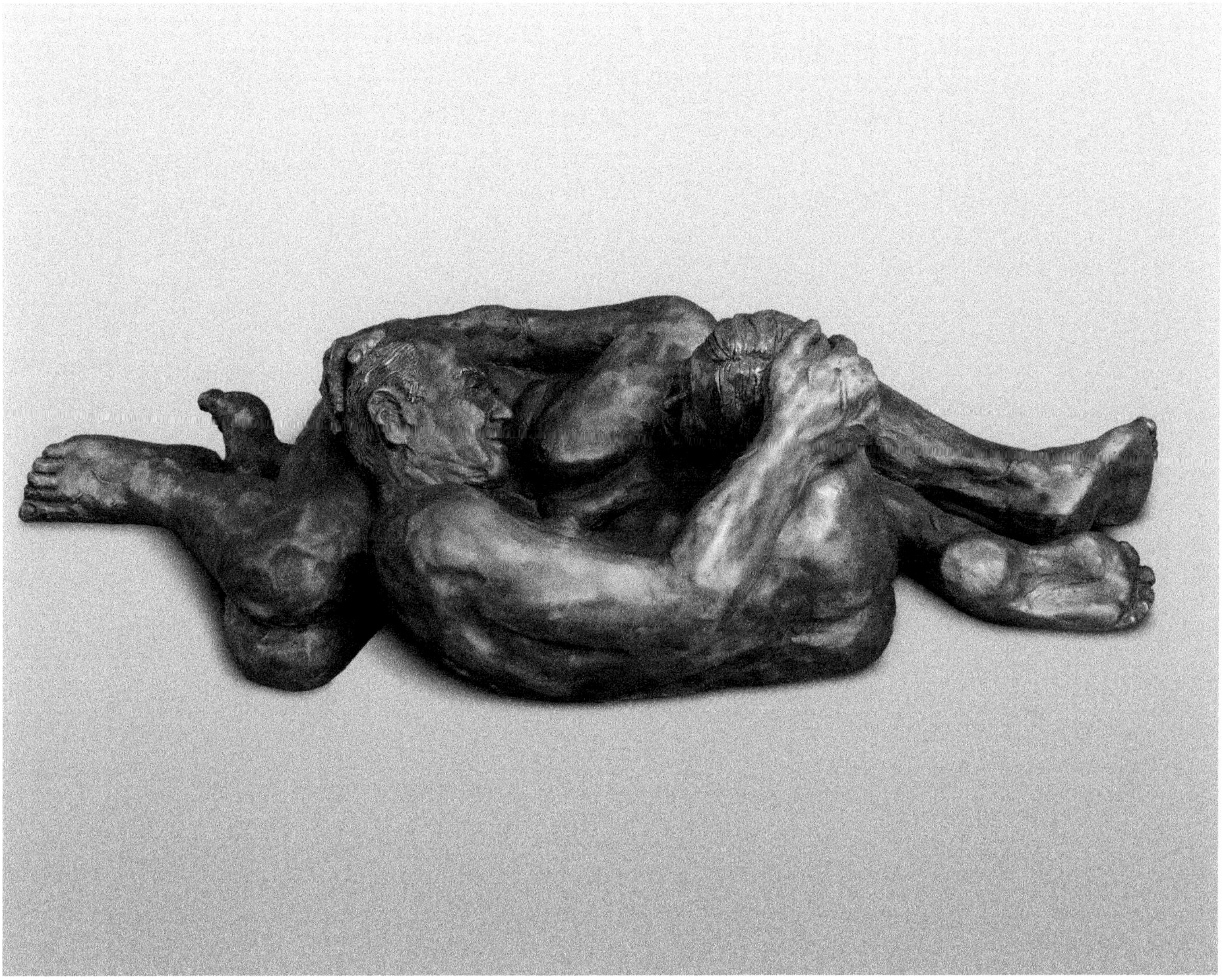

Lovers Reclining

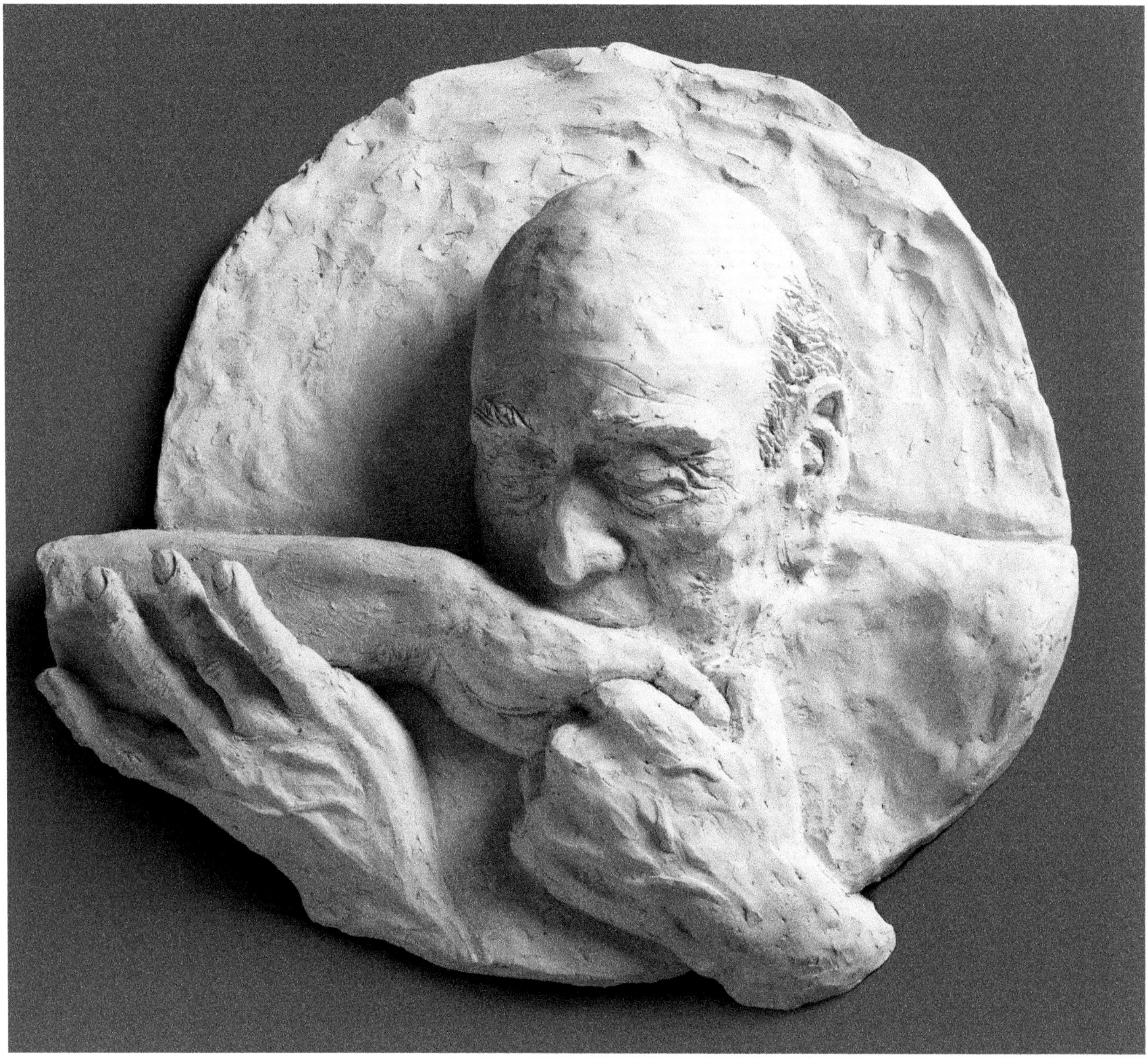

Lover Kissing Hand

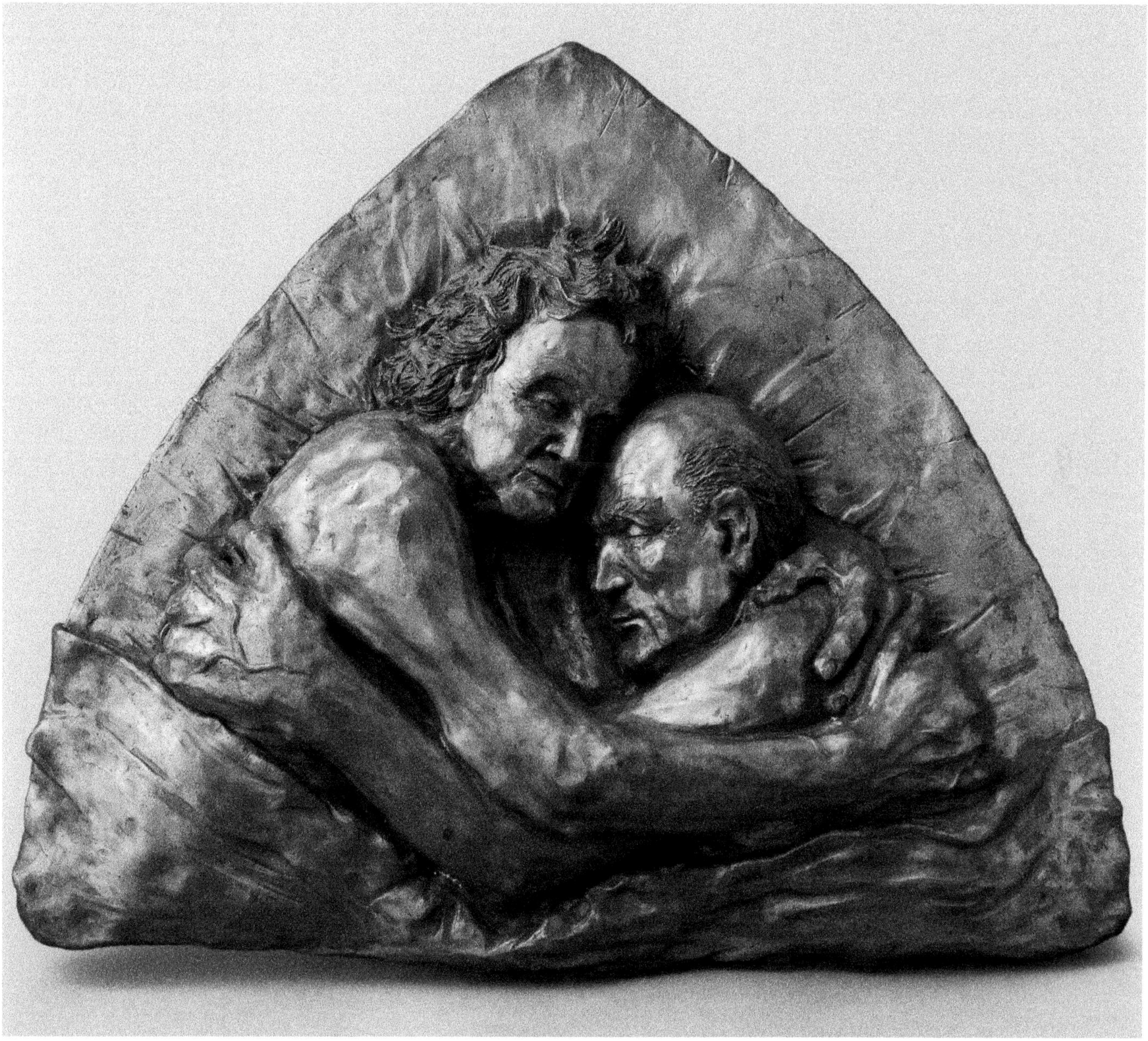

Lovers Embracing

"A curtain of pearls hangs before the hall of jade,
And within is a lovely lady,
Fairer in form than the gods and immortals,
Her face like a blossom of peach or plum.
Spring mists will cover the eastern mansion,
Autumn winds blow from the western lodge,
And after 30 years have passed,
She will look like a piece of pressed sugar cane."

—Han Sahn, Chinese Poet and Recluse

Declining Years

AUNT KITTY AGE 89–97

ALICE

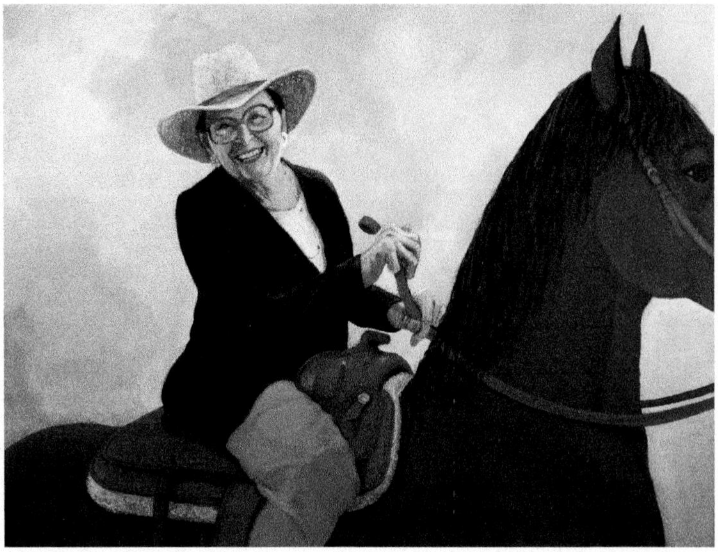

Aunt Kitty at 89

"From the day you are born,

you begin to die."

—Grandfather Semu Huaute, Chumash Indian Medicine Man

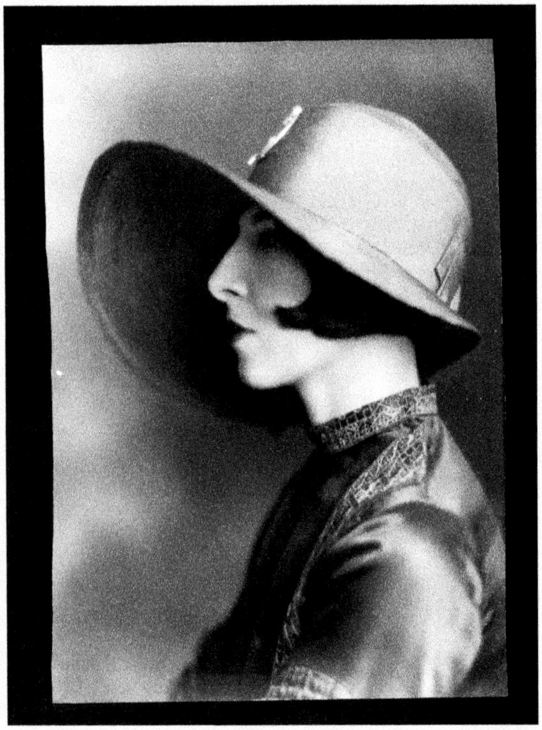

Aunt Kitty at 24

"GROW OLD ALONG WITH ME, THE BEST IS YET TO BE," wrote Robert Browning. But is this true? I have watched family and friends grow old and their declining years certainly seemed to be far from their best. Incontinence, some form of senility, immobility or inability to move around without support, loneliness caused by the death of loved ones, were the on-going experiences that have plagued most of the old people in my life.

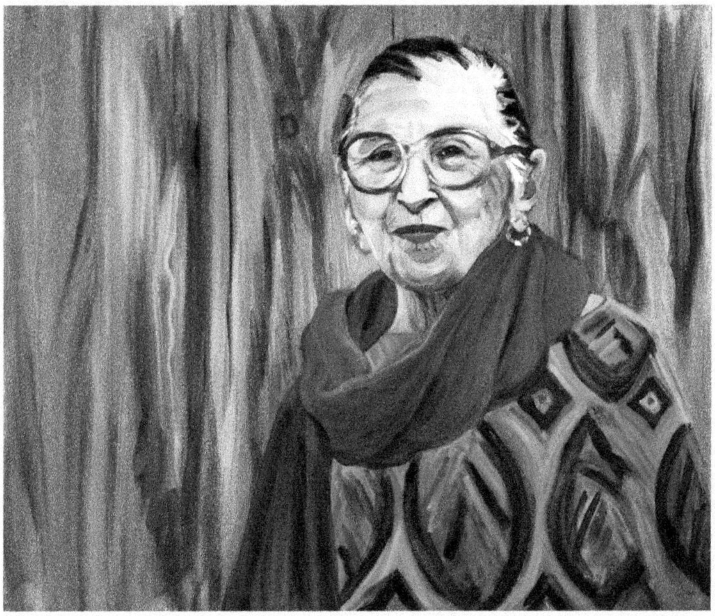

Aunt Kitty at 90

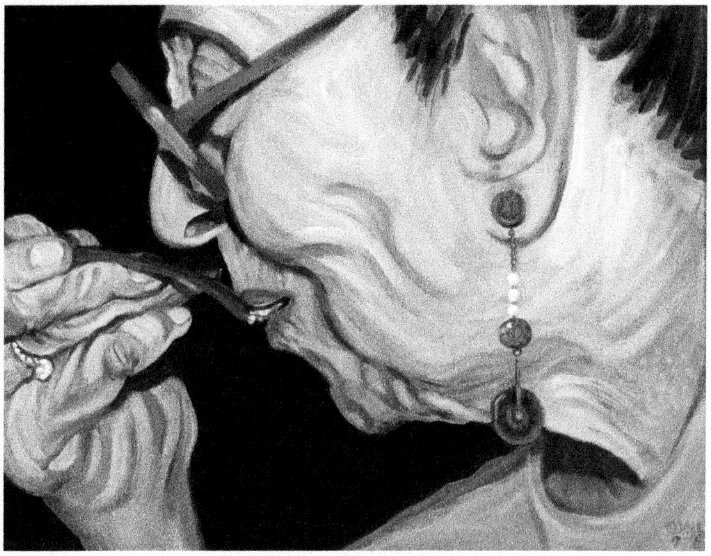

Aunt Kitty at 91

The *Women of Age* and *Naked Truth* series of paintings concerned my search to discover the positive side of growing older and my acceptance of the aging process. To come to completion, I needed to confront two issues that were very difficult for me to contemplate: my fear of the decline in the final years and my terror of dying.

The experience of being caretaker to Aunt Kitty opened the door to further exploration, with paint and canvas, of the phenomena of late old age and the end of life. I always loved Richard's maternal aunt and found her visually fascinating. I began painting her when she was 89, and continued doing her portrait as she aged. Over time, I realized that I had a powerful series that graphically revealed the unfolding drama of the final stages of life.

Kitty had been a very active "feisty old bitch" (as I liked to call her). She was kind, generous, enjoyed everything, and was very adventurous for a woman of her generation. Over her life span she had seen tremendous change. She was born in the horse and buggy era, born before the Wright Brothers flew their wood and fabric glider at Kittyhawk. Yet, she was able to watch on television as men walked on the surface of the moon. How lonely it must have been for her to have lost, one by one, her contemporaries with whom she had shared the experiences of her generation. In many ways, she was a time traveler, a stranger in a strange land.

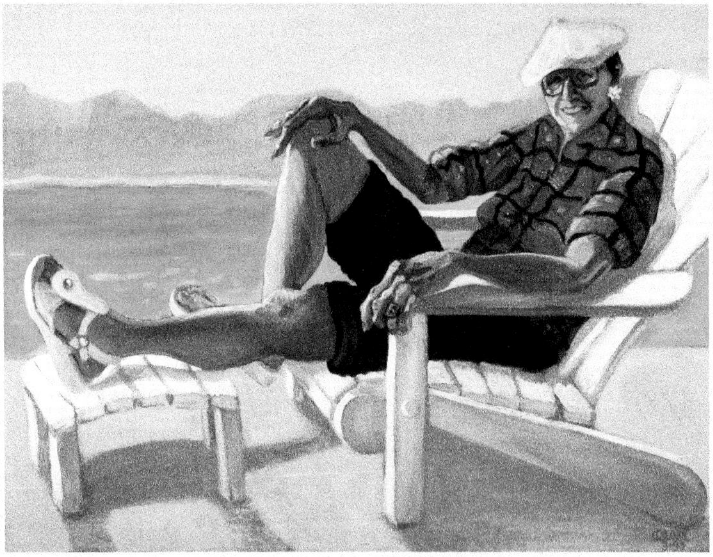

Aunt Kitty at 92

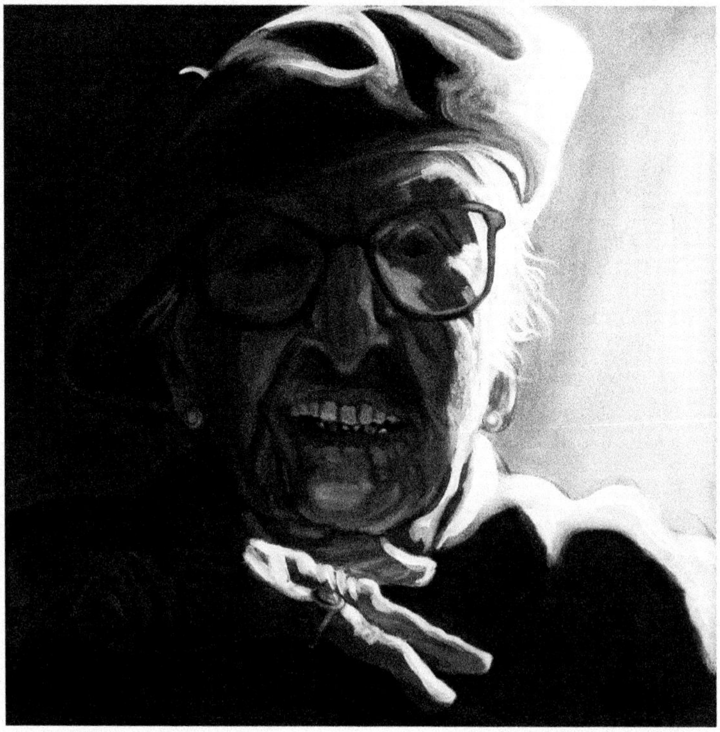

Aunt Kitty at 93

Aunt Kitty drove her car until she was ninety-two. We finally had to take it away because practically every day she called to say that her car had been stolen. In the evening, parking attendants would return her car—the only one left in the lot where she had parked it. How she got home, no one knew. Around the same time, we had to persuade her to move into a retirement hotel, a major change for such an independent woman. After complaining for about two weeks (she said she hated being around so many old people), she just let it go and got into the program.

In eight short years Aunt Kitty went from riding a horse to riding a wheelchair. Each year brought greater deterioration, until, at the end of her life, she was shrunken to a tiny person in diapers, locked in a fetal position, totally dependent on others for her care. Even then, she had a smile for everyone and a "thank you."

Our face and body constantly change as we move through life. Yet, changes in our appearance are less discernable in our middle years. As the sequence of portraits of Aunt Kitty shows, it is shocking to see how quickly deterioration of the body can accelerate in the final years. The changes can be compared to watching the dramatic evolution of a newborn baby into the body of an eight-year-old child ... except that in old age it happens in reverse.

I watched Aunt Kitty physically change as she progressed through her final years. Seeing how she surrendered at each stage, how

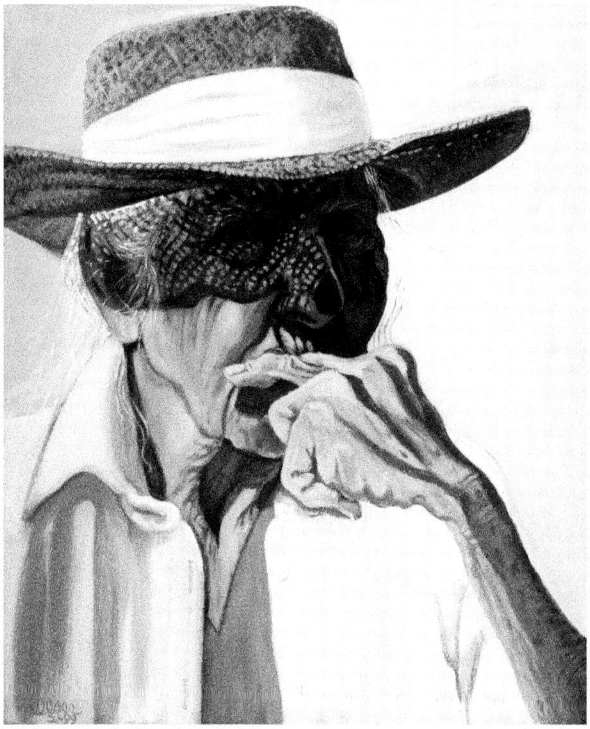

Aunt Kitty at 94

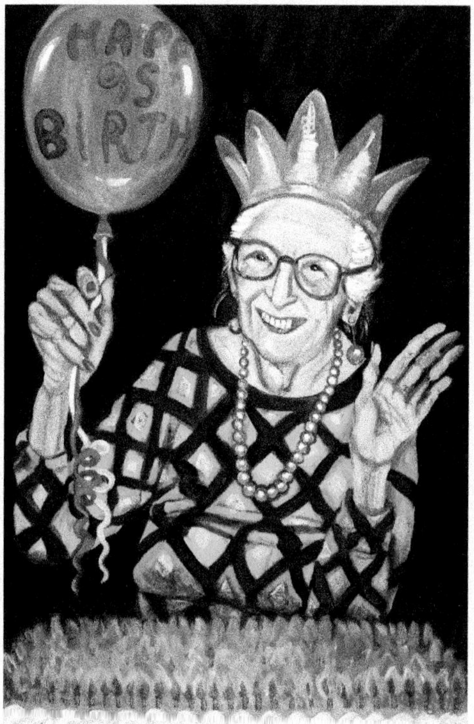

Aunt Kitty at 95th birthday

gracefully and without complaint she let go of each diminishing ability, was a model of how I would like to be as I age and move toward my own death. She didn't look back with regret at how she had changed from what she had been, nor did she obsess about her impaired processes of elimination and digestion, or complain about her aches and pains. She simply accepted her life, her present moment as it was. I recognize that the only way to achieve peace involves surrendering to "what is." When I try to freeze change and struggle to hold onto what is no longer there, I find that this is a recipe for suffering. Surrender is not giving up. It is recognizing the truth of the situation and allowing that truth to be your guide.

Surrendering to "what is" will mean that as I age I must let go of vital parts of my life, just as Aunt Kitty did. As senses dim, strength ebbs, and I am forced to become more dependent on others, the joys of life will inevitably become fewer and far between. It would be unrealistic to hope for a return of former abilities. Old age is a downward trajectory. All of life's important passages—birth, adolescence, graduation, marriage, parenthood, retirement—are passages into life's future. All except old age—the future of old age is death.

So, how am I to deal with these difficult truths of the declining years? Actually, this book catalogues my attempts to do this. Through my art projects, contemplation, and writing, I look my

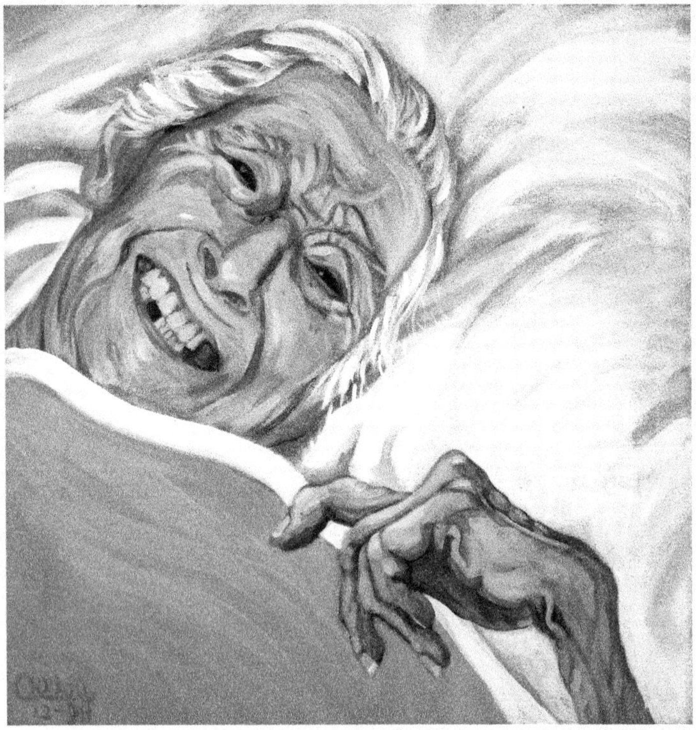

Aunt Kitty at 95

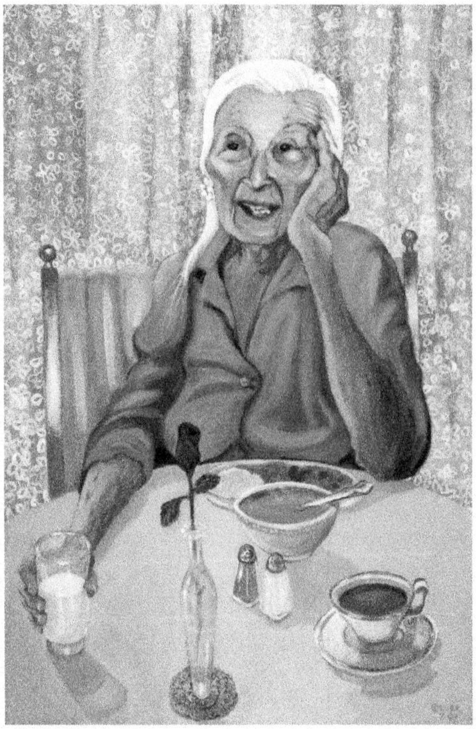

Aunt Kitty at 96

aging and death squarely in the face, rather than hiding from or denying them. I try, to the best of my ability, to allow the truth of the impermanence of my life to enter me. I have spent time with older people, listening deeply to them and absorbing their words and experiences. I work to maintain my precious body which is my vehicle for this lifetime. And, I devote my energies to attending to my spirit—reading uplifting books, keeping the company of spiritually advanced friends and teachers, and practicing such disciplines as meditation, yoga, and prayer. I know that the work I have done has helped to alleviate some of my fear and confusion. Until I am directly faced with disabling health or emotional issues, I can never know for sure, but I firmly believe my experience over the last dozen years has helped to better prepare me for the winter of my life..

Old age and death is a game I know I cannot win. Each day I grow older and the final outcome of the game is never in doubt. Even if I am diligent in the care of my body, it can only delay the inevitable deterioration. The best I can do is play the game well, optimize my moves when life throws a curve, and hope for a good long run. What I can do is treat myself with loving care and hope that the debilities and weakness are staved off to the very end of my life. That is what I would consider a well-played game.

Life is a flawed plan. I agree with the statement, "Youth is wasted on the young." If we could only grow stronger, more flexible,

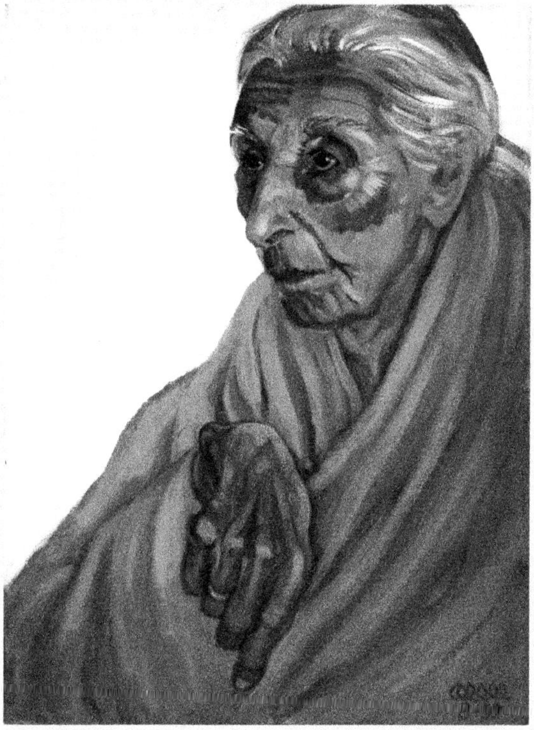

Aunt Kitty at 96

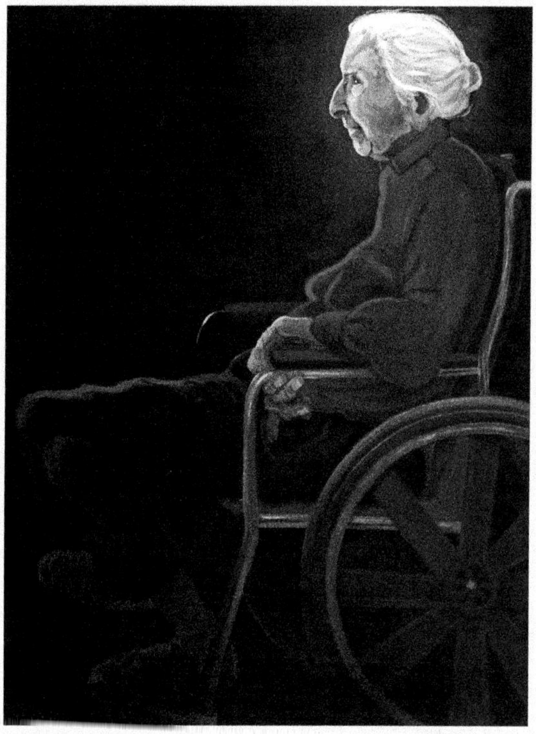

Aunt Kitty at 97

healthier, and more energetic as we grow older, but that is not to be. Since we must decline as we age, I find it imperative to avoid slipping into the trap of negative thinking. It helps to lighten up and maintain a sense of humor about my growing old. After all, there is nothing that can be done, and it is very odd and fascinating to observe myself morph from "girldom" to "ghouldom." My Mom and I used to sing a fifties rock-n-roll song with great gusto about our aging. It was to the tune of "Rock Around the Clock." The only change we made was to the lyrics—we changed the word "rock" to "rot."

Our Last Moments With Aunt Kitty

A FEW DAYS BEFORE AUNT KITTY died, she quietly slipped into a coma-like state. In this final painting, she was "sleeping" peacefully, with only the faintest breath passing through her nostrils. Richard and I carefully tiptoed into her room and quietly bent over her bed. With her eyes closed and without a change in her peaceful state, Aunt Kitty suddenly reached out and grabbed our hands, grasping them tightly. We held onto each other for a short time until her grasp gently lightened and let go. Somewhere in her consciousness she seemed aware of our presence beside her. We exchanged our love and wordlessly said good-bye to each other for the last time. She died a few hours later.

It is an inexplicable feeling to be in the presence of death. One minute Aunt Kitty was alive, breathing and conscious. The next split second her body was still there, but the conscious being who had occupied it was gone. We, the living, were left standing beside the empty shell where Aunt Kitty once lived.

Death is such a mystery. It raises countless questions, but provides no answers. When will I die? What will be the cause of my death? Will it hurt to die? What will become of "me"? Will I go to some other place and see my departed loved ones, or will the "me" with my personal history of dreams, memories, and loves be totally and eternally extinguished?

What, if anything, will remain of my personality after my death is an open question for me. Right now, I enjoy my life and am eager for many more exciting adventures, so for me the thought of death is still a fearful one. My fear of death follows me in the background like a shadow. I don't feel that it is morbid for me to be mindful of my death or the death of those

I love. I want my mortality to be in the open, unhidden. Awareness of my impending death helps me to be ready to die. If I am ready to die, I will be more ready to live.

In our culture, death is a taboo subject. Few are willing to talk about it because they are so fearful. Yet, in many other cultures, death is out in the open, and sometimes even celebrated. One of the most unforgettable images in my life was in India, on the shores of the Ganges River in Varanasi. At this spot, where scores of cremations take place every day, Richard and I were present as the body of a man about my age was carried in and placed on the funeral pyre. We watched transfixed as the corpse, engulfed in flames, was slowly reduced to ashes. While this was occurring, so much life was happening around us … a cow was wading in the water munching on a wreath of flowers from a previous funeral, women were washing their clothes in the river, children were playing, and a puppy was chewing on a human skull at our feet. Death was so close at hand, yet so natural and accepted.

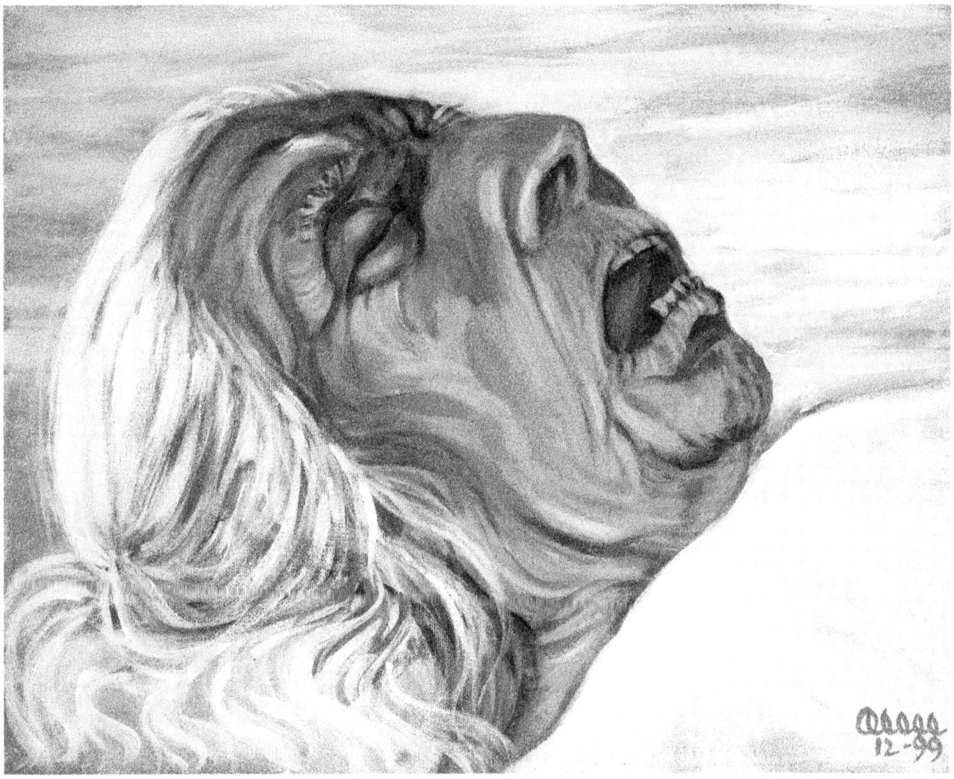

Aunt Kitty dying

My experience with our aged parents and other elders facing death has shown me that most likely my fear of death will change as I move toward the end of my life. Rather than seeing my death as an enemy, I will hopefully come to see it as a friend. I have known a number of elders who accomplished what they needed during their lifetimes. They had nothing left to complete. Their sorrows and accumulated pain had surpassed their enjoyment of life. Uninterested in living longer and ready to depart, they welcomed the angel of death at their door with equanimity. Aunt Kitty was one of them.

"Thus shall you think of all this fleeting world:
A star at dawn, a bubble in a stream;
A flash of lightning in a summer cloud,
A flickering lamp, a phantom, and a dream."

—FROM THE BUDDHA'S DIAMOND SUTRA

Reflections

ON BEING WITH OUR PARENTS
IN THEIR OLD AGE AND DEATH

ALICE AND RICHARD

THE PAINTINGS AND SCULPTURE HERE DEPICT RICHARD'S MOTHER and father, Ruth and Jack, and Alice's mother, Beulah. They were the ones who accompanied us into our middle age. Alice's father, also named Jack, died when she was almost thirteen years old, and her stepfather, Sumner, died in his early seventies. Ruth, Jack, and Beulah all left this world within nine months of each other. Ruth was the first to die, at age ninety-one. Eight months later, shortly before her eighty-eighth birthday, Beulah was gone. One month after that, Jack died at ninety-two.

To perfect the art of aging is to become expert in the art of living. Our parents were our first teachers in that art. They guided us through our youth when we were growing up and they were in the bloom of life. We learned about aging from them when we were in middle age and they were old. Their lessons remain with us to this day.

After we left our family homes to begin our independent lives and to take on other mentors, the relationship with our parents receded into the background. As they aged and needed our help more, we began spending more time with them, increasingly taking over the roles of caretaker and authority. We soon recognized, however, that we needed to approach our relationship with our parents with a softer, more receptive attitude. That sensitivity to their thoughts and feelings would allow us to appreciate the changes they were going through as they aged. It also helped us to realize that they had much more to teach us, and we had much more to learn about aging and letting go of life. Bearing witness to their growing old and ultimately dying provided us with a map of the problems and pitfalls we will most likely face as we age. It also offered us a model, mostly positive, but sometimes negative, of how we can best approach our own aging and death.

Our work with the projects for *The Art of Aging* was a great help to both of us. We were able to better accept our fears and uncertainties and to soften some of the armor that insulated us from our feelings about our own aging. Thus, with less anxiety to blind us, we could be more fully present with our parents.

Our final years with our parents were among the most intimate and rewarding times we ever spent with them. All of us recognized the limited time that remained for us to be together, and we wanted that time to be precious. We felt a sense of renewed affection and family unity.

Of course, being with our parents in their old age was not without its challenges and frustration. A recurring problem for us was dealing with our own impatience. Old people move at their own pace, and getting ready to go somewhere always takes longer than expected. We just had to learn to let go of our expectations and go along at their pace. Another frustration for us came from our parent's understandable desire to hold on to the way things were, even when to

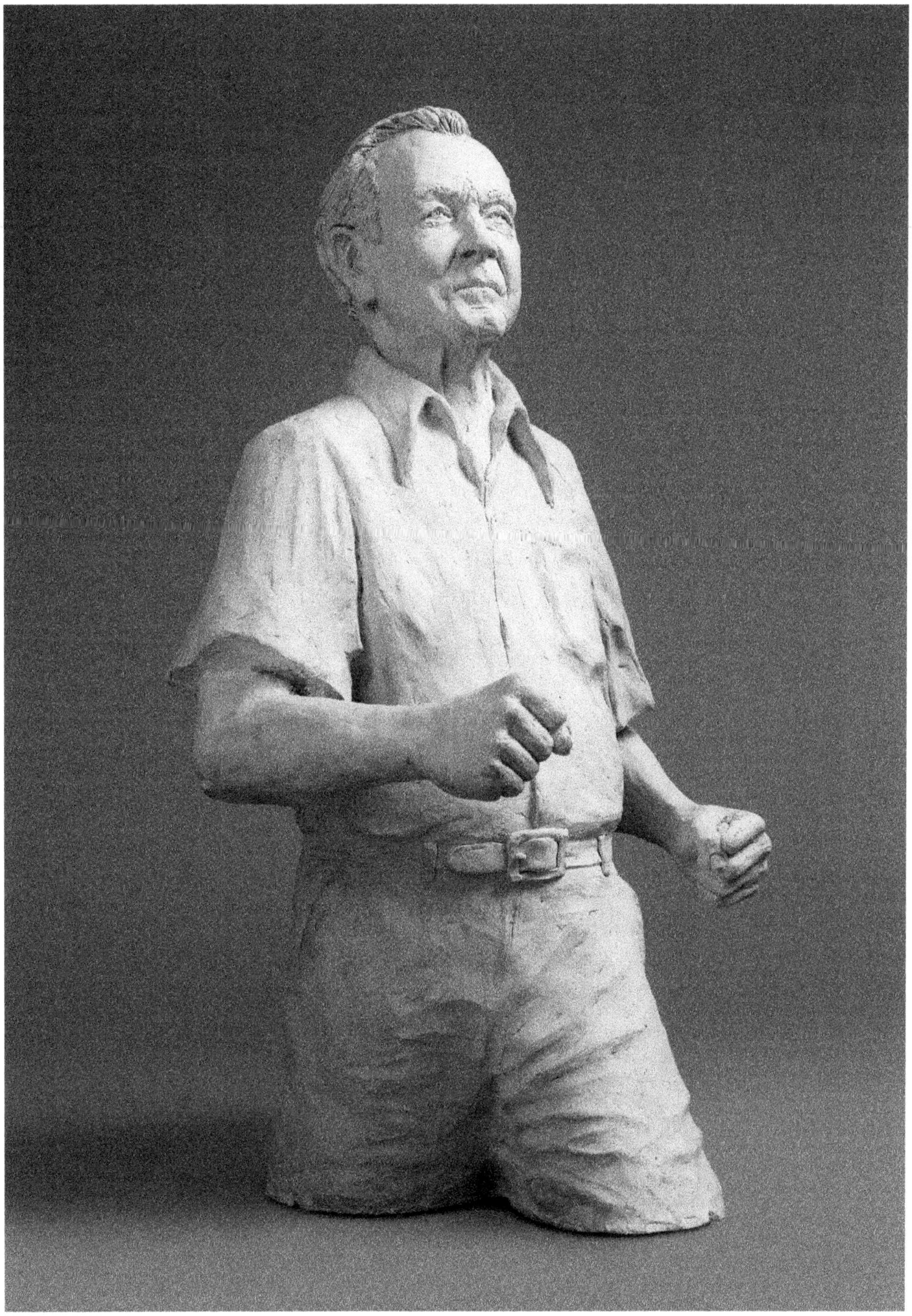

Richard's father, Jack, at 85

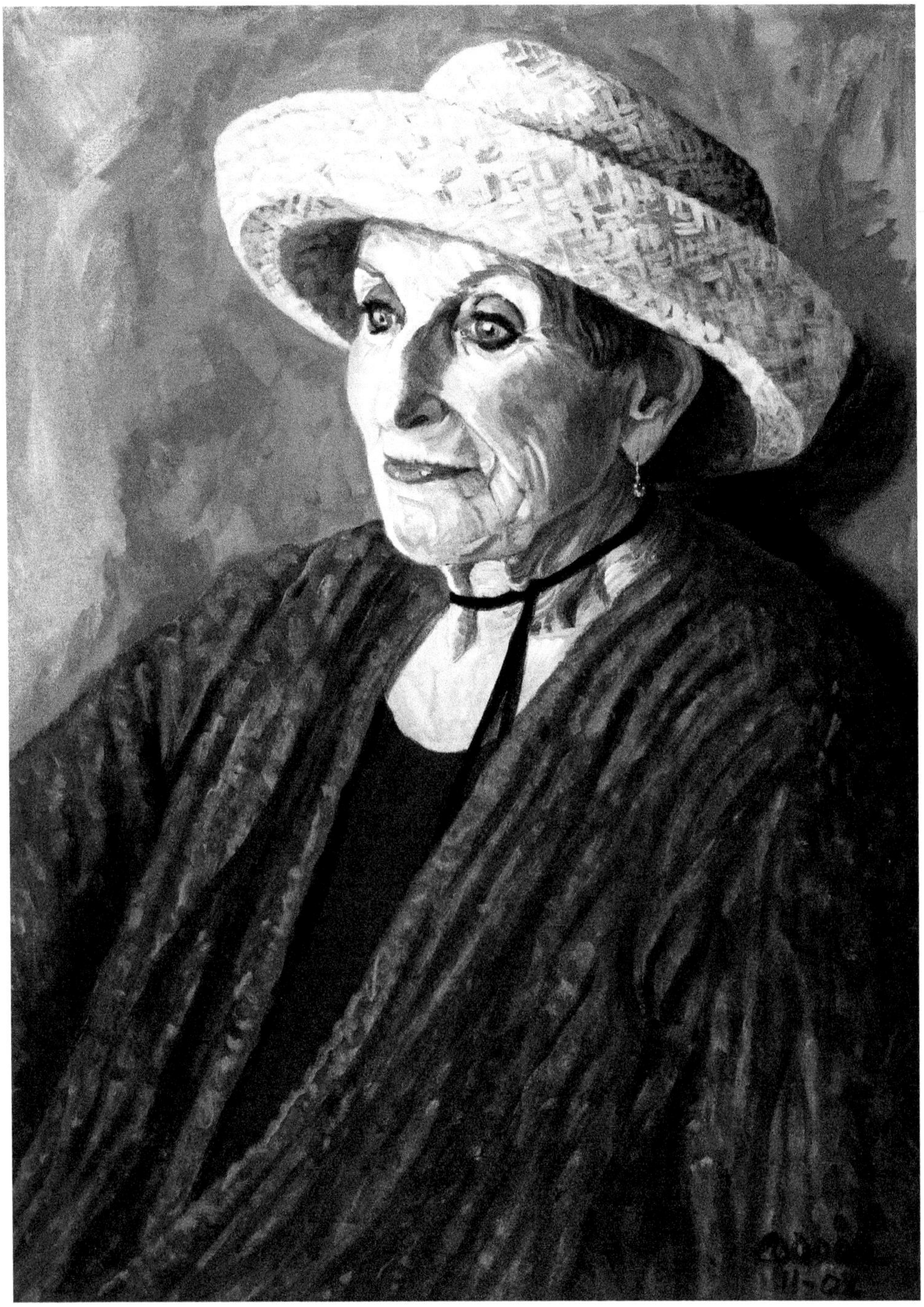

Alice's mother, Beulah, at 85

do so could be dangerous. Richard's father insisted on driving his car even when his ability was impaired by slow reflexes and poor eyesight. Alice's mother insisted on wearing high heels, even after a serious fall. It seemed obvious to us—if you are unsteady on your feet, use a cane; if you can't hear conversations, get a hearing aid. We understood how difficult letting go of independence must have been for our parents, but because of our fear for their safety, their stubbornness put us in the uncomfortable position of lecturing down to them. We hope that when we grow older we will be able to listen to the voice of reason.

As our parents got older and more in need of our immediate help, we made it an important part of our lives to be there to serve them. It was a time to return all the love and attention they had lavished on us when we were young. We knew time was short and wanted to be at peace with them, and they with us. We wanted no unfinished business. Becoming clear with our parents meant working toward letting go of past resentments and releasing judgments and

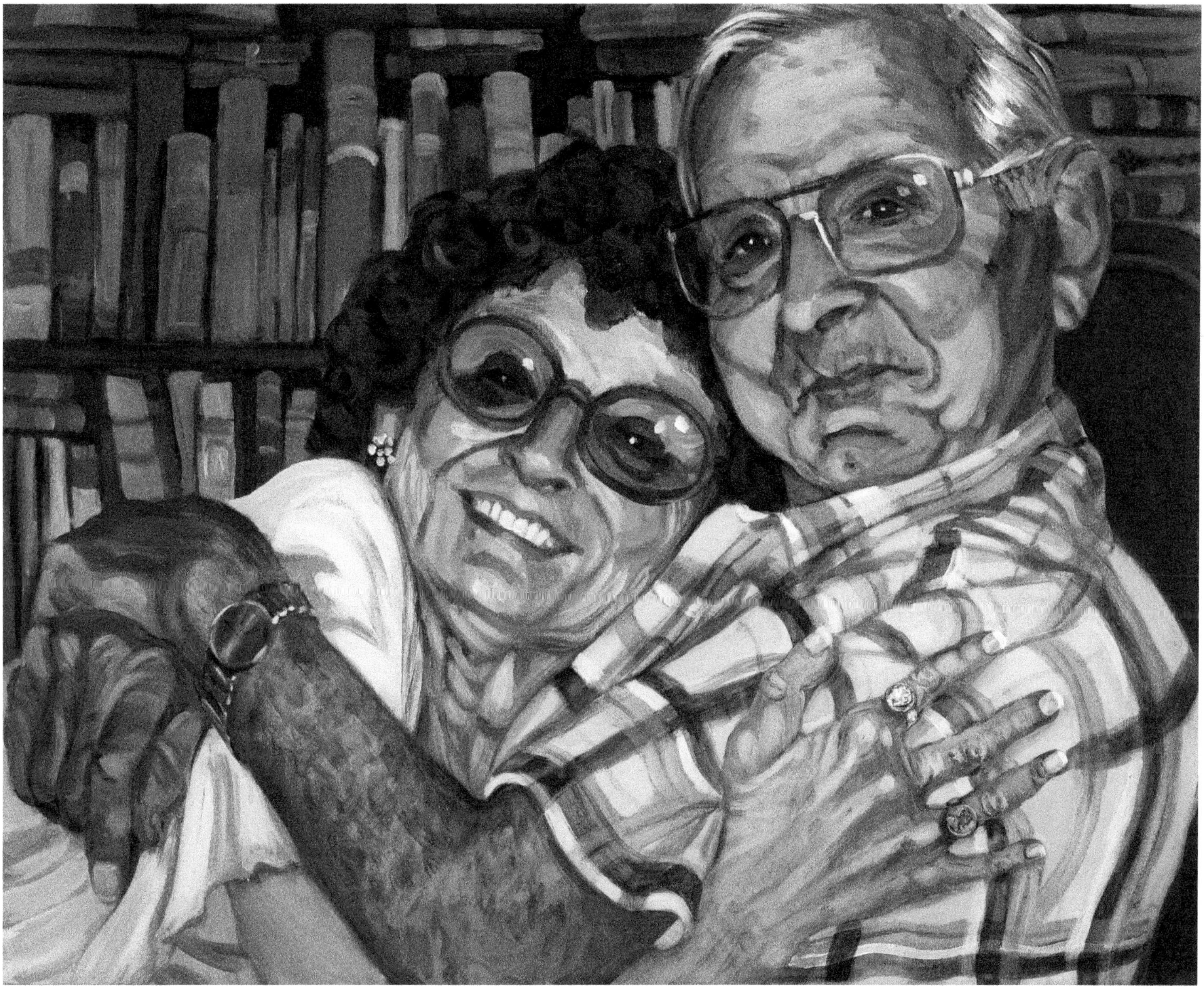

Richard's parents, Jack and Ruth, at 89

irritations we might have felt towards them. It meant letting go of the incidentals and focusing on the essentials—the love we all shared with each other.

We felt that unexpressed grievances we retained from the past were best left unexpressed. After all, our parents were old now and nothing would be accomplished by speaking to them about the past, except to confuse and upset them. In truth, we were loved, maybe not exactly how we wanted or expected to be loved, but we were loved the best way they knew how. If they made mistakes, it was not purposeful. At times they were weak or confused or fearful. They were human.

Our firm intention was to do everything we could to make sure they were

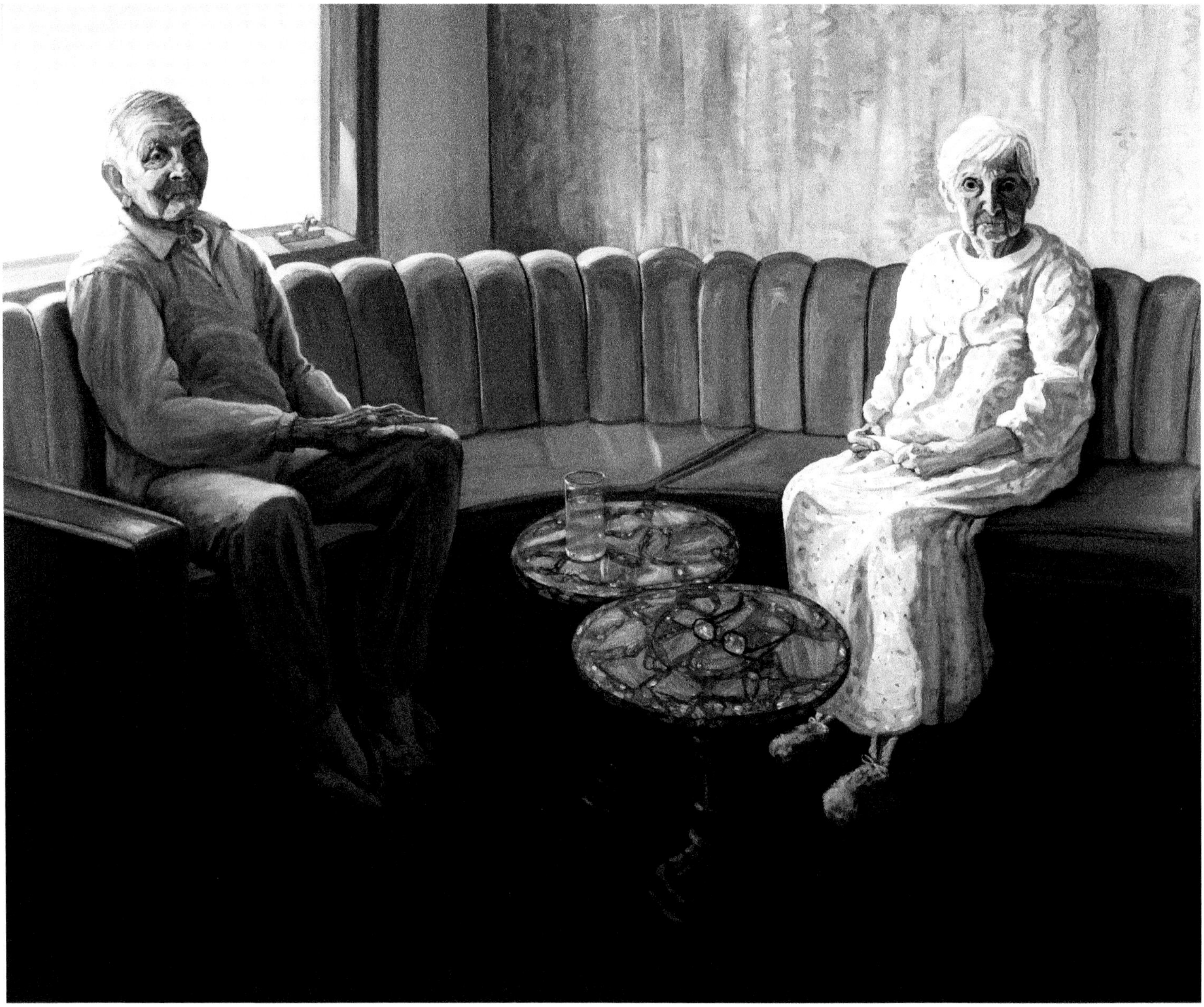

Richard's parents, Jack and Ruth, at 91 at home

comfortable and happy in their final years, and to treat them with love and respect. By the end of their lives, we came to completion with them. When they died, we had no guilt, no regrets, no unresolved feelings—nothing left unsaid. Just mutual love and appreciation remained.

Both sets of parents were close, loving couples with many decades of happy marriage between them. Sumner's passing, and then Ruth's, severed the bond, and dramatically changed the relationships we had with the surviving spouse. They turned to us and shared an openness and intimacy they had previously reserved for their partner. The closing chapter in their marriages signaled a new chapter in their relationships with us.

The death of our parents was a significant event in our lives. To watch death happen, to see each life drain away, to be with the body, and touch the cold flesh of one we love is truly transformational. We can never be the same, never take life for granted in quite the same way. With each parent's passing, we came more in contact with a sense of the reality of our own death and a deeper recognition of the preciousness of life.

Even though they had lived into late old age, and their deaths were expected because of their advanced years, we were still surprised and unprepared. Our grief was not orderly. It came in waves. We might be in the middle of doing something, then, out of nowhere, came a sudden rush of memory and what felt like a blow to the belly and a rip in the heart that left us awash in sorrow. We repeated the usual: "They were ready to go. They lived long lives. They were healthy. They had easy deaths." However, this did little to temper our sadness.

The world changed dramatically with the departure of our parents. While they were alive, we had expended an increasing amount of time and psychic energy in caring for them. There were visits and daily phone calls, issues around health and housekeeping, and ongoing worries about their well-being. We would experience moments of panic if the phone rang at an unusual hour. Then, in quick succession, they all died. We were left with a tremendous empty space in our lives and a heaviness in our hearts. Our lives are filled with other things now, but the emptiness remains. There are so many times when we have the impulse to pick up the phone and call them when there is some news we would like to share. So many times have we had to fight off the instinct to turn down their street when we're driving nearby. We were now orphans. Even though we had parented our own parents in their final years, we were still children in relationship to them while they were alive. Now we are no longer anyone's children. Now, aside from an aged uncle and a few ancient aunts, there is no one from our parents' generation who stands ahead of us in line. Now we have taken our parents' place and have officially become the older generation. The process of caretaking our parents and shepherding them through their deaths was a transition for us, a rite of passage into full adulthood.

Being in the empty houses, the houses we grew up in, surrounded by objects that had been part of our lives and their lives, brought on a flood of memories. We experienced bittersweet emotions—a mixture of sadness at their deaths and sweetness of our life with them. Now, the houses stood quiet and empty of life—a reminder that nothing can undo the inexorable circular movement of the hands of the clock.

Because they died in such close succession, we were faced with the task of liquidating both our parents' households. It was overwhelming for us to sift through lifetimes of accumulation. At first, we saw it as a mountain of "stuff" to be categorized and gotten rid of: "This gets thrown out, this goes to the thrift store, this we can sell at the garage sale, this we'll keep."

After a while, however, the process began to take on more meaning. We realized that each article was a physical remnant of our parents' life. That chair was not simply an object. At the time it was acquired, it was thoughtfully chosen, purchased, carefully placed, and lovingly lived with. That painting, that rug, that vase, that table were all parts of the fabric of their lives. Now many of those things live in our house and are parts of the fabric of our life. We glance around and our memories of our parents come alive.

Surprisingly, the process of pouring over the houses full of possessions allowed us to view our parents in new and deeper ways. Richard found his mother's diary, written when she was an adolescent and young woman. As he read, he was able to see into her innocent and yearning heart. At that moment, she became a multi-dimensional person for him, rather than just a mother and caretaker. Alice found a pile of scripts her father had authored for radio shows in the 1950s, and reading them, could appreciate him more as a unique and creative individual.

Just as our parents' physical bodies had come to an end and would dissipate, now so would their possessions. We, in the process of examining and distributing our parents' possessions, were being witness to and honoring their lives, and adding another layer of finality to their deaths.

Having lived long enough to experience the deaths of our parents and, before them, our grandparents, we are able to view our lives with a wider perspective. We see our lifetime as a point in an evolving continuum, rather than simply as occupying a discrete unit of time. Thus we assume our place in the succession of generations, part of a lineage that encompasses past, present, and future.

From the point in time where we are now, we can look to the past. Stretching backward is an infinite line of ancestors—our respective parents, each of their respective parents, and on and on, back beyond memory. Looking into the future, we see our children growing into middle age, wrinkles beginning to crease their faces. We see nieces, nephews, and cousins who we once knew as infants, then teenagers, now adults, married and now with children of their own. In time these children will give birth, live their lives, and become old.

When our parents died, we inherited each of our families' treasured photo albums. Through faded photographs, we are able to peer into a short period of the past. There, captured in black and white images of our parents and their friends and relatives, long dead, is evidence of a lives lived—of parties, vacations, homes inhabited, pets loved.

There will come a time when nothing will remain of us but images in faded photos, wearing long-outdated clothing and old-fashioned hairstyles, nameless, historyless. Some descendant, sorting through a pile of memorabilia, will blithely toss our photos into the trash. Our once precious possessions, filled with our memories, will end up in that trash heap, or in a thrift store, or an antique shop. This treasured life, where we once resided at the center of the universe, will have no witness.

Is this a tragedy? Not really. It is the way

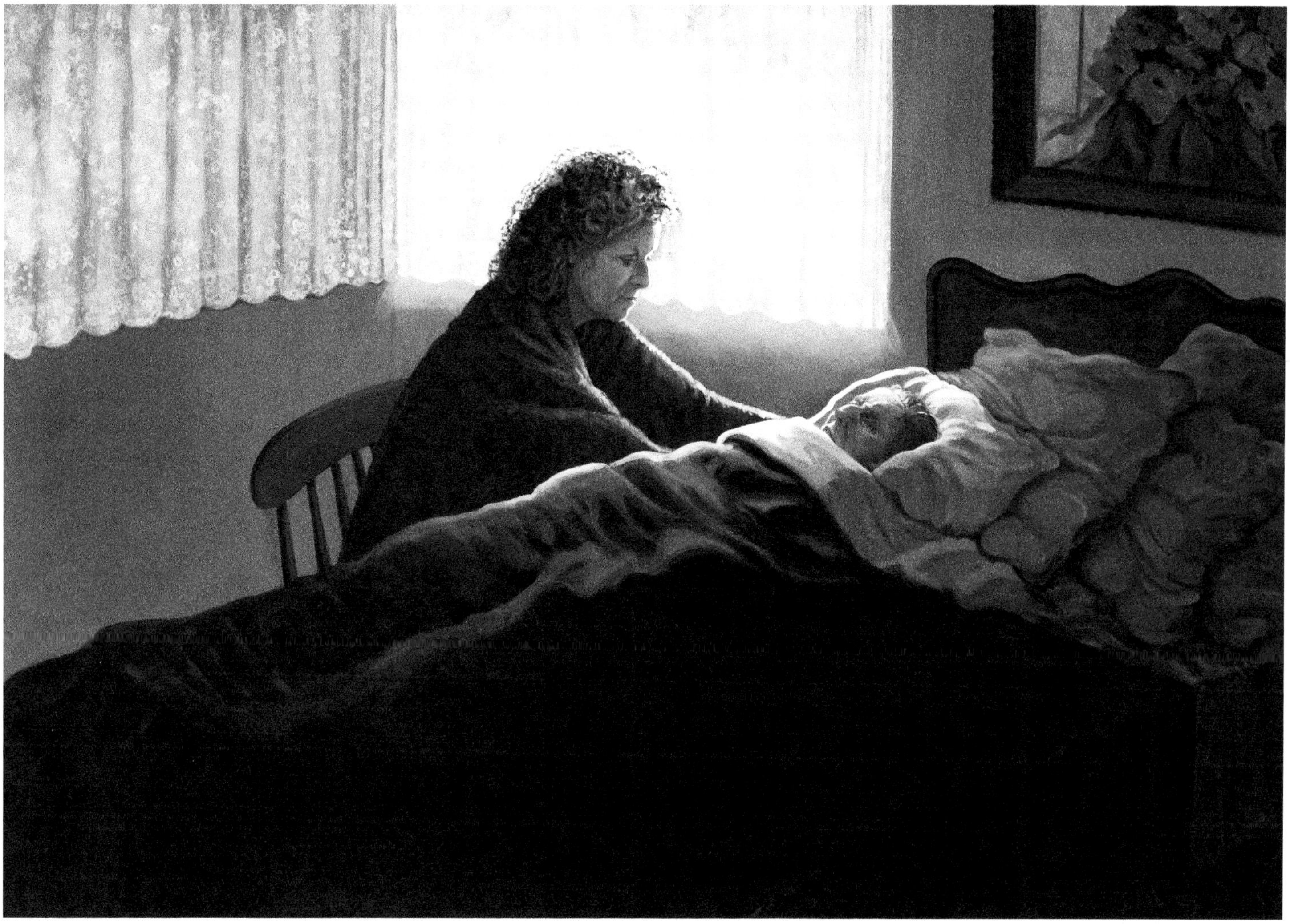

Precious Moments—Alice with her mother at 87 in her last moments

things are—the nature of life—progress, change, impermanence—the continuing cycle of birth, maturity, death. All the universe, visible and invisible, is subject to that process. Creation, maintenance, and dissolution happen at every level—from the birth and death of a tiny insect, to the birth and death of a star.

We take our place with our generation in the continuum, right behind the generation of our parents. The details differ—the Beatles, tie-dye, Vietnam, bouffant hairdos, and bell-bottom trousers replaced the Lindy Hop, big bands, World War II, padded shoulders, and Cary Grant, but the underlying process is the same: the progression of one era to the next. And soon our children will take their place behind us—each generation flowing into the next—in an endless river in which we are merely drops.

To see our lives in this wider perspective, while disquieting, is also comforting—because it is true.

If not now, when?

—Rabbi Hillel

On Becoming Elders

ALICE AND RICHARD

In seed time learn,
in harvest teach, in winter enjoy.

—William Blake

"OLD"—THE WORD HOLDS SO MANY NEGATIVE IMAGES AND connotations—decrepit, stale, useless, decaying, passé. Contrast that with "young" —fresh, vibrant, new, active, passionate. Yet, there is the opposite. Youth can be naïve, immature, shortsighted, inexperienced. And, the old can be wise, dignified, venerable, enduring, authoritative, having depth of character and mature judgment. Without minimizing the legitimate merit of "young," as we age, we are coming to a greater appreciation of these positive values of "old."

At this writing Richard is sixty-five and Alice is sixty-eight. When we started our art projects we were in the old age of youth. Now we are in the youth of old age. Having lived through the spring, summer, and fall seasons of life, we now leave autumn behind and are entering winter.

So, how do we really feel about becoming senior citizens? Truth is, it is meaningless to put a number on how old we feel. Only when we blow out the candles on our birthday cakes do the numbers of years we have lived become relevant. The numbers can be disturbing. We recently attended Alice's fiftieth high school reunion. That's half a century! Alice has only twelve more years until she is eighty! Eighty seems really, really old ... and twelve years is so short.

How did we get there so quickly? We were kids just a minute ago. As we have gotten older, it seems like the hands of the clock are accelerating—spinning. Months go by as if they are weeks, the years as if they are months. We are astonished when an event we are sure occurred only last year really happened three years ago!

They say that the mirror doesn't lie, but day-to-day changes in our appearance are difficult to recognize. We were recently viewing videos of a vacation we took several years ago The first time we viewed them shortly after the trip, we thought we looked so old. This time we were surprised at how young we looked!

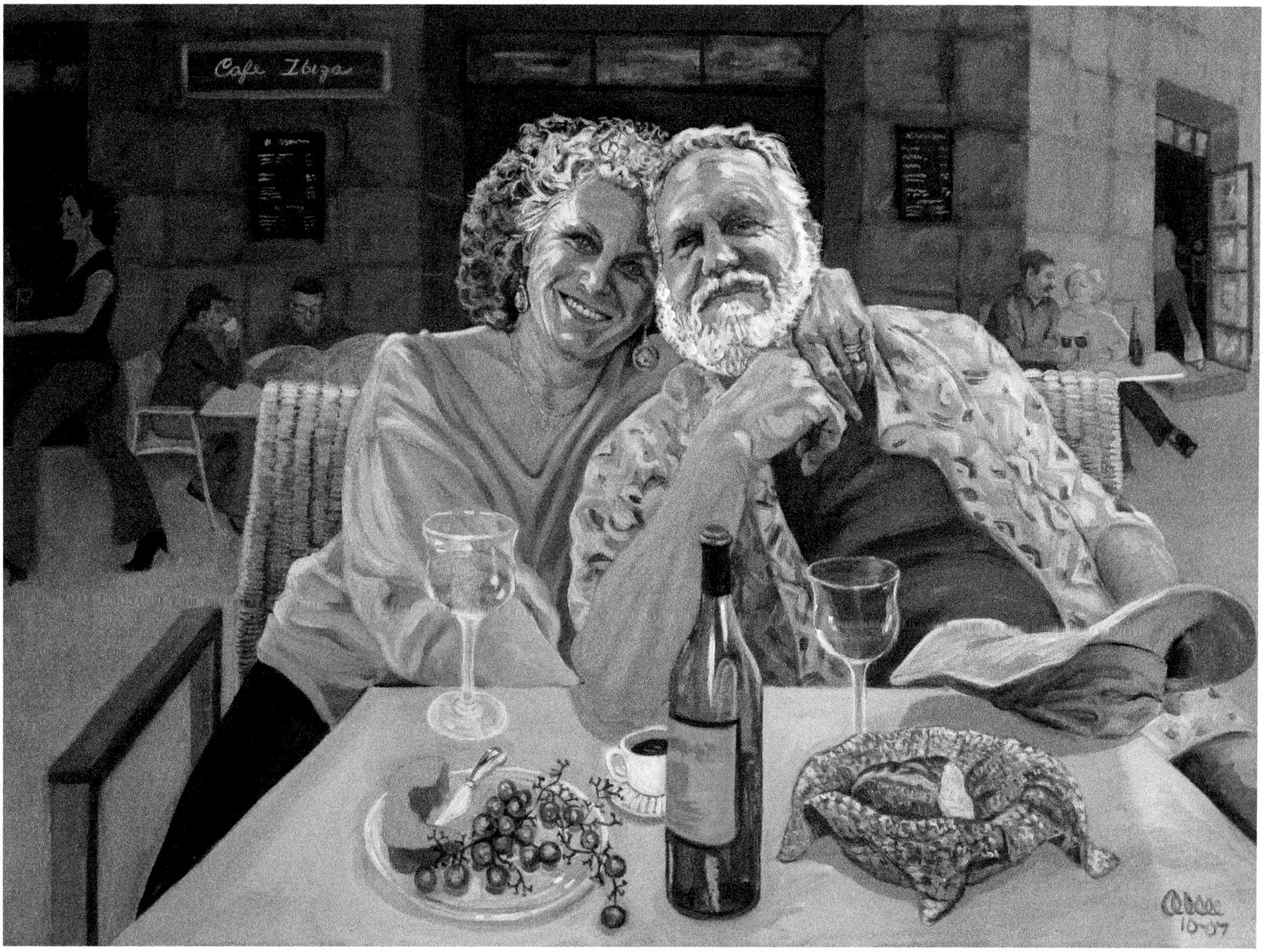

Alice and Richard

Inside, we feel kind of ageless—neither young nor old, and both young and old. The innocent child we once were, the rebellious adolescent, and the dutiful adult still reside in our aging bodies. However ageless we feel inside, the world at large views us differently. The "elderly person" involved in the traffic accident reported by the newspaper turns out to be younger than we are. To the young ticket takers at the movies where we buy our senior citizen tickets, we must look ancient. Senior citizen's discounts aren't the only advantage of being older. Paradoxically, while elders tend to be marginalized in our society, it seems by virtue of our grey hair, we are accorded a bit more deference and respect from younger people. While it is a relief to be offered a seat, or given help carrying heavy loads, it is a bit uncomfortable that someone sees us as needing assistance. It is also very sweet—and appreciated.

Our long personal histories have provided us with a larger perspective on life.

We have been schooled from kindergarten to college, had adolescent crushes to failed marriages, and, finally, built an enduring, loving marriage with each other. We have seen the entrance of children into the world and watched them grow into adults and have children of their own. We have had diverse employment from menial jobs to responsible positions. We have witnessed the illnesses of friends and family, and have experienced the demise of all our parents, grandparents, and several friends. We have watched the world go through a parade of changes—styles of fashion, developments in technology, trends in music and dance, and more. We have lived through momentous world events, and have seen the coming and going of the famous and infamous. All the years, memories and experiences are just part of "life's soup" that has made us who we are today.

At this time in our lives we have never felt happier or more at peace. We are relatively healthy, have most of our "marbles," share deep love and, through having "cooked" long enough in "life's soup," achieved a modicum of wisdom. These are truly our "golden years." If we could freeze time, this is one of our favorite times of life to be alive. However, we are beginning to feel the first drafts of winter coming on. Ahead, we see the specter of progressive debilitation, powerlessness, and loss—and we are afraid. Old age is certainly not for "sissies." Will one, or both of us fall ill? Will we become dependent? Will our minds be impaired? Who will be the first to die? It is not for us to know the answers to these questions now. We will learn as our lives continue to unfold. After all, we are still "works in progress," hopefully with much more to experience and learn.

Throughout the production of our art projects we have met amazing and inspiring elders. They have given us hope that despite the difficult trials that come in the latter stages of life, we, too, can have a rich life harvest in our old age. Working against this hope is our cultural conditioning. We were born into a society that is in horror of growing old, a society that views aging as a tragedy and a curse, a society that spends untold billions of dollars every year trying to hide or delay the evidence of aging. So afraid of aging is this society that monsters, ghosts, and zombies in the horror movies we scare ourselves with exhibit the unmistakable signs of late old age—bony fingers, wrinkled skin, sparse, wirey hair, and long, jagged teeth. All of our lives we have been fed society's fears, judgments, and negative beliefs. We have ingested and assimilated these thoughts and feelings without ever being able to critically analyze them.

Only now that we have entered into the doorway of old age are we able to begin accessing what it means to be an elder and impartially evaluate those youthful judgments and negative beliefs. What we see now when we view ourselves through aging eyes is very different from what we saw when we looked at elders through the prejudice and fears of our youth.

What we in our youth feared most, and still fear, about growing old is loss—loss of our looks, loss of our passion, loss of our health, our independence, each other, and, eventually, our lives. These losses are real and impactful, and without a doubt will eventually make our sunset years the most challenging period of our lives. The losses so far, though relatively insignificant, have been teaching us humility. In our prime, we were radiant, strong and attractive. Not so true anymore. If we live on to late old age we will end up being shrunken and frail. The aging process, year after year, forces us to burn up our pride and vanity. Over time, the weight of those years wears us down and transforms our youthful arrogance to humility, and our humility to compassion.

Loss is the most visible part of growing old, but not the most meaningful part. If we can look beyond loss, or rather integrate and accept the losses, we can add depth and meaning to our lives. Our intention is to treat each loss we experience not as a defeat but as a challenge—to make us deeper and more resilient. That depth and resilience unfolds more when we fully encounter our aging mind and body, accepting the inevitable changes as they occur. Accepting with grace change that cannot be changed—isn't that part of what wise aging is about? Isn't that part of what life is about? If we try to fight the changes, pursuing only the easy, the pleasant, the status quo, while resisting difficulty, pain, and change, we inevitably expend enormous energy resisting life—because life includes difficulty, pain, and change. Opening ourselves to experience the suffering as well as the pleasant is the only way to experience our fullness.

We realize that as scary as aging can be (and it can be scary if we let our minds fast forward ten or twenty years into the future), we cannot allow our anxiety to interfere with our present experience. Ignoring, covering up, or lying to ourselves about the process of rotting that is occurring in our mind and body will take us away from reality and cut off our aliveness. The rot offers valuable insights. Every element of our aging process has its truth and richness. As we find ourselves in transition from mature adulthood into old age, a natural preparation is occurring within us on many levels, consciously and unconsciously, to move us on to this next stage. Our bodies lead the way—physical disabilities, energy waning, senses dulling, memory eroding. The message is very clear. What is happening is that our body and mind are becoming less relevant. What then? We are being called upon to turn within and focus more on our soul. Our final destination is spirit, and our aging body can help move us closer to a spiritual perspective.

The process that is occurring here—spiritual potential awakened by declining energies in the body—is only one example of lessons that are occurring on many levels as people enter old age. Every loss a person experiences contains a potential gift. For each door that closes, a window opens to a panoramic view of greater depth and meaning. As the bloom of youthful beauty fades, we can become more open to discover our inner beauty. As "romance" wanes, a deeper, more mature, and expansive love can take its place. As we become more dependent on others, we can learn to receive with grace. As we withdraw from being "useful"—being a parent or wage earner—we are more able to just "be," without compulsion to compete or prove ourselves to others. As our ability to be in control of our world diminishes, it becomes more appropriate to relax, let go, and surrender to the natural flow. As we become aware that our time is running out, we are more inclined to embrace and savor each moment. What precious gifts these are. They help us to drop useless baggage like superficiality, petty pride, greedy ambition, jealousy, and impatience. These gifts represent freedom—freedom to be our own authentic selves, without the need to impress, acquire, or conquer. The losses and hardships of aging then turn into blessings.

If we could, would we go back in time? There are moments, especially if we are feeling creaky, when we could be tempted. Sure, it would be nice to have a young, lithe body and a wrinkle-free face. But given the choice of returning to a young body while being stuck with a post-pubescent mind, or of remaining in our older bodies with our present mental makeup—no contest. We have gained so much value from our aging, and are comfortable with who we have become. We have achieved a measure of inner peace and surrender. We don't have time for the angst, trauma, and drama that we had in our earlier years.

Our life experiences have changed us, and caused us to reorder our priorities. Things that were of vital importance even a few years ago seem to matter less now. Prestige, power, accomplishments, possessions—we leave these to the young. We find great joy in the smaller things, things grounded in the present moment, like reading together in bed, enjoying times with family and friends, and walking arm-in-arm in the evening. Our pace has slowed, and this is a good thing. In the past we sought to be filled by things external to ourselves and felt pressured to go, to see, to do, to have. Now, we take more time to savor—to look and touch and taste our experiences. We find this much more satisfying. This slowing down, which has happened naturally as we age, allows us the opportunity to pay attention to our moment. Without attention, life rushes by in a blur, and we live less than a full life.

Many things that were appropriate in life's spring and summer have become inappropriate in our fall and winter. We don't need to stand up with our hands in the air in the front car of the roller coaster. At the same time, we don't need to go in the opposite direction and become paralyzed—so obsessed with safety and comfort that we are reluctant to pursue the unknown. There is still adventure in our souls.

It seems as if almost daily we get reports that some friend or acquaintance has died or has contracted a horrible disease. This puts us in touch with our own vulnerability, and a real sense that our clock is running down. Minor physical and mental symptoms that would have escaped our awareness when we were younger take on greater significance. A pain in the belly or a lingering cough may signal "the beginning of the end." A moment of forgetfulness may indicate the onset of Alzheimers. A routine physical holds a bit more anxiety than it did ten years ago. It is not that we have become obsessed with our bodies. We are just more vigilant. The human body is a miraculous machine, but the parts start to wear out after awhile.

In our youth we felt invulnerable, as if no harm could touch us. We had unquestioning trust in our body's powers of healing. Physical ailments were always transitory, injuries would heal quickly, illnesses passed in a short time. But now, some of the symptoms we are experiencing might be the beginning of chronic problems that we must deal with for the rest of our lives. Now, we are feeling a bit more fragile. We take fewer chances and demand less of ourselves. Instead of always telling our bodies what to do, we started listening. Our bodies speak more insistently the older we get—too much greasy food, and our stomach lets us know; a little too much exertion, and our muscles tell us to ease off. We have less energy, tire more easily, feel like napping in the afternoon. These and other physical changes are signposts. And, the signs are clear—we are getting old—it's really happening to us! There is nothing we can do to control it. The clock keeps ticking and we can't stop it or slow it down.

There is no denying, our future is abbreviated. (We jokingly call this "circling the drain.") This realization brings a sense of urgency. In the past, we had gotten into the habit of putting things off until tomorrow. We recognize now that we have fewer tomorrows. We can't indulge in lengthy detours, or expect second chances. This influences countless thoughts and decisions. We don't have time to consider long-term financial investments, and when we buy flowers and trees to plant on our property, we opt for the mature specimens. If there is something we want, or something we would like to do or accomplish—why wait? Soon enough we will be too old to participate in or enjoy many things we take for granted now. We don't want to arrive at the end of our lives full of regrets—for chances wasted and opportunities not taken. The wisdom of Rabbi Hillel's compelling question keeps reverberating in our minds, "IF NOT NOW, WHEN?"

While our bodies and minds have matured, so have our spirits. The big questions we touched upon in our youth, we revisit now with increased depth and urgency: "Who am I and what am I?"; "What is the meaning of life and my place in the cosmos?" The years have given us a panoramic perspective, so our answers have greater depth. We have come to perceive that our true identities lie beyond what we usually identify as our self—our personality, gender, occupation, history, even our mind and body. This search for our true identity and the significance of our existence is no mere intellectual exercise. It is part of an ongoing process of "summing up," looking within and attempting to make sense of our time on earth. As we move deeper into old age, we surmise that our explorations will play a larger role.

We have acquired a sense of respect and awe, and a feeling of humility. When we look at the complexity of our bodies and our senses, see a sunset or watch a bird in flight, we know there are miracles at work. In these moments we are imbued with a sense of the sacredness of our lives and everything around us. More than ever before, we have a feeling that we are part of an immensity that is far beyond the limits of our comprehension. This immensity resides within us, as well as without. It is beyond change and beyond time. Therefore, it is the only part of us not subject to change and time. So, while our bodies and our personalities may age, our essence, which is the ground of our being, remains immutable.

This essence, this immutable ground of being, is what draws us now. When we leave the world we will be as naked as when we entered. Our accomplishments will be meaningless and our possessions useless to us. What better way to spend some of our remaining time than to turn inward and upward and explore the eternal and infinite energies that the great sages spoke of and wrote about. We are drawn to follow in their path.

This does not mean that we are about to enter a monastery or wander alone in the desert. Our path will be to attempt to simplify our life—to let go of clutter, unneeded objects, unproductive relationships, old resentments, and other emotional baggage. Doing so will free up energy and leave room for our souls to grow.

When we look back at our lives, we feel a poignancy bordering on sadness as we realize how much of our journeys are already complete. In our youth we had "ten miles behind us and ten thousand more to go." We felt there were infinite possibilities and unlimited challenges. We've taken on some of those challenges and avoided others, realized some of those possibilities and failed at others. We've fulfilled some of our dreams and after years of postponing, have let go of others. Now, much of our life stories have already been written, and cannot be altered. Our challenge is to be able to look back at those failures and unrealized dreams with a shrug and a smile. As Alice's mother, Beulah, said on her deathbed, "It is what it is."

This attitude of self acceptance has come easier over time. In the past we had read self-help books and eagerly attended self-improvement courses. Now we have befriended ourselves and come to peace with who we are. There is no one to impress, not even ourselves.

More and more children and young adults are coming into our lives—usually sons and daughters of friends and relatives ... and their children. Lately, we seem to regard them, especially the young ones, with an extra amount of tenderness. Perhaps because they are so recently entered into this world, in contrast with us, who are closer to the exit. Being of a grandparent's age, we have a wider vision of what their futures might hold. A mixture of love and heartbreak, pleasure and pain, success and failure awaits them. Our hearts are touched by their sweet innocence. It is unfortunate that we will be able to experience only a small portion of their life. We are curious as to where their life path will lead them.

We take delight in the fresh enthusiasm of the young people in our life as they explore and discover the world. Their joy in discovery serves to remind us to open our eyes and ears and resist the tendency of numbness that comes from having "been there, done that." Any artist of life must make room to explore, and to be touched by the new. To cease to explore is to stagnate, and stagnation is more lethal than any disease.

Each generation tells its story with their own fashion, language, music, and hairstyle. This is good because it is not the similarities that add spice and enliven us, but the differences. Even though other generations seem foreign to us, it helps to remember that the differences between all generations are mostly on the surface. Underneath, all of us want the same thing—to be safe and healthy, to love and be loved, to prosper, to protect our loved ones. With that understanding, the generation gap narrows and disappears for us.

From our position as elders, we recognize that we have a responsibility that extends beyond our individual lifetimes. We want the world our children will inherit from us to be better—kinder, safer, more abundant, and free—than the one we inherited from our parents. Unfortunately, we are not in a position of power and influence where our actions can touch multitudes. But we are able to affect those with whom we come in contact—one person at a time. By simply treating others as we wish to be treated, we will be doing what we can to make the world a better place.

We have come to see this simple kindness as an essential key to happiness and fulfillment. There are as many pathways to live a good life as there are people. Some find fulfillment in their search for God or for the Infinite. For others, happiness is found in enjoyment—fine food, travel, pleasing surroundings, good friends, and lovers. Still others find their joy in intellectual pursuits or in physical fitness. There is no right or wrong, but we believe that no matter which way someone chooses to live their life, it cannot be complete without a healthy dose of kindness and generosity. Whether it is giving a gift we know will bring joy to someone, spending time with a sick person, feeding the hungry by contributing to charity, these acts of kindness toward others will make our own lives more satisfying and meaningful. The more we serve others, the more we fill our own cup. Returning to others the bounty we have been given is both an expression of our abundance, and recognition of our reaching full maturity. In youth we received, in maturity, we give back.

We have been thinking in terms of what we will leave as our legacy, something that will mark our brief existence on earth. Aside from financial endowments, we want to leave a piece of ourselves that will endure. Our art is part of our legacy. So is this book. At the same time, we realize the idea of a legacy is vanity, and has very little meaning. A few years after our death, who we were and what we have done will have been long forgotten. The only thing that has real meaning is what we are doing with our life now. Today really is the only day that matters. Yesterday is a memory, tomorrow is a dream. Past and future are nothing compared to the living moment.

Having hindsight, we wish that when we were younger we were awake enough to realize how incredibly precious time is. We have so little of it. The years pass by so quickly, and once gone can never be recaptured. Every minute that passes is a minute less of life—and each minute life leaks away like sand in an hourglass. Knowing this as we do now, we would have worried less, judged less, used more of our time to slow down, smell the roses, and celebrate everyday miracles. And, most of all, open our hearts more to love. There is nothing more precious than love, and more precious than the love that is received, is the love that is given. Looking back at the peak moments in our lives, we see that the times we felt most alive and fulfilled were invariably times when we were giving our love.

We don't know if there is a grand plan. What we know for sure is we are born, grow old and die. Ultimately, all we have in this life is time. We cannot foretell how much or how little is left. Like the game of musical chairs, we never know when the music will stop and how the game will end for us. Because the future is uncertain, many mornings we greet each other with a cheery, "We made it another day!" And many evenings, before we fall asleep, we say, "If we don't see each other again, it's been a good run!"

Because all we have in life is time, the most important question we can then ask ourselves is, "What shall I do to fill up my remaining time?" Or, "How shall I spend this next hour, this day, this year ... knowing it may be my last?" This question becomes more urgent as our remaining time becomes shorter. It cannot be satisfactorily answered by the mind—with words. It must be answered with action, with how we live. With this increasing sense of the preciousness of time, we make it our goal to live consciously each and every day with as much integrity, generosity, humor, forgiveness, and love as we can muster. This means conducting our lives in such a way that when our time comes to depart, we will have no regrets and can leave with a clear conscience and a sense of completion. Day by day we try to do this. This is our art in aging.

In a sense, the whole of our life is our work of art. Although we use paint and clay and words as our artistic medium of expression, our true art is in how we live day by day—how much of ourselves we give to those that we love, the care we take in our work, how we behave with integrity in the world. This is creative work, full of improvisation, discovery, and imagination. Our life/art piece is still a "work in progress." In fact, not until our life is over, is that art piece complete.

What happens to this precious work of art we have spent our entire life creating? Who cares! When we die, it is no more. The joy comes from the act of creating the art piece, not from whether it endures after we are gone. Life is about the journey, not about arriving at the destination.

When all is said and done, we are left with the feeling of gratefulness. Each morning we awaken is the renewal of the gift of another day of life. We are grateful for this gift of time and for the gift of this body, this mind, this spirit, for each other and all the beings in our life. We are grateful for the opportunity to live, even if for an infinitesimal moment, on this beautiful earth. Yes, there is pain and suffering, dissolution and defeat. And yes, in the end we will be nothing but dust. But what a miracle and blessing to be alive.

We are just two people, lost among billions of others, carried along on the surface of a round, spinning clod of earth, orbiting a gigantic fireball, the whole thing streaking through dark, endless space. Each day approximately 365,000 new lives enter the world to join the 6,500,000,000 people already here. On the same day, 150,000 depart. The immensity is mind boggling and leaves us feeling very small and insignificant. In contrast, here we are, intently immersed in our precious daily lives. We live in our sweet little house, feel excruciating love for each other, extend our love to our family and friends, and also the cat. On pleasant evenings, after a good meal, we sit outside on our patio discussing the world situation, while petting the cat on our lap, and slapping at mosquitoes as the sun goes down. We hope, we fear, we yearn, we weep, we laugh. It is all so, so beautiful.

"What if we couldn't wait
to be old, like a child can't wait
to be an adult?""

—Nader R. Shabahangi, PhD

Afterword

ALICE AND RICHARD MATZKIN AND THEIR ART—A LOVE STORY

ALICE AND RICHARD

"Every artist dips his brush in his own soul,
and paints his own nature into his pictures."

—Henry Ward Beecher

WE MET AT A FRIEND'S HOUSE IN 1982, AND AFTER OUR FIRST DATE were never apart. It was love at first sight. Immediately we felt comfortable with one another, as if we had known each other all our lives. We recognized that in each other we had found a friend, partner and helpmate, as well as a lover. Within a few days of meeting we began to live together. A few months later we traveled to India, where we were blissfully married. Now, well into our sixties, we remain gratefully so to this day.

It was this love for each other that rekindled our creative juices and inspired both of us to return to our respective artistic pursuits. We had both abandoned art years before, Alice to raise a family and Richard to pursue a career in counseling. Our coming together in love was a catalyst. We experienced a creative frenzy—each sparking and invigorating the other—and it remains so after a quarter of a century.

We live in the foothills outside the small hamlet of Ojai in Southern California. Our home sits on an acre at the end of the road, surrounded by fruit trees and backed up to the Topa Topa bluffs. We share a bright studio lined with windows and skylights. Working in the same studio space is a blessing. We enjoy working together and welcome and appreciate each other's opinions and observations. People find this surprising, given that producing art is such an intensely personal pursuit—fraught with all sorts of opportunities for esthetic differences, emotional vulnerabilities, and ego clashes. However, we have brought our love for each other into the studio with us. We are not in competition. We trust each other and have a healthy respect and admiration for each other's talent. We are tuned in to the other's art and can offer complementary ideas and perceptions toward the works-in-progress. We have followed the same process in creating this book.

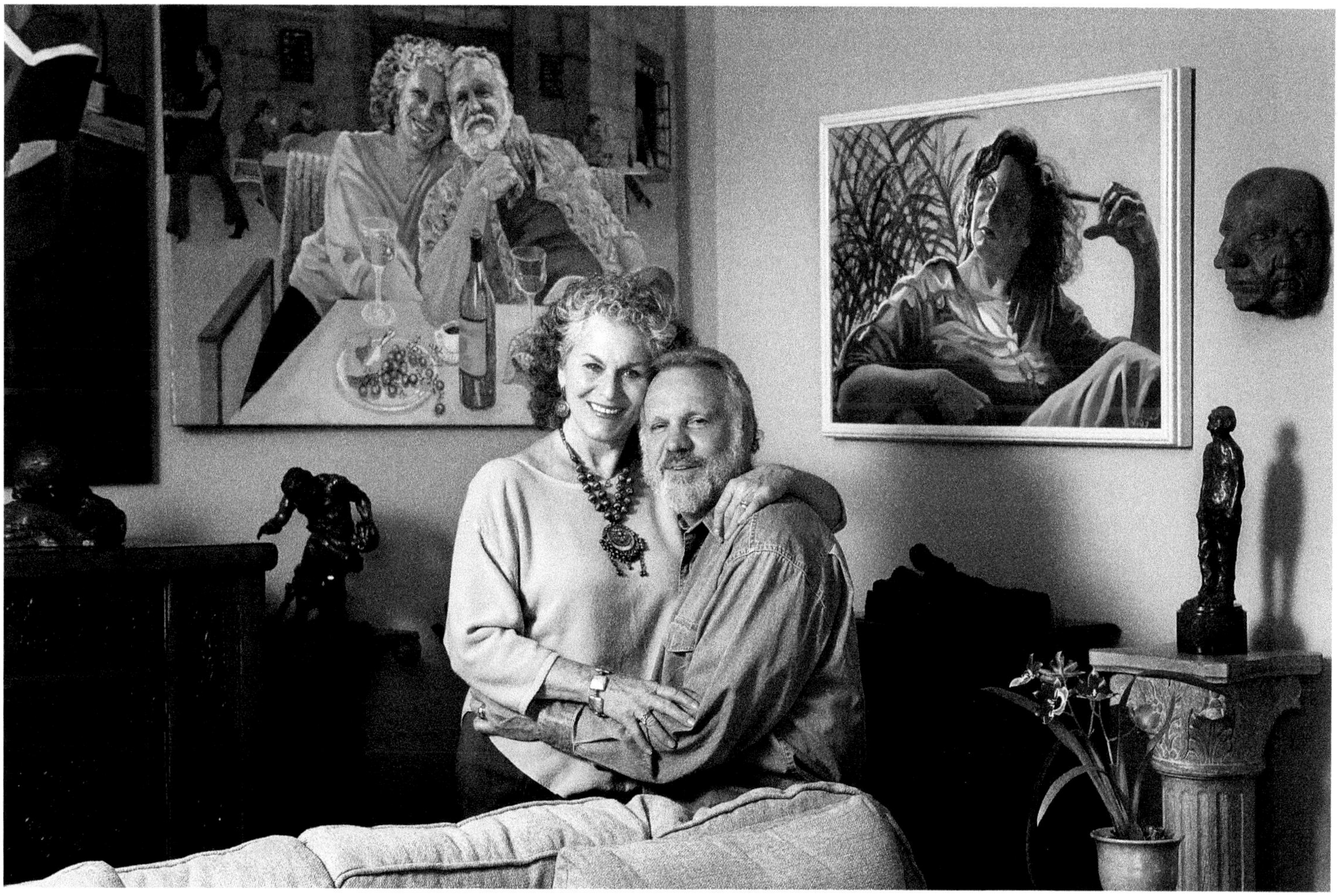

Alice and Richard and their art

Though we are distinct individuals, think and express ourselves very differently, and create in different media, our experience of aging is amazingly parallel. Our intention is to have this project be a shared creation. And so, in this spirit, we tell each other's story.

Richard

As a child, Richard was always drawing and painting. In junior high school his talent was recognized with a scholarship to the prestigious Otis Art Institute in Los Angeles, his only formal training. Around the same time, he was introduced to jazz and took up drums. Rhythm was always a natural part of him, and for many years music overtook his interest in art. He played a lot during the 1960s and '70s with well-known jazz and blues musicians, and even had a recording contract with a major label. Growing tired of the music business, Richard decided he wanted to explore psychology, so he gave up drums and earned a master's degree in that field. While art and music lay fallow, he worked in a variety of venues in counseling and education. In the late seventies he "dropped out" to live and study in an Eastern spiritual community. At the time we met and fell in love in 1982, he was working in a psychiatric hospital.

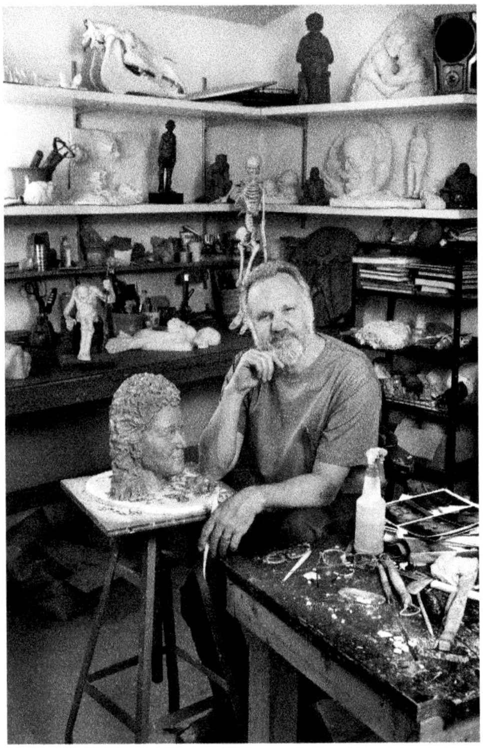

Richard Matzkin and his art

With our love as inspiration, Richard began to revisit his natural artistic talents, which had lain dormant for two decades. He started playing the drums again and began writing. Then, for some reason, I decided to sign him up for a sculpture class, and he agreed to go. His natural ability to create form from a lump of clay was evident from his first touch of the material. In fact, he could have taught the class! In a few months he learned the basics of building and firing clay, and then was on his own.

Richard has always had the instinctive ability to form in clay what his eyes see. Because he has great visual memory, he rarely works from photographs or reference material. He works quickly and viscerally, forming and kneading the clay with energy. The old bodies of his subjects hold

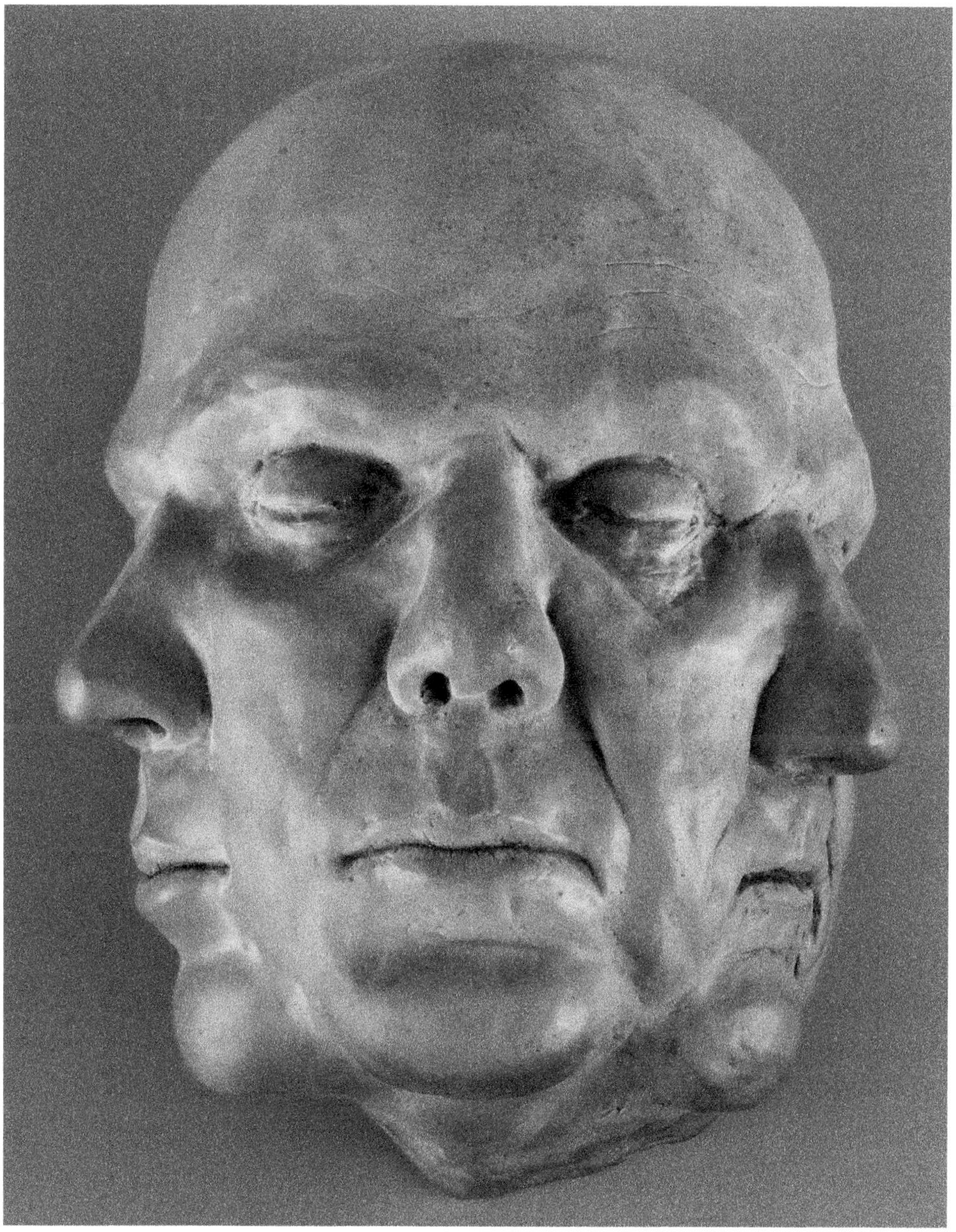

Evolving Self Portrait. This self portrait illustrates my changing face. It is divided into four quadrants beginning age 20 to 40 to 60 and projected into the future at 80.

personality and character. A seasoned soul inhabits those bodies and rough clay is the perfect medium for Richard to bring out that soul.

There is often a spontaneous element in his work. In the sculpture *Old Man Watching TV*, the weight of the figure forced the chair that it was placed on to sag. Richard didn't repair this because the sag was in keeping with the collapsed figure. Another piece fell to the ground as he was hollowing it out. After the first reaction of horror at the squashed figure, he was delighted with what the force of gravity had done to improve the form.

I wouldn't call Richard's work beautiful in the usual sense: balanced form, graceful flowing lines or smooth finishes. What he is about is capturing the emotion in the figure. Because of that emotional quality, most people find it hard to be neutral when looking at the figures he makes. The response can be unpredictable. I've seen people's faces light up into smiles or break into tears, as well as recoil in disgust.

Whether the viewer is attracted or disturbed by his sculptures is of little consequence to Richard. He says, "As long as people are touched by these pieces, whether positive or negative, I am pleased."

Richard likes to surround himself with things that are old and weathered (like me). Ancient farm implements in the orchard, old-fashioned hand tools, and tin signs tacked onto the walls of the barn, a sun-bleached cow skull in the studio and, on the bathroom drain board, fossils that are millions of years old. This predilection for the old, the imperfect, the weather beaten, and the impermanent is reflected in his art.

Alice

WHEN WE FIRST GOT TOGETHER there was very little indication that Alice had any talent or interest in art, other than a few small oil paintings bearing her signature, dating from the early sixties, which were stored in the garage. Alice never had formal art training. She had taken some art classes with a teacher named Ron Blumberg for a while and painted mostly still life in oil using a palette knife. In 1964, after the birth of her son Jason and, eighteen months later, her daughter Angela, she substituted creating art for creating a family. Then, around 1985, Alice decided to bring along her old set of paints and a canvas when we went on vacation to Northern California. We arrived at a deserted beach in early morning and Alice set up her easel. She painted from morning to sunset. This was the beginning of the re-emergence of her passion for painting. A short time later, she was fortunate to find Alex Vilumsens, who was the perfect teacher for her at the time. Alex's "right brain" style of teaching fit with Alice's spontaneous nonintellectual approach.

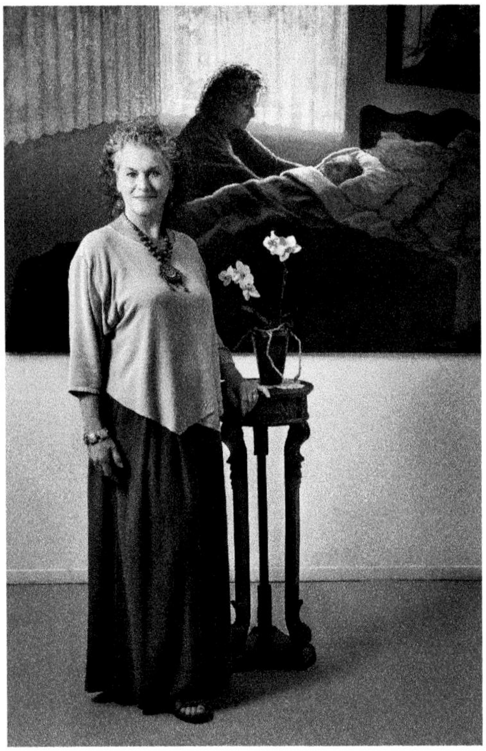

Alice Matzkin and her art

Alice switched from oils to acrylics. She gravitated from painting diverse subjects to painting portraits exclusively. She loves people, and that love is translated to canvas. She does not attempt to obtain a realistic image of her subjects. "That's why we have cameras," she says. It is the essence of the person she wants to reveal. She has the unique ability to capture a soul, as well as a likeness.

Alice works from photographs because people can be relaxed and more natural posing for a snapshot than posing motionless for a long period of time. She is adamant about using her own photos because she feels that the photography is an essential part of the creative process. She will often take scores of photographs of her subjects. Sometimes she creates composites—a hand from one photo may be combined with the body from another and the head from still another. She quickly sketches the outlines of her subject on canvas with a large brush and paint, trying to capture the energy as well as the form. Then she starts adding detail with color.

Alice's choice of color is instinctive. She says, "The color chooses me." She doesn't consciously think, "This purple needs more red," rather, her brush is guided intuitively to the paint. The colors her brush chooses are sometimes unusual and sometimes downright weird. She may make a lip blue or an eye purple, but it works. In fact, the unique color combinations are not usually visible unless you stand close to the canvas. But they are felt.

Alice probably spends as much time sitting and staring at the work as she does actively painting. Her staring can take unusual forms. At times she will take the canvas outside and view it from a far distance. She feels the work should look good close up as well as from far away.

There is a mirror standing in the corner of the studio, and Alice occasionally will look into it to observe the progress of the painting. She wants the portrait to look like her subject even when the image is reversed. The mirror can show flaws in proportion and provides a fresh perspective.

Alice often will paint at dusk as the room is getting dark. The semidarkness shows the relationships between the lights and darks almost as if the painting were in black and white. This way she can see the contrasts in color values more clearly.

I love to visit the studio every half hour or so, especially when Alice is beginning a painting. It is amazing to see how rapidly she progresses. Usually she captures a face within a few minutes. At other times, especially near the completion of the painting, she may work for several days on a single finger.

Alice works with total concentration over long periods of time. She has been known to work from morning to midnight totally unaware of the passage of time. Often I will prepare meals for her and she will eat in the studio so that interruptions are minimized. Of course she will always stop for the occasional shoulder and neck massage.

People often ask Alice how she knows when she is finished with a painting. Her answer is, "When in that moment I don't know where to put my brush next." After the final brush stroke there is occasion for staring and more staring at the painting. If it passes muster, she'll add her signature, and then I'll hear the worried lament, "What am I going to paint next?"

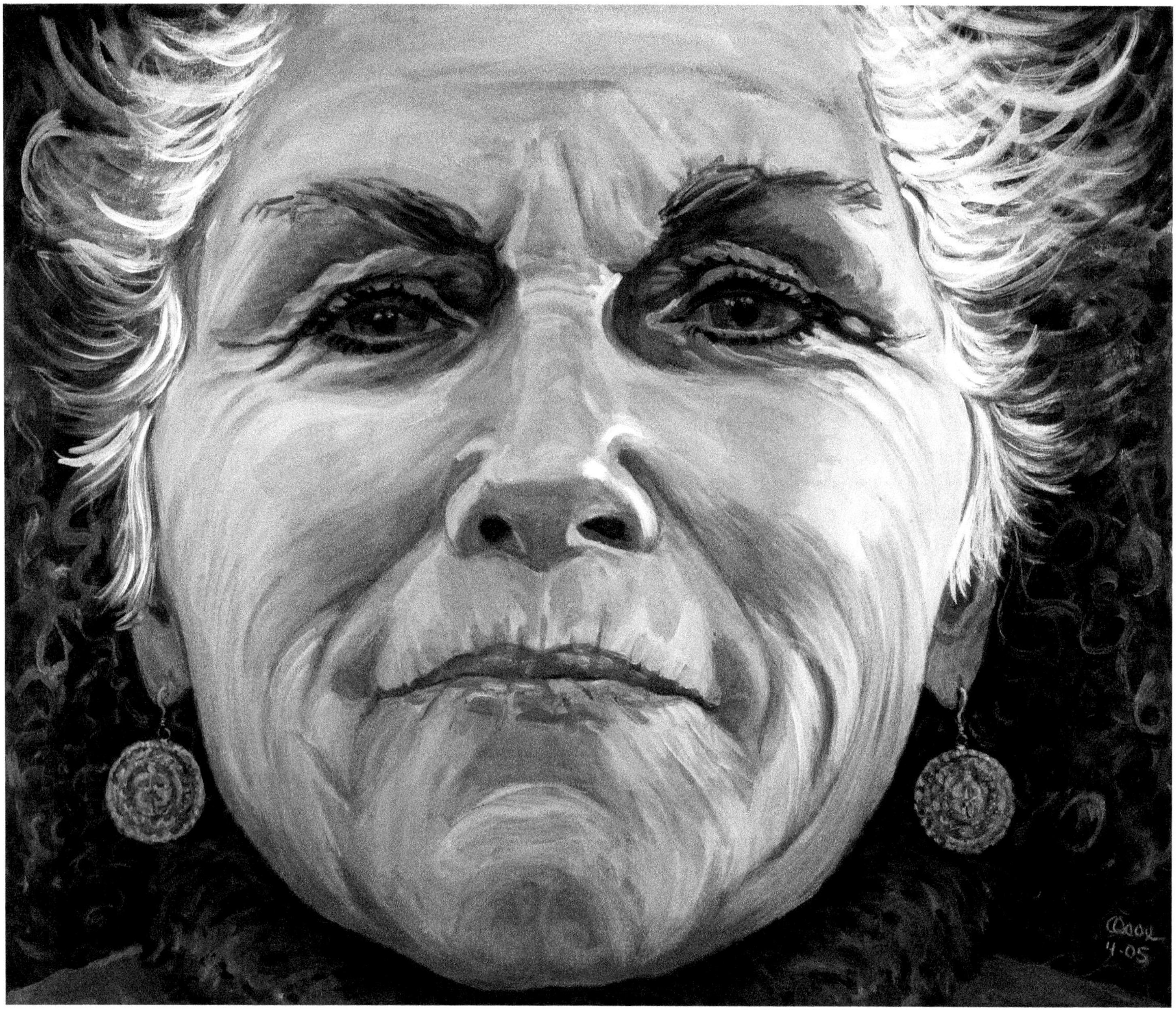

Self portrait of Alice at 65. This enigmatic self portrait is an honest depiction of my face without hiding the wrinkles.

About the Authors

Richard Matzkin was born in 1943. He is a sculptor, musician, therapist, and writer. His sculpture has appeared in a book published by UNESCO and a monumental equestrian work can be found in the train station in Camarillo, California. He has had numerous one-man shows and his emotional sculptures are in collections throughout the United States.

Alice Matzkin was born in 1939 and has painted most of her life. She has two paintings in the permanent collection of the National Portrait Gallery of the Smithsonian Institution, one of Beatrice Wood at 100, and one of Betty Friedan. Her portrait of Chelsea Clinton hung in the White House during the Clinton administration. Her entire collection from the *Naked Truth* series of paintings appeared in *Ms. Magazine*. She and her *Women of Age* series were featured on television's *The Oprah Winfrey Show.*

The Matzkins share a studio next to their home in the hills above the hamlet of Ojai, California. For the past dozen years their work has focused almost exclusively on older people.

PERMISSIONS AND CREDITS

All paintings were photographed by Kristin Altimus.

All sculptures were photographed by Michael Butler Photography, except *Old Man and Baby, Old Baby, Lovers in Bed,* and *Lovers Spooning*, photographed by Rob Clement from Rashneon Photography, and *Old Face* and *Embrace*, photographed by Alice Matzkin.

All photographs of Alice and Richard are by Donna Granata, *Focus on the Masters Series 2008.*

The photograph of Alice with Beatrice Wood on page 22 is by Richard Matzkin.

Cover painting by Alice Matzkin—*Beatrice Wood at 105, nine days before her death.*

Page 33: Betty Friedan by Alice Matzkin, acrylic on canvas, 1995, currently on view in *20th Century Americans: The American Search for Justice;* courtesy National Portrait Gallery, Smithsonian Institution; ©Alice Matzkin.

Sculpture molds were made by Reije Andersson Fine Art Studio and Robert Wenszke of Artisan Bronze did the casting and patinas.